MORE THAN JUST A GAME

Columbia Histories of Modern American Life

Columbia Histories of Modern American Life

The books in this new series are concise interpretive histories focusing on major aspects of the American experience since World War II. Written by leading historians, the books draw on recent scholarship to create a lively and interesting account of the subject at hand. The books are written accessibly with a general reader/student audience in mind. Each volume includes an excellent bibliography and a detailed index.

Religion in America Since 1945: A History, Patrick Allitt

MORE THAN JUST A GAME

Sports in American Life Since 1945

Kathryn Jay

Columbia University Press   New York

Columbia University Press
Publishers Since 1893
New York   Chichester, West Sussex
Copyright © 2004 Columbia University Press
All rights reserved

Library of Congress Cataloging-in-Publication Data
Jay, Kathryn.
  More than just a game: sports in American life since 1945/ Kathryn Jay.
        p. cm. (Columbia histories of modern American life)
  Includes bibliographical references and index.
  ISBN 0–231–12534–8 (cloth, : alk. paper)
  1. Sports—Social aspects—United States—History—20th century. I. Title. II.
Series
  GV706.5.J39 2004
  796.357'0973'09045—dc22
                                                    2004044498

∞
Columbia University Press books are printed
on permanent and durable acid-free paper.
Printed in the United States of America
c 10 9 8 7 6 5 4 3 2 1

Contents

Illustrations follow p. 112

Acknowledgments

When I first started this project, I was living in a guesthouse in a lower-middle-class neighborhood in Mexico City. I arrived in Mexico just as the 2002 World Cup competition got underway and watched the city's excitement level grow as fans—and *everyone* was a fan—followed their team's fortunes. Because of time-zone differences, Mexico's pivotal first-round game took place at 6 A.M. local time, and so, along with about twelve other sleepy fans, I roused myself from bed to watch the national team and its wonderfully named leader Cuauhtemoc Blanco tie a lackluster Italian squad and secure a coveted spot in the second round of the competition. The city exploded with energy: the traffic, never good, was snarled for hours as fans ran in circles around the Angel of Independence, a statue that commemorates the country's freedom from Spain and is unfortunately situated in the middle of a busy street. Every newspaper published a special edition with photographs from the game, and restaurants and bars across town endlessly replayed the game for several days.

Perhaps it was a bit more excitement than in a comparable U.S. city—especially considering the Mexicans hadn't actually *won* the Cup but only advanced to the second round—but it did not seem that far from American celebrations for sports victories. The televised coverage of the game, however, was another story. There was no halftime show with flashy graphics and excited announcers, no recaps of other World Cup matches currently in progress, no running scroll at the bottom of the screen, no specially made commercials featuring World Cup tie-ins. Instead the fifteen minutes between the halves featured endless replays of the sole Mexican goal interspersed between equally endless, and poorly produced, commercials for Lala bread, Powersex energy powder, Nextel phones, and dishwashing soap. I could hardly believe my eyes. This was not the United States.

To continue my soccer odyssey, I visited Brazil just two weeks after the country's team had won the World Cup. Yellow and green flags flew everywhere, and Ronaldo remained the man of the hour. But the attention of the people of Rio de Janeiro had already turned to the semifinals of the Libertadores Cup and the fortunes of Fluminese and Flamingo, two of the most successful local teams. Rio de Janeiro alone hosted four teams, and seemingly everyone was a fan of one of them. Attending a party hosted by a group of Brazilian feminists, I explained that I was writing a book on American sports and suddenly found myself hearing about how one woman became a fan of the Vasco da Gama team because of the team's history of hiring black players, how another had always rooted for the Botafogo squad because her father did, and how a third thought Flamingo would take the Brazilian title this year. At least I think this is what they said, since my Portuguese language skills are nearly nonexistent and their English sometimes faltered. But we were talking sports, so it hardly mattered.

Long before my Latin American soccer experiences, sports had played an important role in my life. I played softball from the moment my small town in Texas established a league for girls. I got to stay up late to watch the Boston Red Sox–Cincinnati Reds 1975 World Series and cried with happiness when Carlton Fisk hit his famous just-inside-the-foul-pole homerun. I rooted for the "Luv ya, Blue" Houston Oilers, especially Earl Campbell, Billy "White Shoes" Johnson, and the dashing Dan Pastorini. I read Dave Campbell's *Texas Football* magazine from cover to cover and every year picked my favorite high school stars so I could follow their careers, including Garth Ten Napel, an all-Conference linebacker for Texas A&M, whom I liked more for his name than anything else. I adored Cesar Cedeno, Dickie Thon, and Jose Cr-u-u-u-u-u-z of the Houston Astros, and lived and died with the team in the baseball playoffs of 1979 and 1986. And I watched the University of Houston's Phi Slamma Jamma fall apart in the 1982 NCAA Championship on a tiny black-and-white TV. Obviously, my sports memories are shaped by a particular time and place, but they speak to the role of sports in creating memories and shaping identity. Though I haven't lived in Texas for nearly fifteen years, I still root for the Astros and the Texas Longhorns—something made easier by the Internet—and I moaned when the Oilers up and moved to Tennessee. The teams I root for are a critical part of why I continue to think of myself as a Texan.

My interest in sports also led me to teach a regular sports history course at Barnard College. In this, I received heavy encouragement from my department chair, Bob McCaughey, who believed that a course on sports history had merit and might draw a wider range of students to the study of history. Over the past six years, my students have pushed me to rethink my assumptions about the role of sports in American society. In particular, I would like to thank the students in a seminar I taught on sports since 1945, especially Kristen Aiken, Richard Cacioppo, Nicole Cohen, Yael Fisher, Scott Hopson, A. J. LaRosa, Jason Magnus, Erika Rose, and Ryan Wilner, whose astute papers added to my knowledge of recent sports history. Rich, Nicole, and Yael also served as research assistants for this book, doing yeoman work in the Columbia University libraries, as did Nicole Conway during the summer of 2002. Sarada Callison also proved especially helpful in researching Title IX, and Phillip Wallace spent hours helping to compile the book's index.

While I am responsible for all of its mistakes, both the conception and execution of this book benefited tremendously from the help of James Warren at Columbia University Press. Jamie has been an excellent editor, striking just the right combination of enthusiastic encouragement and (very) mild scolding. He would make a great Little League coach. Photo editor Elyse Rieder and manuscript editor Michael Haskell were also very helpful in the book's later stages, while assistant editor Plaegian Alexander ably took care of the many little details.

Members of my family also offered constant assistance and support. My mother Shirley Christian has cheered my interest in sports my entire life, whether driving me to practice every afternoon when I was a child or asking regularly, "So, is the book finished yet?" over the past two years. Max Friedman offered choice tidbits from sports movies, while Martin Friedman and Elena Servi Burgess graciously found sport-related poems and thought hard about the book's possible title. Finally, my partner Elisabeth Jay Friedman lovingly read every word and offered insightful suggestions that improved the book. In taking me along to Latin America for six months, she allowed me to experience sports—and a host of other things—in an entirely different context, which helped to sharpen my thoughts on American sports. Finally, she had complete faith in my ability to finish this project, even when I wasn't so sure myself. We make a great team.

MORE THAN JUST A GAME

Introduction

*I*n modern American society, sports are far more than just a game. This is made abundantly clear by the sheer number of sports-related metaphors that dot the English language and are "brought into play" across a wide swath of public life. When politicians debate the question of affirmative action for minorities, both sides speak of a level playing field. Some teachers want to raise the bar in testing, but many of their students would rather punt on taking exams. Good corporate managers acknowledge the need to regularly touch base with their subordinates in order to ensure employees don't drop the ball when working with a client. In any arena, a poor quality product or a poor effort is bush league, while a top earner is an all-star and a rank beginner a rookie. We admire people who can't be counted out, those who get up off the mat and try again despite adversity, but we also encourage our friends to know when it's time to hang 'em up. In a different realm, adolescent males yearn to get beyond first base in their sexual explorations and dream of scoring with beautiful women.

Sports saturate our culture as well as our language. By the end of the last century, Americans had spent millions on Nike's Air Jordans, Champion sweatpants, Reebok T-shirts, and New Era caps, eager to look like jocks even if we rarely moved off the couch. Sports were so central that from Massachusetts to Alabama, state legislatures proved more ready to cut teacher salaries than to pare the budget for intercollegiate sports. Cities around the country founded midnight basketball leagues, convinced by policy makers who declared sports a dependable method for converting budding gang members into productive citizens. And sports channels proliferated, as did sports-related Internet sites and radio programs, making sports a ubiquitous part of everyday life. Today, rooting for a favorite team or a favorite star remains a central pastime for a significant percentage of the American public, whether grandmothers keeping the faith in their Red Sox caps or grown men waving "terrible towels" at Pittsburgh Steeler games or small boys crazy for Tony Hawk. While all this enthusiasm has often been dismissed as a harmless pastime or mere silliness, no history of modern American life is complete without an examination of sports. Over the past sixty years, sports became a multibillion-dollar industry that is a central lens through which we view the world, helping many Americans to create a sense of personal identity and community and allowing us the space to discuss often contentious issues.

"America, rightly or wrongly, is a sports crazy country," said President Bill Clinton in 1998, "and we often see games as a metaphor or a symbol of what we are as a people."[1] This book tries to make some sense of why that is and how it came to be in the period between World War II and the turn of the century. I pay close attention to the development of sports—just how did the National Basketball Association go from a podunk regional league to an international powerhouse, for example—and to the accomplishments of many great players and teams, but I also attempt to place sports in a broader social and cultural context. In the professional ranks, baseball, football, and basketball get the most consideration, though the stars of golf, tennis, stock car racing, and extreme sports earn their moments of scrutiny. On the collegiate level, football and basketball dominate the narrative, in part because the level of funding they receive dwarfs all other intercollegiate sports but also because these two "major sports" have had such a powerful impact on how Americans think about the college "experience" itself. Analyses of the Olympics and the growing appetite for recreational sports round out the study. Some of this information is not new. Many scholars have written with great insight on American sports, and this book depends heavily on their analyses. At the same time, I have included stories and details from a wide range of sources,

especially local newspapers and sports magazines, to deepen the interpretation and to explore issues that have not yet received extensive
coverage by other scholars.

Winning, often at any cost, has profoundly shaped the sports we
play and the sports we watch in the decades since World War II. Americans like winners. "In this country, when you finish second, no one
knows your name," said basketball coach Frank McGuire. "Every time
you win, you're reborn," claimed the NFL's Vince Lombardi, "when
you lose, you die a little." And basketball coach Bill Musselman, who
compiled a 78–180 NBA record, nevertheless maintained that "defeat
is worse than death because you have to live with defeat."[2] Sure, Americans root for the underdog, but even then we are hoping that the little guy will rise up and smite the big guy, take him down a peg, symbolically enact what many are of us unable to do in our daily lives. In
other words, Americans want the underdog—picture the gawky freshman Steve Nash calmly draining free throws to lead the fifteenth-
seeded Santa Clara Broncos to an upset over number-two Arizona in
the 1993 NCAA tournament—to be a winner, at least for one night.

This urge to produce winners need not be understood as negative.
When Branch Rickey signed Jackie Robinson to a major league baseball
contract, the decision sprang partly from a realization that Major
League Baseball's color line was morally wrong, but it was also true that
Rickey saw Robinson, and by extension other black players, as a cheap
labor pool that would help his club achieve more victories on the field.
The pressure to win was what finally drove Southern schools to integrate their football and basketball teams in the late 1960s and early
1970s. As the most likely apocryphal but nonetheless revealing story
goes, not until Sam "Bam" Cunningham scored four touchdowns in a
42–21 University of Southern California rout over the University of
Alabama in 1970 did Alabama coach Paul "Bear" Bryant finally decided
to recruit a few of the many great African American players from the
South. Finally, the need to beat the Soviet Union in the Olympics
spurred the United States to allocate more money for women's
Olympic teams in the late 1950s and early 1960s. Gold medals won by
female athletes counted just as much in the final standings, a fact that
helped to overcome a century-long opinion that women should be
cooperative, not competitive, when they played.

On the other hand, the desire to win has led to repeated scandals in
college football and basketball, as alumni and coaches collude to produce a team that can win in the cutthroat atmosphere of Division I
intercollegiate sports. Paying athletes to play and cutting corners in

other ways was commonplace among athletic departments in the 1950s, when coaches such as Bryant regularly left hundreds of dollars at potential recuits' homes, and it remained so in the 1990s, when a record five schools in the Southeastern Conference (SEC) faced major NCAA penalties for recruiting violations and other infractions. The emphasis on winning has also encouraged some athletes to use performance-enhancing drugs to shave a second off their race times or to add bulk and muscle to their frames. St. Louis Cardinal slugger Mark McGwire admitted that he used a testosterone-boosting compound called androstenedione during the year he broke Roger Maris's home run record. While the substance was legal in Major League Baseball (MLB), the National Footbal League (NFL) and the International Olympic Committee (IOC) had banned it, and no one could guess at its long-term effects on the human body. Fans are not exempt from the mania for victory, and citizens have spent millions in taxes and approved outrageous bond deals to attract professional teams to their cities, all to have a winning team wearing jerseys emblazoned with their city's name. A victorious sports team can be more appealing than improving housing for the poor, adding city services, or paying city workers a higher wage.

This need to win has created a fascinating duality in American sports. In general, Americans tend to overlook the sometimes seamy underside of the sporting world as long as teams and athletes are winning. We celebrate athletes as national heroes and regard sports as a place that teaches all the best qualities of citizenship, especially integrity, reliability, and a sense of responsibility. In the next breath, however, the problems of sports—cheating, drugs, violence, and an overweening emphasis on financial gain—are bemoaned as representing the decline of the nation itself, with sports serving as a sort of public barometer of ethical values and decency. As should be clear, in the United States, sports are rarely *just* sports.

This book looks closely at the ways that sports have both mirrored and shaped American culture since World War II. Important issues of race, gender, class, and national identity have been worked out on the country's sporting fields, as athletes and teams became symbols of the larger social forces transforming American society. Yet Jackie Robinson's integration of "America's national game" was more than symbolic. Because professional baseball was a much-watched national industry, Robinson's on-the-field achievements helped to bring changes in other realms and inspired civil rights activists to fight harder for integration in other arenas. Two decades later, when African American players rebelled against the way they were treated by college coaches, their claims of racial discrimination and overt prejudice drew on existing civil rights and black power movements and echoed an ongoing national debate on the treatment of African Americans. But because Americans cared about college sports, when black athletes spoke out, they had a bigger platform from which to influence public opinion. Sport does more than imitate social realities; it produces them.

Sports also became a place to sort out Cold War rivalry and express national pride, particularly at the Olympics. "Wouldn't it be great?" asked Olympic wrestler Terry McCann in 1960. "Wouldn't what be great?" a teammate replied. "If we beat the Russians," said McCann.[3] In the years between 1945 and the fall of the Soviet Union in 1991, concrete examples of "beating the Russians" were hard to come by, a reality that made sports a critical site for articulating Cold War tensions. When an American wrestler pinned a Soviet, or the United States triumphed in the overall gold-medal count, American superiority found rare clarity of expression. The connection between Olympic victory and national dominance had an impact on sports, of course, contributing to a win-at-all-costs attitude and reinforcing the association between athletics, civic development, and national pride. Americans began to sing the national anthem before sporting events during World War II and never stopped. After the attacks on New York and Washington D.C. on September 11, 2001, many baseball teams added a rendition of "God Bless America" to the traditional seventh-inning stretch, a development that seemed normal at the ballpark, though it would have been out of place at the theater, the opera, or any other public entertainment.

Sports have played a particularly important role in shaping gender expectations in the United States. Athletes such as slugger Mickey Mantle and quarterback Joe Montana embodied a particular vision of masculinity that many have yearned to emulate. Like many other male stars, both were attractive family men, hard working, powerful, tough, and able to overcome pain to achieve their goals. By the early 1950s, participating in sports had become a societal expectation for young men and muscles a critical marker of manhood. Young women, in contrast, aspired to be "some of the prettiest coeds on campus [who] dance and lead the cheers at halftime."[4] Or they longed to be model Cheryl Tiegs, whose 1978 nipple-revealing mesh swimsuit turned *Sports Illustrated*'s annual swimsuit issue into a national obsession. These commonplace attitudes made sports an unlikely site for social change, but when women began to demand their opportunity at bat, the results created a social revolution that reverberated far beyond the field.

Television made the link between sports and identity that much stronger. When female or minority athletes appeared on television, they reached a bigger audience and challenged more assumptions than they could without the medium. Televised games also created a visual association between winning teams and the cities they represented, making local teams even more vital to city identity. Coach Vince Lombardi and the on-the-field success of the Green Bay Packers in the early 1960s put the city on the American cultural map. Television made sports into spectacular entertainment, turning local games into national, and sometimes global, events and, in this way, reshaped how Americans understood the meaning of sports. Of course, the money that television revenues provided to owners also had a profound impact, helping to transform postwar sports into a multibillion-dollar business and solidifying the link between athletics and the consumer appetite. When the Houston Rockets signed the seven-foot-five-inch Chinese star Yao Ming, he became an instant corporate star in the United States, pitching Apple computers and Visa credit cards with an easy grin. At the same time, his presence extended the NBA's reach in China and created new fans for the game across the world.

One example should help to make the complexities of modern sports clear and demonstrate this book's approach to placing sports in a broader social and cultural context. Lance Armstrong was a brash twenty-five-year-old in 1996, just coming into his own in the world of cycling. He had won a stage of the Tour de France, the world's most prestigious bicycle race, and had made enough money on the European cycling tour to buy a Porsche sports car and an expensive home on a lake near Austin. But he wasn't feeling well. One of his testicles was slightly swollen, he felt like he had a constant case of the flu, and he suffered through crushing headaches. Still, he kept training and riding, finishing sixth in the 1996 Olympic time-trial cycling competition despite his physical condition. After coughing up blood one night and realizing that his testicle "was horrendously swollen, almost to the size of an orange," he finally went to the doctor and learned that he had testicular cancer, which had spread to his lungs and his brain.[5] Doctors gave him less than a 40 percent chance of surviving, and, as he later found out, they were being optimistic. After brain surgery to remove cancerous lesions and four rounds of chemotherapy that left him retching, wasted, and nearly immobilized, Armstrong's doctors deemed him cancer-free. He had beaten tough odds to become a cancer survivor.

It was an incredible accomplishment, but most Americans knew nothing of Armstrong's victory over death. He competed in a sport, after all, that few Americans followed or even understood. Most people thought of cycling as a weekend recreation, not an ultracompetitive sport that required years of rigorous training and the willingness to endure enormous physical pain. But Armstrong not only beat cancer, he also returned to professional cycling and won the 1999 Tour de France, a three-week-long marathon of racing that demands superb physical conditioning and a wide range of biking skills. Armstrong made his mark on the Sestrière, a harsh mountain in southern France, blowing away his competition in a ferocious climb to the top. The following year, he won the Tour again, and then again and again, wearing the yellow jersey that signaled victory for five consecutive years.

It was an incredible story of mental fortitude and gritty determination, and corporate America went crazy for Armstrong, despite the oddness of his sport in the mind of most Americans. In 2001, he garnered more than $5 million in endorsements and more than doubled that figure the following year. In addition to being a stunning example of the human spirit's will to win, Armstrong was an attractive young white man with a sweet smile, a beautiful wife, and a newborn son. Together, it was a package that could be used to sell almost anything—Nike shoes, Oakley sunglasses, Coca-Cola, Bristol-Myers medicine, Penguin-Putnam books, American General life insurance, Subaru automobiles, the United States Postal Service. Still, more than just the corporate world found Armstrong irresistible; Americans loved him, making his 2000 autobiography a bestseller and supporting his work in the fight against cancer. By 2002, Armstrong ranked fifth among the world's most appealing product-endorsing athletes.

Most people—especially advertisers eager to use his image—presented Armstrong as a strong-willed, hard-working hero, but a minority saw him, without evidence, as a cheater in a sport that rewards cheating. It is hard to preserve a sense of innocence in modern sports. For all of Armstrong's success—or maybe because of his success—accusations of illegal drug use dogged him. Though the cyclist had passed every drug test he was given, he admitted that "it's a war I will never win. Even if they found a foolproof test for everything, which I would love, these guys are always gonna come up with something. . . . I think if I pass all those tests, they're still gonna say, 'It's *something*—the seaweed, the chemotherapy.' "[6] Part of the suspicion stems from the numerous cases of doping that have been uncovered in the professional cycling community, which has one of the highest rates of illegal-drug use of any major sport. The assumption is that because Armstrong wins, he must be tainted. No one, the argument goes, can win without performance-enhancing drugs if everyone around him is doping. Ironically, even these ugly accusations became fodder for an advertisement, when Nike filmed the cyclist riding in the rain and then giving blood to tour doctors. "Everybody wants to know what I'm on," Armstrong said in a voiceover. "I'm on my bike, busting my ass six hours a day. What are *you* on?"[7]

Some scholars, and more than a few television commentators, have argued that modern sports have been spoiled by exactly the same phenomena that made Armstrong a household name: the overwhelming need to win and the way sports and sporting heroes have been recreated as consumer products to be bought and sold. "There's a monetary value placed on heroism," claimed Olympic swimmer Mark Spitz. "You show me a hero in America today, and I'll show you a millionaire."[8] In this view, whatever was once "pure" about sports is now gone. This may be true, and this book will take a close look at the impact of consumerism on postwar sports. Yet Armstrong's story resonates in American culture despite the hype and the product placement, and his triumphs are about more than claiming multiple victories at the Tour de France. Sports remains a place where transcendent moments are possible, and this book will explore the ambiguities that arise when commerce and heroism meet.

1. Sports, the American Way

Nineteen forty-one was a difficult year. Though the United States was not yet at war, newsreels, the radio, and newspapers bombarded the American public with news of Germany's attack on the Soviet Union and the constant bombing of Great Britain. At home, the Great Depression had eased, but many Americans continued to struggle financially. Yet the catchphrase of the summer of 1941 had nothing to do with either war or the economy. Instead, the question—asked at local bars and hair salons, at the country club and the parish church, by schoolkids, old men in the streets, even young mothers pushing strollers—was "did Joe get a hit today?" For more than two months of the hot, hard summer of 1941, from May 15 to July 17, New York Yankee center fielder Joe DiMaggio got at least one base hit in each of the fifty-six games he played. DiMaggio's streak even inspired a hit song. The refrain of "Joe, Joe DiMaggio! We want you on our side!" neatly captured the hero status that "Joltin' Joe" had achieved.[1] Joe's achievements were part of a golden season on the baseball field. His midsummer hitting streak won DiMaggio Most Valuable Player honors, despite the fact that Boston Red Sox outfielder Ted Williams hit .406 for the season. Forty-one-year-old Lefty Grove earned his 300th career win. The Yankees won the World Series against the Brooklyn Dodgers in five games, their ninth championship in sixteen years.

The star-studded 1941 baseball season would be the last hurrah for top-level play until after World War II. When the Japanese bombed Pearl Harbor on December 7, 1941, Detroit Tiger star Hank Greenberg was the first major league player to enlist, on December 9. Like hundreds of thousands of other young men in the months following the attack, he saw it as his patriotic duty to defend the United States against the threat posed by the Axis powers. Greenberg, from a middle-class Orthodox Jewish family in New York City, was perhaps more politically aware than many ballplayers. Already a idol to many Jews because of the home-run power that helped earn him MVP honors for the 1940 season and for his unwillingness to listen to anti-Semitic slurs, by the late 1930s Greenberg had come to see his homeruns as political statements, arguing that "if, as a Jew, I hit a home run, I was hitting one against Hitler."[2] Bob Feller, Cleveland's emerging pitching star, said he was "outraged about Pearl Harbor and what Hitler was doing in Europe" and also enlisted immediately, joining the United States Navy and serving aboard the battleship *Alabama* in the Pacific.[3]

Other players followed Greenberg and Feller's lead after the 1942 season, with approximately sixty-five starters disappearing from major league rosters. In February 1943, for example, DiMaggio traded his $43,500 annual salary from the Yankees for the $50 a month earned by army enlisted men, while Williams joined the Marines. These enlistments, along with that of heavyweight boxing champ Joe Louis, made front-page news, part of a wartime propaganda effort that urged individual sacrifice for the larger good. Williams had won baseball's Triple Crown in 1942, leading the American League in batting average, homeruns, and runs batted in (.356, 36 homers, 137 RBIs). His enlistment was a professional sacrifice that could be easily measured and thus evocatively represented the unseen sacrifices of millions of American men. In exchanging baseball's baggy pants for a khaki Army uniform, sports stars such as DiMaggio and Williams also took the luster of their sporting success and buffed it into a shining symbol of American patriotism.

The real sacrifice of some major stars enhanced an existing association between playing sports and being a "good American." Greenberg, for example, reenlisted after his first tour of duty and eventually served in the military from 1941 to June 1945. He was sent to China to establish bases for B-29 bombers. Williams served three years during World War II then another two years during the Korean War. More than five hundred major league players spent time in the military, including thirty-two Hall of Famers. Just as the military and the American government benefited from the wartime service of famous sports stars, sports benefited from being so closely associated with the wartime effort. Games remained entertainment, but they were more than frivolity and fun.

These attitudes developed from late-nineteenth-century ideas about muscular Christianity, spread in particular by the Young Men's Christian Association and by President Theodore Roosevelt's claim that when young men "hit the line hard" in football, they then developed into powerful leaders, ready to conquer the world and rule it well. By the turn of the century, the notion that men expressed their vigor of mind and spirit through their bodies was commonplace. Bold and decisive action—doing something daring—became a key marker of manhood. Postwar ideas about sports built upon these long-held attitudes. But rather than seeing sports primarily as a way to create good Christians or Anglo-Saxon leaders, by the early 1940s, many viewed sports as the perfect medium for creating good American citizens. Sportswriter John Tunis, who wrote more than a dozen sports-related children's books, believed that the way sports were played in different countries affected the development of democratic, fascist, and communist societies. Tunis compared the football huddle to the New England town meeting and baseball games to the working of democratic governments during crisis moments. Unlike the harsh discipline of sports programs in Nazi Germany, which Tunis contended had turned young men into compliant followers susceptible to Nazi doctrine, sports in the United States reflected all the positive values of the country—hard work, democracy, and the opportunity for individual advancement.

Like Tunis, many people came to believe that the ways that Americans played sports both reflected their culture and, ultimately, shaped it as well. In other words, DiMaggio's hitting streak may have been terrific entertainment during a difficult historical moment, but it also represented something great about the United States. Particularly because DiMaggio was the son of Italian immigrants, his baseball abilities stood as an illustration of the American melting pot and the great American myth that hard work and talent led to success.

The idea that sports was integral to the "American Way" had both radical and conservative implications in the decades after the war.

Sometimes the "American Way" was shorthand for the philosophical values of equality, democracy, and tolerance, all of which had far-reaching consequences for social justice and social change. In this context, the most commonly used sports metaphors were fair play and a level playing field. African Americans used these ideas to question whether the United States could be a democratic and equal country if blacks were barred from major league baseball. If sports truly represented all that was best about American society, then African American athletes deserved the right to compete fairly; they deserved an equal opportunity in sports, and by extension, in the rest of society. More often, however, the "American Way" of sports meant winning. Getting ahead and coming in first were part of the proof that the United States was the best country on earth. Despite its emphasis on the "all-American" nature of sports, this interpretation found easy association with the business side of sports. Winning cost money. In both cases, playing sports reinforced traditional gender norms, becoming the space in which boys learned how to be men.

This "all-American" vision of sports would also be sorely tested in the years immediately after World War II, especially by gambling and cheating scandals in college sports. Nevertheless, the rhetoric of sports as a great melting pot of American values held firm. Divided into four sections, this chapter looks at the developments and contradictions in sports after World War II. The first section explores the impact of war and its aftermath on the development of professional sports. Though every sport felt the strain of World War II, they all grew bigger, more popular, more commercial, and more professional in the years immediately after the war. The second section looks at popular attitudes about the meaning of sports. If sports had been simply entertainment, they could never have become so central to American society. Instead, sportswriters, promoters, coaches, and even college presidents presented sports as physical representations of the "American Way." This widespread mind-set generally ignored, sometimes with difficulty, the trend toward a more commercial and professional sports, preferring to celebrate the amateur athlete as the best America had to offer.

The last two sections explore the interactions between these concurrent developments—sports as a booming entertainment industry and sports as the maker of men and an example of all that was best in America. The third section of the chapter examines the radical implications of seeing sports as a bastion of fair play and a symbol of the American melting pot. Jackie Robinson's appearance in a Brooklyn Dodger uniform in 1947 reverberated far beyond the ball field and signaled the beginning of a slow dismantling of Jim Crow attitudes and laws in American society. The fourth section explores what happened when the image of sports as character building collided with win-at-all-costs elements of the "American Way." Could collegiate sports build character and be major revenue producers at the same time?

THE DEVELOPMENT OF PROFESSIONAL SPORTS

Just five weeks after the Japanese attack on Pearl Harbor, President Franklin Roosevelt wrote what has come to be called the "green light letter" to baseball commissioner Kenesaw Mountain Landis. Landis had asked whether major league baseball should shut down for the duration of the war. In response, while noting that the final decision rested with the owners who ran the game, Roosevelt encouraged owners to continue because he felt the game was "thoroughly worthwhile" and that "it would be best for the country to keep baseball going," both as a morale booster and for its entertainment value.[4] The president, undoubtedly busy with a two-front war, also took time to suggest that baseball hold more night games to ensure that defense workers would be able to attend. Roosevelt's letter guaranteed that America's national pastime would continue for the duration, with owners carefully deflecting any criticism by presenting the game as a key element in homefront patriotism. Games were postponed for D day, the Allied invasion of Normandy on June 6, 1944, and for the death of President Roosevelt on April 12, 1945. Indeed, without star ballplayers, making baseball an appealing consumer product required the trappings of patriotism. Teams held special games to raise money for war bonds and armed-service relief funds, featured military bands and marching soldiers as part of the pregame entertainment, and wore special uniforms and printed special programs in an effort to draw fans to the ballpark. And by the end of the war, it was accepted practice to perform the national anthem before every game. For fans, paying to see a game held the promise of both entertainment and a show of patriotism.

In his 1942 letter, Roosevelt admitted that the loss of players might lower the game's quality, but he was optimistic that this would not dampen the sports' popularity. All those patriotic rituals proved critical to maintaining baseball as an entertainment product since the level of on-field play plummeted during each of the war years. Despite the game's connection with the war effort, attendance at baseball games dropped significantly. Clubs averaged just under 7,500 fans per game from 1941 to 1945. In part, this was because too many fans were on active duty or working long hours in defense plants or juggling several jobs to take advantage of a booming economy after so many years of hard times. But the quality of play discouraged many fans. As more and more baseball players were called up to serve, team owners turned to increasingly inferior replacements to keep the national game going. These replacements ultimately included players such as Joe Nuxhall, a fifteen-year-old pitcher signed in 1944 by the Cincinnati Reds, and Pete Gray, a one-armed outfielder who played seventy-seven games in the 1945 season with the St. Louis Browns. But despite the severe manpower shortage, the substitutes did not include African Americans, even though Negro League greats such as Satchel Paige and Josh Gibson were available. Stadiums dropped rules segregating fans by race, but Major League Baseball resisted integration on the field. In 1944, the Browns, traditional doormat of the American League, won their only pennant with a roster full of players classified 4-F. The level of play had sunk so low by the end of the war that one writer said that he couldn't imagine either the Detroit Tigers or the Chicago Cubs winning a single 1945 World Series game. Of course, Detroit and Chicago were the two teams playing in the Series.

With so many athletes serving their country, other professional and college sports also struggled during war. In professional football, the Pittsburgh Steelers and Philadelphia Eagles combined their struggling franchises in 1943 to create what fans called the Steagles. The Brooklyn, New York, and Boston franchises similarly merged in 1945 to be called the Yanks. Franchises lacked players because, by 1943, 376 NFL players were on active duty in the service. Team rosters were cut from thirty-three to twenty-eight per game. And the Cleveland Rams disbanded for the 1943 season because the team's two owners were in the military. In college football, 190 small colleges gave up football for the duration of the war, and major university teams saw their schedules severely curtailed and their rosters diminished by military enlistments. In one patriotic example, thirty-one players took the oath of enlistment into the Naval Air Corps at halftime of the 1942 Cotton Bowl. Like many other traditional rivalries across the country, the annual "Big Game" between the University of California and Stanford University was cancelled from 1943 through 1945 because of Stanford's difficulties in fielding a team. In college basketball, travel restrictions and military call-ups also played havoc on teams. The University of Utah Utes, who won the 1944 NCAA tournament, did not even have a regular season gym in which to play. Their conference had suspended play and the Army had taken over the Utah field house. Most of the Utes' eighteen victories came against service teams in church gyms. No golf tournaments were held in 1943, while both the Masters and the U.S. Open were cancelled in 1944 and 1945. And the baseball record book was not published in 1944 because of a nationwide paper shortage.

There was one notable exception to the personnel struggles that vexed college and professional sports. The All-American Girls Professional Baseball League (AAGPBL), started by Chicago Cubs owner Philip Wrigley in 1943, enjoyed abundant talent during its eleven years in existence. The baseball owner and chewing-gum mogul knew that women's sports could draw a crowd. Women's softball had been a proven moneymaker during the Great Depression, especially in the Midwest, with as many as 30,000 fans attending championship games at Wrigley Field in Chicago. League directors tried to hire famous managers, including retired Hall of Famer Jimmie Foxx, to pull more fans to the ballpark. Four midsized cities near Chicago hosted teams in the first year: the Racine Belles, South Bend Blue Sox, Kenosha Comets, and Rockford Peaches. Two more teams were added in 1944, and the league grew to eight teams—all in the Midwest—by 1946. Racine won the league's first championship, with Gladys "Terrie" Davis taking the first batting title with a .332 average. The league was evenly balanced and almost every team eventually won a championship, with the Kalamazoo Lassies taking the final title in 1954.

Women's baseball proved immediately popular, drawing an average of 2,000 to 3,000 spectators per game, with an estimated 10,000 at a Fourth of July doubleheader in South Bend, Indiana in 1946. The teams were the main summertime sports entertainment in their Midwestern locales because minor league baseball was nearly shut down by the high number of military call-ups of its players. The idea of female ballplayers was more accepted during the war since 5 million women joined the labor market between 1941 and 1944, with 19.5 million women earning wages in 1945. Female factory workers assembled guns and built tanks, making good money and upending traditional ideas about what constituted women's work. Ballplayers earned between $45 and $85 per week for the 108-game season that ran from May through September. The demands of war production allowed women new freedoms outside the home, and the AAGPBL took advantage. And like major league baseball, the women's league presented itself as a form of patriotism, labeling its players the girls next door, the kind of women that soldiers dreamed about when they were far from home. Before every game, the teams assembled down the first and third base lines to form a "V for victory" salute for the war effort followed by the national anthem.

The league started as fast-pitch softball with some modifications, including allowing runners to lead off first base and a larger playing field. Then, gradually, the ball grew smaller and overhand pitching started in 1947. In addition to slightly different rules and a larger ball than the men's game, there were other differences in the All-American Girls Professional Baseball League. League officials "wanted the girls to conduct themselves as ladies at all times, but to play like men," according to Helen "Gig" Smith of the Grand Rapid Chicks. And Wrigley himself insisted "that the women would have to look like women and act like women."[5] To protect feminine virtue during road trips, each team included a chaperone in addition to the manager and fifteen players. Women might enter a traditionally male sphere to play ball, but league officials presumed they needed to be watched over while on the road, an assumption that would have been ridiculed if anyone had suggested chaperoning the New York Yankees when they visited Boston. AAGPBL players were also required to maintain a high level of feminine behavior. Every player attended evening charm-school classes, where they learned proper etiquette and personal hygiene. And in addition to uniforms, gloves, and bats, each woman received a beauty kit as part of her equipment. Because playing baseball challenged traditional notions of femininity, how players looked and behaved off the field mattered. Despite these limitations, AAGPBL players took pride in their abilities and the high level of competition. Many mourned when the league failed in 1954, doomed by competition from television and other sports as well as a reassertion of traditional gender roles for men and women.

When the war ended, fans flocked back to ballparks and stadiums. Fittingly, Hank Greenberg was the first major leaguer to return from the war and play in a game, on July 1, 1945. Despite missing more than four years, Greenberg hit a home run in his first game back. Thanks to the off-the-field military efforts of men such as Greenberg and the owners' wartime patriotic appeals, major league baseball had survived the years of World War II with its reputation as the American national game enhanced, even if attendance had dropped. With major stars returning from the service, fans proved eager to be entertained, to once again appreciate the on-the-field talents of great players. Between 1945 and 1949, attendance at ballparks more than doubled, jumping to an average of almost 16,000 fans per game in 1950. Going to a game represented a return to normal and a vindication of what the United States had fought for during the war. It also helped that baseball enjoyed a virtual monopoly on professional team sports. Neither professional football nor basketball had a national reputation at the end of the war, overshadowed by baseball, horse racing, and boxing on the professional level and intercollegiate football and basketball on the amateur level. The great horse Citation, who won the 1948 Triple Crown, garnered more publicity than any pro basketball player; Sugar Ray Robinson, the terrific middleweight boxer, earned more headlines in New York City than the NFL's New York Giants. But baseball was king, and the seasons immediately following World War II offered spectators both impressive individual performances and spine-tingling pennant races.

Ted Williams returned from the service to win the MVP award in 1946, and his sterling performance helped the Boston Red Sox easily win the American League pennant. St. Louis Cardinal outfielder Stan Musial, who had emerged as a superstar during the 1943 and 1944 seasons before serving in the Navy during 1945, answered the critics who claimed his statistics had been inflated by inferior competition by leading the National League with a .365 average. The Cardinals won the National League pennant, their fourth in Musial's four full seasons, and went on to beat Boston in the World Series. Though the Red Sox won the American League pennant in 1946, prewar order was restored the following year when the New York Yankees were again World Champions. The Yankees won titles in 1947, 1949, 1950, and 1951, though the biggest story in New York City during the late 1940s was the emergence of Brooklyn Dodger Jackie Robinson as a league star and fan favorite.

In one of the game's most extraordinary seasons, the Boston Red Sox, New York Yankees, and Cleveland Indians battled until the final day of the 1948 season for the American League pennant, with American League MVP Lou Boudreau leading the Indians to the pennant. Musial won his third National League MVP but missed winning the Triple Crown by one homer, batting .376, with 131 RBIs and 39 homeruns. DiMaggio, despite battling injuries, led the American League in home runs with 39 and RBIs with 155. The Indians then beat the Boston Braves in the World Series. Nevertheless, attendance at the park gradually leveled off after 1950 and did not catch up to the average of the immediate postwar years until the 1990s. In the early 1950s, attendance dropped from high of 20.9 million total fans in 1948 to 14.3 million in 1953. Baseball remained the most visible game in town but other attractions, especially the new medium of television, increasingly cut into its audience.

Major League Baseball was a lucrative business for owners, although, legally, baseball remained a game, not a business. A 1922 Supreme

Court decision held that professional baseball was "still sport, [and] not trade," and was thus exempt from federal laws regulating interstate commerce.[6] This decision allowed baseball to maintain what was called the reserve system, which bound players to the teams which signed them for the duration of the players' careers. Though a player's contract might run for only one year, his team reserved the right to sign him for the following year or trade him to another team. The 1922 decision was tested several times after World War II, including a 1946 suit brought by Danny Gardella, who had been banned for playing in the Mexican Leagues while he was owned by the New York Giants. Every legal challenge failed or, like Gardella's, was settled out of court by the league, meaning that the owners maintained almost total control and could keep players' salaries low even as their own profits increased.

Some of the profits came from broadcasting. Every team had a radio contract, made possible by a 1938 legal decision that held that sports teams owned the exclusive "rights" to their games and could sell them to broadcasting companies. And as early as 1946, New York Yankee owner Larry McPhail sold the rights to Yankee games to DuMont Television Corporation for $75,000, making the initial foray into what would prove to be a huge moneymaker for owners. Smaller market teams were unable to command similar prices with either radio or television, meaning that the development of broadcasting rights helped big-market teams such as the Yankees dominate the game both on the field and in off-the-field publicity. Indeed, a New York City team won every World Series between 1949 and 1956.

Major League Baseball was highly centralized, with clearly kept records, organized seasons, stable teams—no team had changed cities since 1903—and widespread press coverage on a both local and national level. The same could not be said for either professional basketball or football in the years immediately after the war. Professional football was only several years removed from semiprofessional status when World War II came to an end. The league began as the American Professional Football Association in 1920 (it was renamed the National Football League in 1922). The league started with the majority of its teams in smaller Midwestern cities, including the Akron Pros, Canton Bulldogs, Green Bay Packers, and Decatur Staleys, and was considered a working-class sport. The Staleys moved to Chicago under the new ownership of George Halas and became the Bears. The Bears helped to stabilize the entire league when, in 1925, they signed University of Illinois superstar halfback Red Grange to a professional contract. Widespread press coverage of Grange's every move, combined with the

Bears' East Coast tour, brought much-needed publicity to the league and a certain level of respectability.

Still, though there were a few stable franchises, including the Bears, the Packers, the New York Giants, and the Chicago Cardinals (now the Arizona Cardinals), many franchises came and went in the league's first twenty-five years. The league instituted a college draft in 1935, but the first player drafted, Heisman Trophy winner Jay Berwanger, never played in the NFL. And it was not until 1936 that teams played the same number of games per season. Still, players such as Washington Redskin quarterback Sammy Baugh and Packer end Don Hutson gradually helped to transform the pro game into exciting entertainment for fans. When Hutson and Baugh first entered the NFL, pro football was a game heavily oriented to the run, with teams using the forward pass only in desperation or on special surprise plays. When Hutson retired in 1945 after catching a then astounding 488 passes in his career, the forward pass had become a major part of every NFL's team offense.

The stellar play of players such as Hutson, Baugh, and Philadelphia Eagle Steve Van Buren helped the league survive the war years with continued fan interest. By the end of 1945, the league appeared to be on the verge of financial success despite the need to combine some teams during the war. This encouraged the rise of a rival league in 1945, the All America Football Conference (AAFC). The AAFC challenged NFL teams in three cities but also brought franchises to cities that had never hosted professional football, including Miami, San Francisco, and Los Angeles. AAFC began with eight teams, including the Cleveland Browns, who won the league championship for four consecutive years. The Browns had replaced the NFL's Rams in Cleveland. The Rams had moved to Los Angeles, even though the team's closest competitor was more than 2,000 miles away. With only one game per week, football teams could be located in cities over a broad geographical distance, particularly with the development of transcontinental air service in the years immediately following the war. Both leagues wanted to claim the possible profits of the rapidly growing West Coast city. The Rams, San Francisco 49ers, and Los Angeles Dons became the first West Coast–based major-league sports franchises in the United States. The AAFC lasted just four seasons, but its three most successful teams, the San Francisco 49ers, Baltimore Colts, and the Cleveland Browns—averaging 57,00 fans per game—joined the NFL.

The Browns, under the direction of coach Paul Brown, continued their winning ways, taking the NFL championship in their first year in the league. The Browns faced a significant rival in the Los Angeles

Rams. The Rams became the dominant offensive team in the league, with hometown star Bob Waterfield, who had starred at UCLA, and Norm Van Brocklin at quarterback, along with receiver Elroy "Crazy Legs" Hirsch and running backs "Deacon" Dan Towler and Tank Younger, who were among the first African American players to integrate the league. Behind their stars, the Rams won a division title in 1949 and Western Conference championships in 1950 and 1951. New talent emerged as more college stars decided to sign with the NFL. Three-time college all-American Doak Walker led the league in scoring in 1950, his rookie season. Walker's abilities helped to carry the Detroit Lions to back-to-back championships in 1952 and 1953. By 1952, the NFL was fairly stable: total attendance reached 2 million, and franchises found widespread local support. With teams in major cities on both coasts and a powerful, centralized league office under the direction of Commissioner Bert Bell, the NFL edged ever closer to big-league commercial success in the early 1950s. Still, as late as 1956, *Sports Illustrated* offered its readers fifty-five feature stories on baseball and fewer than five on professional football. Baseball remained unchallenged as America's game.

Professional basketball was even more "minor league" than the NFL. While professional basketball has been played in the United States since 1896, with the first professional league in 1898, the roots of the current professional game grew out of the Midwestern Basketball Conference (MBC), founded in 1935. Early professional basketball was an unstable proposition, with the best teams forced to barnstorm in order to survive. Three great teams, the Boston Celtics, the Harlem Rens, and the Philadelphia Sphas (which stood for the South Philadelphia Hebrew Association), dominated competition in the 1920s and early 1930s, but for the most part, professional and semiprofessional basketball teams enjoyed regional, not national, fame, and played an important part in the leisure activities of urban, ethnic communities. Teams such as the Irish Brooklyn Visitations and Polish Detroit Pulaskis were community institutions, and most pro players were from ethnic and racial minorities—Irish, Jewish, African American, Polish.

The MBC, which changed its name to the National Basketball League (NBL) in 1937, was the first successful and sustained professional league. The league survived during the war despite the loss of many players to the military, and the Fort Wayne Zollner Pistons, started in 1939, emerged as the class team of the league. Because the Pistons were a company team, players held jobs in the plant doing defense work and were thus exempt from military service. At the end of the war, the league expanded from eight to twelve teams and attracted a large number of college stars, especially from the Midwest and West, as new players. The 1947–48 season was the high mark for the NBL. Its players were college stars with wide name recognition and the league had six strong franchises in Minneapolis, Fort Wayne, Indiana, Rochester and Syracuse, New York, and Oshkosh and Sheboygan, Wisconsin. However, the league's Midwestern, midsized-city roots left it little room for growth, and it faced a new and dangerous rival in the Basketball Association of America (BAA).

The BAA had been started in 1947 by big-city arena owners who wanted to fill seats and turn a profit when hockey teams were not playing. Madison Square Garden owner Ned Irish and Walter Brown, who owned the Boston Garden, needed entertainment to fill open dates. All the teams in the fledging league were on the East Coast and in major Midwestern cities, all much bigger than the cities represented by NBL teams. One mark of the difference between the competing leagues was that every team in the BAA represented a city, rather than a company or a businessman. Eleven teams, including the New York Knicks, Boston Celtics, and Philadelphia Warriors, competed in the first year, which proved a financial disaster for the league. While the Knicks' debut in Madison Square Garden attracted 17,205 spectators for the first professional basketball game in the Garden since 1929, average league attendance hovered at about 3,000 fans per game. Four teams, in Toronto, Cleveland, Detroit, and Pittsburgh, dropped out after the 1947 season. The second season, with eight teams, including the new Baltimore Bullets, proved not much better financially. In addition, several teams struggled in arenas aimed primarily at more profitable hockey teams. The court was often slippery because of the ice underneath, and the arena was cold and sometimes foggy.

One clear example of the small-time nature of professional basketball was the decision of the 1946 college player of year, seven-footer Bob Kurland, to forego both leagues and instead take a job with the Phillips Petroleum Company and play for the company's Amateur Athletic Union (AAU) team. Kurland had outdueled George Mikan in college, but it was Mikan who became pro basketball's first superstar big man, turning the Minneapolis Lakers into perennial contenders. When the original barnstorming Boston Celtics joined the Basketball Association of America, baseball and hockey were all that mattered in Boston. The Celtics lost their opening game on the road to the Providence Steamrollers, but they need not have worried about negative publicity since the *Boston Globe* buried the story under an account of local high school football. The other Boston newspaper did not even mention the Celtics during the BAA's first two seasons. Smaller cities—with less competition for fans—proved more receptive to professional basketball. The Rochester Royals, who won NBL championships in 1945–46 and 1946–47, enjoyed sold-out crowds and prominent newspaper coverage in their hometown.

Despite its popularity, the NBL could not survive against the larger markets of the BAA. Several team owners in the NBL were eager to join the newer league: Indianapolis Kautskys owner Fred Kautsky ran a large grocery store, while the Fort Wayne Zollner Pistons were run by the owner of largest piston company in the United States. Both businessmen preferred that their teams play opponents from New York and Boston, where there were excellent advertising opportunities, rather than smaller venues such as Oshkosh, Wisconsin, or Akron, Ohio. As a result, in 1949, ten teams from the BAA and seven from NBL merged to became the National Basketball Association (NBA). The league's decision to give the home team the entire gate receipts helped to doom smaller-city teams, and the NBA underwent a serious winnowing process in its early years, from the seventeen teams in 1949 down to just eight by 1954: the Knicks, Celtics, Philadelphia Warriors, Minneapolis Lakers, Milwaukee Hawks, Syracuse Nationals, Rochester Royals, and Detroit Pistons. Basketball's maturation as a sport played by professionals demanded the development of a centralized league monopoly, a commitment to the marketplace and commerce, and franchises in large cities.

Although the development of the NBA meant that basketball had a stable professional existence, it was not yet in "the big leagues" in terms of fan popularity and newspaper coverage. The New York Knicks could often only play eighteen home games per season at Madison Square Garden because college basketball was a bigger draw and Ned Irish was reluctant to settle for the smaller crowds that the Knicks would attract. The NBA remained much less popular than the college game until the late 1950s, in part because in the late 1940s and early 1950s, pro basketball was a rough, sometimes violent game marked by offensive stalling, frequent player brawls, and endless fouls. "You've got to give it right back to them with a basket or a punch," Mikan explained about opposing players, "or they'll pound you right out of the league."[7] In a 1949 game between Boston and New York, referees called one hundred fouls and broke up three fistfights. Most players continue to shoot two-handed set shots and, though jump shooters were emerging, slam dunks remained rare. Marginal players made about $4,000 per year in 1950, journeymen between $5,000 and $7,000, and only eight stars earned five figures, with the highest salary at $17,500.

While radio play-by-play coverage of games was common, professional basketball rarely appeared on television. The NBA signed its first small TV contract in 1953. Because there was no shot clock, lesser teams could hold the ball for long periods, preventing the better team from scoring, but making for a boring exhibition for fans. A 1951 game between the Fort Wayne Pistons and the league champion Minneapolis Lakers ended with a final score of 19–18, with Fort Wayne holding the ball for up to three minutes at a time. This did not make for good television. A 1954 change in the rules about fouling and the implementation of a twenty-four second shotclock remade the game and encouraged greater fan interest. For the 1954–55 season, scoring jumped from an average of 79.5 points per game to 93.1. These changes in the NBA, along with its focus on professionalism, filling arenas in major cities, and building a name-brand product on a national level, represented progress for the game. There was more money, more college stars joining the league, more coverage. There was even a television contract. But the changes of the postwar period came at a cost. Smaller towns and ethnic communities that had closely followed teams made up of local players lost the opportunity to compete within a formal professional league structure.

THE MEANING OF SPORTS: DEMOCRACY, MASCULINITY, AND THE MELTING POT

John Tunis wrote ten children's books between 1938 and 1946, tackling subjects such as racism, ethnic prejudice, and anti-Semitism within the context of sports. In *All-American*, published in 1942, one high school ballplayer explains to a teammate that "calling names like peasants and clunks and all that is no good. It's no good in the United States. There aren't any peasants in this nation. There are just citizens, one as good as another and no better than the others, you and Goldman and Keith and all the rest of you."[8] The playing field, with its emphasis on teamwork, taught the lessons of pluralistic democracy, in other words, and sticking up for a teammate required that players ignore differences in class, race, and ethnicity. Tunis's somewhat idealistic idea about possibility of teaching social justice through sport also argued that true democracy in sports required the inclusion of African American athletes. (Equal opportunity did not extend, however, to women, who generally were cheerleaders, girlfriends, or mothers in children's sports novels.) Fitting in, getting along, being a good teammate—these ideas formed the backbone of thousands of books and stories for boys in the 1940s and 1950s. The team was the central unit of adolescent life. Whether written by Tunis or Clair Bee, who wrote twenty-three Chip Hilton novels in the 1940s and 1950s, or the writers who reported on sports for such magazines as *Collier's* and the *Saturday Evening Post*, the overwhelming message was that sports demanded and developed character while helping Americans of different backgrounds find common ground.

After World War II, many Americans continued to believe that sports was a melting pot that provided the children of immigrants and working-class families great opportunities for success. Some teams proved the perfect embodiment of this ideal. The 1948 Olympic weightlifting team, which took four of the six gold medals in the weightlifting events, included athletes from seventeen different nationalities, "men who were brown, white, yellow, and black, men who represented many of the popular religions in the world today. Jewish, Catholic and all the branches of the Protestant churches."[9] One of its members was Tommy Kono, a Japanese-American from California whose family had spent the war in an internment camp, and who was perhaps the most successful American weightlifter of the late 1940s and 1950s. According to Bob Hoffman of the York Barbell Company, which supported and trained the team, the success of weightlifters such as Kono represented a "nation where every man has a square deal. Where all men are born equal, where every boy has the possibility of becoming president, of being a champion athlete, a great business success, doing as he likes to find his road to strength, health, happiness, and success."[10] Of course, Hoffman ignored the internment of Kono and his family during the war in order to celebrate the "square deal" that sports offered. To be a winner in sports was to be a winner in life. Like the message conveyed in children's books, Hoffman and others claimed that when men worked together on the field or in the weight room, they naturally learned American values. Games did more than just foster democracy, they taught it.

Certainly, just as in the late nineteenth and early twentieth centuries, sports remained an important cultural venue for many immigrants, serving as a public ritual of inclusion as well as a space in which minority groups could prove their worth to themselves and to a white, Anglo-Saxon majority. This was true for both ethnic groups and religious minorities and, especially after the integration of professional sports in the late 1940s and early 1950s, for African Americans as well. Jews rooted for Greenberg, Italians sent mounds of fan letters to DiMaggio, Poles thrilled to the exploits of Musial, whose Polish immigrant father worked in the Pennsylvania mines. Joe Louis, the great heavyweight boxing champion, was a 1930s icon of black masculine strength and ability. Poet Maya Angelou remembers her entire rural community gathering around the radio to listen to Louis fight, and when Louis beat a white man in the ring, it "proved that we were the strongest people in the world."[11] Angelou's Southern home town was not alone in this conviction, and massive celebrations broke out in African American neighborhoods whenever Louis won a fight.

Like ethnic ballplayers such as DiMaggio, who in the late 1930s was almost always described as an Italian star, Louis' image as an American hero solidified when he joined in the Army in 1942. Wartime calls for pluralistic patriotism—setting American tolerance in opposition to the horrors of German ideology about race—made casual ethnic slurs less acceptable and began the transformation of ethnic heroes into American heroes in the mainstream press. By the time he retired from the Yankees in 1952, DiMaggio was portrayed not as an Italian ballplayer but as a child of immigrants who found success through sports. He had been transformed into an assimilationist figure—the classic all-American superstar.

Though the mainstream press increasingly shifted its reporting focus away from questions of ethnicity or race, ethnic and racial communities continued to celebrate minority superstars as symbolic representations. Catholic newspapers routinely covered the exploits of all the major Catholic stars in both the professional and amateur ranks, and the University of Notre Dame football team became perhaps the most visible cultural representation of Catholic power in American society. The Fighting Irish had become a national powerhouse under Coach Knute Rockne in the early 1920s. An innovator on the field, Rockne created a more wide-open offense that enabled his teams to beat the traditional powers of the East. Off the field, he manipulated the media better than most, signing Babe Ruth's publicist, writing a syndicated column, and running annual summer football camps for adolescent boys eager to experience the Notre Dame magic. By 1927, 120,000 spectators crammed into Chicago's Soldier Field to watch Notre Dame play the University of Southern California. In those years, social critic Frederick Lewis Allen claimed that "more Americans could identify Knute Rockne as the Notre Dame coach than could tell who was the presiding officer of the United States Senate."[12] By the mid-1930s, Notre Dame had set a tone of masculine spirituality that pervaded the dreams of thousands of aspiring Catholic schoolboys.

The school's national reputation was enhanced by Hollywood in 1940, when Ronald Reagan and Pat O'Brien starred in *Knute Rockne—All American*, a fictionalized account of the coach and his team that forever gave American culture the phrase, "win one for the Gipper." Notre Dame's standing as a Catholic cultural icon in the immediate postwar period was not hurt by the fact that between 1946 and 1949 the football team did not lose a single game. For many American Catholics, the school's victories on the gridiron signaled the rise of Catholic influence in society.

Catholic attitudes pervaded football in other ways as well. In Chicago, the top Catholic-school football team and the top public-school team competed for city bragging rights in the annual "Prep Bowl." Vince Lombardi, who would become the well-known coach of the Green Bay Packers in the early 1960s, started his head coaching career at St. Cecelia's High School in Englewood, New Jersey. Lombardi became the Saints' head coach in 1942, and, after an opening loss that season, his teams went undefeated for the next four years. Catholicism and football were inseparable at St. Cecelia's when Lombardi coached there. Players suited up for their game on Sundays, then attended Mass and received communion. Afterward, the school's teaching sisters stood outside and handed out sacramentals—little red felt hearts that represented the sacred heart of Jesus—that players tucked into their jerseys or football pants. Then before the game, Lombardi gathered his players together to recite the Lord's Prayer. After games, if the team had won, they rode together to the Sisters of Charity Convent, where the nuns would file out and listen as the team sang the school song. Lombardi equated loss with sin, arguing that the idea of a good loss "was just a way to live with yourself. It's a way to live with defeat."[13] The attitude that losing was sinful sounds harsh, especially since every contest can have only one winner. However, Lombardi simply added a veneer of spiritual urgency to the prevailing idea that sports were the most effective way to teach boys the values and qualities that would make then good citizens—and good Catholics.

His ideas about the meaning of football combined a postwar emphasis on citizenship and teamwork with earlier beliefs that sports created strong bodies and thus strong Christian men. Lombardi believed that "football was a lesson in life." Young men would "get knocked down, but they had to drag themselves up and take another hit and do it right."[14] While football was a harsh and sometimes violent game, he argued that getting ahead in American society, especially as a member of a religious or ethnic minority, required a similar willingness to struggle and sacrifice physically and mentally. For Lombardi, and for thousands of high school and college coaches, the money and energy spent on sports could be justified because they taught young men self-discipline, obedience, self-awareness, and the meaning of hard work. And for working-class boys of every religious background, they could also prove an obvious way to better their social standing. Vince Promuto, who played professional football for the Washington Redskins in the late 1950s, was from the "Little Italy" of the Bronx, a tough neighborhood where "your social status was won with your fists."[15] His father ran a garbage-collection business, but Promuto's athletic abilities earned him a scholarship to Holy Cross University, making him the first person in his neighborhood to attend college.

In a fight against what came to be called "godless communism," the physical expression of religious belief was a potent weapon against forces that seemed to threaten American society. In this way, sports came to occupy a central role in the making of moral, upright, good American men. When sports fans rooted for stars based on their religious faith, or when coaches maintained that sports promoted a combination of faith and citizenship for players, they reflected what Will Herberg would call, in the mid-1950s, a "triple-melting-pot." In his 1955 essay, *Protestant, Catholic, Jew*, Herberg claimed that the three major American religions provided an important sense of group identity, so that religious identity had become "both genuinely American and a familiar principle of group identification." Religious belief, much like rooting for a sports team, expressed faith in "the American Way of Life."[16] When a Catholic schoolboy in New Jersey knelt to say the prayer of the rosary after a boxing victory in the local Catholic Youth Organization (CYO), or when a Southern football team knelt in prayer after the game, or when the yeshiva teams of Reuven Malder, the son of a Jewish scholar, and Danny Saunders, the son of a Hasidic rebbe, played baseball in their yarmulkes in Chaim Potok's *The Chosen*, each expressed the pluralistic nature of American society. To play sports was part of becoming an American man, whether Jew, Catholic, or Protestant.

AFRICAN AMERICANS AND THE DESEGREGATION OF SPORTS

This idea was true for African American men too, though segregation often kept them from playing on teams with white Americans before the war. The fight against the Nazis in World War II made overt expressions of American racism more suspect, and in sports, as in other areas of life, African Americans used wartime ideology and their own record of wartime service to agitate for integration. Prior to integration of team sports, of course, African Americans turned especially to track and boxing stars—Jesse Owens and Joe Louis, for example—but the symbolic importance of being part of a team made the fight for full integration of special importance.

Heavyweight boxer Louis was the great black star of the late 1930s and 1940s. When Louis beat James Braddock in 1937, he became the first black heavyweight champion since Jack Johnson, twenty-two years earlier. Before his 1938 rematch against German Max Schmeling, Louis even met with President Roosevelt, who allegedly told him "Joe, we need muscles like yours to beat Germany."[17] Adolph Hitler had proclaimed Schmeling a icon of Aryan supremacy, so both world leaders viewed the match through the lens of national identity. Of course, this conceit had long been commonplace. What was unusual was that a black man would serve as a representative of the entire United States. Louis had been knocked down and defeated by Schmeling in 1936, but this time over 70,000 watched as he flattened the German boxer in the first round. The fight lasted a mere 124 seconds.

Louis's fists signified America's international power in 1938, but the fighter also served as a compelling figure of African American achievement, encouraging a newfound assertiveness in the fight against inequality. His promoters carefully crafted the boxer's image to make him palatable to white audiences, presenting him as a humble family man who was a "credit to his race." For African American fans, however, Louis's raw power and his ability to knock out white opponents in the ring resonated as profoundly as his public image. Who could say that Louis was any man's inferior, at least in the ring? And if Louis could beat white men, then perhaps other African Americans were equal as well. He held the heavyweight title until 1949, defending his title so often that his opponents became known as the "bum of the month," so black fans had plenty of opportunities to celebrate.

Louis's public image only improved during the war. After donating the purses of two fights to the Naval and Army Relief Funds, Louis enlisted in the Army as a private in 1942. Used by the Army to promote patriotism, he never saw combat in his four years of service. Instead, he fought in staged exhibitions for the troops and went on morale-building tours. Louis was no dummy. Realizing that he could entertain white soldiers but that he and other black soldiers could not fight in integrated units, Louis also used his fame to agitate for equal treatment for black soldiers within the service. After the war, he returned to professional boxing in a rematch with Billy Conn, whom Louis had knocked out in 1941. When reporters asked him how he would handle Conn's quickness in the ring, Louis replied, "He can run but he can't hide."[18] Then he knocked out Conn in the eighth round.

As the heavyweight champion, Louis was a potent emblem of racial pride. But while he fought white boxers, the structure of his sport meant that he was never part of an integrated team. Because it is a solitary sport, an African American could be a boxing champion without upsetting traditional racial norms. In addition, boxing had many fans but was not America's national game. For all these reasons, the integration of baseball ranks as one of the most evocative developments in postwar racial relations. Some scholars have argued that Brooklyn Dodger Jackie Robinson is one of the most important figures in twentieth-century American history. This again points out the centrality of sports to American cultural ideals and also makes clear how important baseball was in the 1940s. As we have seen, MLB's efforts to wrap itself in patriotism during the war only increased the notion that this was America's game, a manifestation of all that was best about the United States. Long-standing cultural myths presented the game as fostering both social integration and democracy, a truism that immigrant boys such as DiMaggio seem to embody when they "made good" through their talent and dedication. Other professional sports would sign black players immediately after the war, but only Robinson's signing and first year attracted such national attention. Only Robinson—and perhaps young Larry Doby, who joined the Cleveland Indians in 1947—served as a physical representation of shifting racial attitudes and the triumph of American democracy and tolerance.

Common wisdom held that the game was open to anyone with talent, no matter their background. Putting aside that fact that *all* women were shut out of the game, baseball's color line mocked these ideas of equality within the game. One-armed Pete Gray could briefly roam the outfield for the St. Louis Browns, but African American players were forced to play in their own league for inferior pay and under inferior conditions. In a smaller sign of changing attitudes, MLB did sign almost forty Latin American ballplayers during the war. The look toward Cuba, Puerto Rico, and the Dominican Republic that started during World War II constituted the beginning of a trend, but, given the "black-and-white" nature of American race relations, the signings attracted little attention.

Black activists pushed hard for integration during the war. Wendell Smith of the Pittsburgh Courier pushed owners to let black ballplayers try out for teams. Sam Lacy, another of the most persistent voices advocating integration, broke color barriers of his own when he gained entrance to the Baseball Writers Association in 1948. Lacy was the first African American writer to be admitted. Negro League owners, who had an investment in maintaining the status quo, nevertheless proposed adding one all-black team to the majors, thus integrating the league if not individual teams. But the war itself and American wartime propaganda made the segregation of America's national pastime an increasingly uncomfortable irony. The language of the "American Way" could be radical in its implications, as Tunis understood. True democracy, whether on the field or in general society, demanded equal opportunity. For sports, and for the United States, to live up to its stated creed, African Americans would have to be included.

The first public hint that MLB might be changing its stance was in fact linked to the wartime service of African American soldiers. Happy Chandler, newly elected as the league's commissioner in 1945, told a reporter for the *Pittsburgh Courier* that if an African American "can make it on Okinawa and Guadalcanal, hell, he can make it in baseball." He added that "I don't believe in barring Negroes from baseball just because they are Negroes."[19] Chandler's remarks were far removed from those of the previous commissioner, Landis, who was adamantly opposed to black players in the major leagues and ruled the league with an iron fist.

Brooklyn Dodgers' president Branch Rickey had already decided to sign a black player when Chandler made his statement, partly because he believed it was right and partly because he saw it as an opportunity for profit on and off the field. For Rickey, the untapped black talent pool seemed to have the potential to make the Dodgers world champions. After scouting the Negro Leagues for what he called his "noble experiment," Rickey settled on Robinson, then the shortstop for the Kansas City Monarchs. Though Robinson was not the best player on his Negro League team, he had attended college, playing baseball, basketball, and football at UCLA. He had served as an officer in the army during the war and was a married man with what Rickey considered good religious values. In the patronizing language of the day, Robinson was a "credit to his race." These qualities, as much as Robinson's on-the-field abilities, made him Rickey's choice.

Rickey understood that Robinson would be scrutinized on and off field. He grilled Robinson so hard, trying to prepare him for the worst and most humiliating treatment, that Robinson found himself "chain gripping my fingers behind my back" to keep from responding. Rickey stipulated in Robinson's contract that the player could not fight back against his tormentors for two years. "I want a player with guts enough not to fight back," said Rickey.[20] This would not be easy for Robinson. A proud man, he was not someone who "knew his place" and non-chalantly accepted racial injustice. While in the Army, he had been brought before a court-martial for his refusal to step to the back of an Army bus.

Ironically, America's national pastime would start the process of integration in Canada. Robinson signed a minor-league contract with the Montreal Royals in 1946. Many fans jeered Robinson, particularly in Southern cities such as Louisville and Baltimore, and opposing play-ers taunted him with racial slurs from the dugout. Nevertheless, his performance on field was stellar, and he joined the Dodgers in 1947, the first black player to play major league baseball since Moses Fleet-wood Walker in 1889.

The twenty-eight-year-old Robinson's charismatic personality, out-standing play, and ability to turn the other cheek despite constant racial slurs made him a superstar, popular among both black and white fans. Sam Lacy recalled that fans would wait patiently after Dodger games for Robinson to appear. Some wanted autographs, other "simply wanted to touch him. It was as though [he] had suddenly been trans-formed into some kind of matinee idol." For black fans, he overshad-owed even Louis as the "savior" of the race. One sportswriter remem-bered the huge number of black fans who came to Robinson's games, eager to applaud his every move. "A tall middle-aged black man stood next me," he said, "a smile of almost painful joy on his face, beating his palms together so hard they must have hurt." In black communi-ties across the country, even in places where no major league teams played for thousands of miles, the universal question was: "How'd Jackie make out today?"[21]

Robinson made out pretty well. Despite the intense pressure of the season—he faced vicious verbal abuse from opposing dugouts, received regular death threats, and was hit by more pitches than any other player in the game—Robinson batted .297 and stole twenty-nine bases. At the end of the season, *Sporting News*, which had strenuously opposed integration, voted him baseball's first-ever "Rookie of the Year."

It is hard to underestimate the ultimate effect of Robinson's inclu-sion into the "national game." When a black man took the field with white teammates, rather than facing off against a white man in the ring or even running next to him in a race, the idea of integration suddenly seemed possible. Robinson was part of a team. As a second baseman, he was also one half of a double play combination with shortstop Pee Wee

Reese, a Southerner from Kentucky. Together, Robinson and Reese showed thousands of Americans a working model of racial integration. This is certainly the story Americans told themselves. Newspaper accounts viewed Jackie Robinson's 1947 integration of baseball as an example of the best American virtues of tolerance and democracy while attributing past and continuing discrimination against African Americans to "Southern values" antithetical to a national consensus. Rickey even earned comparisons to Abraham Lincoln for his decision to sign Robinson.[22] Robinson's stirring success on the field made it possible for Americans to ignore both past discrimination and ongoing racism within American society in general and baseball in particular.

The two owners who proved most aggressive in bringing black players to the majors were Rickey and Bill Veeck, the owner of the American League's Cleveland Indians. They were also the game's two most aggressive marketers, eager to find new angles to sell baseball to the public. For Rickey and Veeck, hiring black ballplayers, whether morally right or wrong, made good business sense. During Robinson's rookie year, African American fans at Ebbets Field in Brooklyn increased by 400 percent, part of the almost 2 million people who watched the Dodgers play that season, a new record. These swollen attendance rates justified Rickey's decision as sound. Other owners would spend the next decade trying to decide whether signing black players could result in more wins and thus increase attendance, or whether white audiences would fail to identify with the team and thus reduce attendance and revenues.

One side effect of Robinson's integration of the major leagues was the rapid destruction of the Negro Leagues. The league, always financially marginal, though hugely popular in black communities, could not compete once the major leagues began to recruit a few black players. In the year after Robinson signed with Dodgers, attendance at Newark Eagles games dropped from 120,000 to 57,000 for the season. The next year it was down to 35,000. The Negro National League folded in 1951, and the Negro American League survived with only six teams. By 1960, only the Indianapolis Clowns, where a young Hank Aaron got his start, were left from the many Negro League teams. The Clowns survived by becoming an entirely barnstorming unit, the Harlem Globetrotters of baseball.

Most black owners received no compensation for the players who went to majors. Rickey, for example, paid Kansas City Monarchs owners Tom Baird and J. L. Wilkinson nothing for the rights to Robinson, arguing that the Negro Leagues were closer to booking agencies than to leagues and so deserved nothing for players. He smartly realized that owners would not dare protest, at least not protest too loudly, because they would be accused of blocking the advancement of black players.

African American players trickled slowly into the major leagues. In 1948, three years after the Dodgers signed Robinson, there were only four African Americans in MLB: Robinson and Roy Campanella played for the Dodgers, Doby and Satchel Paige for the Indians. There were other Negro League stars, including Josh Gibson and James "Cool Papa" Bell, but MLB owners rejected them because of their ages or fears that these players would not be able to withstand the pressures of integration. It would be another ten years before all clubs had at least one black player.

Baseball earned most of the attention, but other professional sports also began to hire black players in the postwar era. In professional football, African Americans had played on NFL teams during the 1920s and early 1930s but were "unofficially" excluded from the league from 1934 to 1946. Desegregation came again in 1946, though the national public barely noticed. The Los Angeles Rams, under pressure from officials of the publicly owned Los Angeles Coliseum, signed Robinson's former UCLA teammate Kenny Washington and another former UCLA player, Woody Strode. Neither player saw much action in 1946. Washington had been an all-American halfback for his senior season in 1939, but the color line in the NFL held firm through the war, leaving Washington to coach part-time at UCLA and play semiprofessional ball in California. By the time he played for the Rams, Washington was seven years removed from college and had suffered several knee injuries. The blazing speed that had made him a college star was largely gone, but Washington nevertheless led the league in yards per carry in 1947 (7.4 yards) and scored the year's longest touchdown run, going ninety-two yards against the Chicago Cardinals. With the Rams unwilling to give him much playing time, Washington retired after the 1948 season.

Though the reintegration of professional football was largely lost amid the hoopla of Robinson's integration of the national game, the signing of Washington and the other black players did receive significant coverage in the black press. In the AAFC, the Cleveland Browns voluntarily signed fullback Marion Motley and tackle Bill Willis in 1946 and proved much more willing to integrate the players into regular team play. Motley in particular was vital to the Browns' success, averaging 8.23 yards per carry in 1946 and 5.7 yards over his eight seasons in the AAFC and the NFL. As with Washington, segregation forced

Motley to wait for his opportunity in professional football. He was twenty-six and working in a local steel mill when he earned a tryout for the Browns. Though their teammates were cordial, Motley and Willis faced constant racism and violence on the field. Opposing players would step on their hands and arms after a tackle or kick them in the groin during a pileup. Motley remembered that this abuse went on for several years, until their tormentors "found out what kind of players we were. They found out that while they were calling us, 'niggers,' I was running for touchdowns." In addition, since Motley started for the Browns on both offense and defense, where he played linebacker, he could promise his abusers that "if I don't get you now, I'll get you later."[23] Unlike Robinson, the nature of the game made it acceptable for Motley to hit back.

Motley, a bruising 6 foot 1 and 240 pounds, and Buddy Young, who stood only 5 foot 4 and relied on speed and quickness to succeed, were the top two African American stars in the AAFC. Motley earned 4,712 yards in his eight-year career with the Browns. Young joined the AAFC with six other African American players in 1947, and in the three years before the AAFC merged with the NFL, he rushed for 1,452 yards. The undersized but speedy Young prompted comedian Bob Hope to quip that "I'd heard of black magic. Now I've seen it."[24] In addition to his play as a halfback, Young specialized in exciting punt and kickoff returns, often dazzling crowds with his ability to elude tacklers in the open field. While Young could recount experiences like a trip to Baltimore where he was met by fans in blackface outside the locker room, he continually maintained that professional football helped African Americans conquer prejudice and encouraged white Americans to rise above bigotry. Nevertheless, Jim Crow laws often forced Young to stay in separate hotels during team trips to the South and Midwest.

Despite the on-the-field success of players such as Motley and Young, only twenty-six African Americans played in the NFL and AAFC between 1946 and the start of the 1950 season. Most, like Strode of the Rams, were token players who rarely played in games, were cut once the season started, or had only one-year careers. As in baseball, certain teams hired black players with much more frequency than others, especially the Browns and Rams, as well as the San Francisco 49ers and New York Giants. Football's racial pioneers never captured the national imagination. Unlike Robinson, they were rarely invoked as symbols of democracy and equality in action, except in the black press, which provided constant coverage of their exploits and made them racial heroes.

Professional basketball had the most fluid racial policies of the three major team sports. Although African American players were never well represented, they played sporadically throughout the 1940s in the NBL. Four players, including former Harlem Rens star William "Pop" Gates played at times during the 1946 season, but none returned for the 1947 season, perhaps because of Gates' on-court fight with a white player. Black basketball players were also well represented on the national stage by the all-black Harlem Globetrotters, who toured the country playing college all-star teams, local all-star squads, and even NBL teams. The Globetrotters, founded in 1926, were hugely successful after World War II. In 1948 and 1949, for example, they played, and beat, the defending NBL champion Minneapolis Lakers and their star big man, George Mikan. The 1949 victory came in front of an enthusiastic crowd of 21,866 at Chicago Stadium. In 1950, Globetrotter owner Abe Saperstein started a barnstorming tour called "the World Series of Basketball" in which his team played a series of games against the year's best college players. The Globetrotters finished the tour's first year with a 11–7 record against a college team that featured Bob Cousy, and the eighteen-game roadshow attracted an attendance total of 181,364.

Despite these clear indications that African American athletes could play against NBA-caliber players, the NBA was the last of the three leagues to integrate. In 1950, Walter Brown of the Boston Celtics drafted Duquesne University's Chuck Cooper in the second round of the draft, later stating that the team did not care "if he's striped, plaid, or polka dot! Boston takes Charles Cooper."[25] Buoyed by the Celtics decision, the Washington Capitols then drafted Earl Lloyd late in the same round and the New York Knicks signed Nat "Sweetwater" Clifton away from the Globetrotters later in the summer. Lloyd would be drafted into the army after only seven games with the Capitols, but Cooper averaged 9.5 points and 8.5 rebounds in his first season, and Clifton was a role player on a Knicks team that made the NBA finals. Like the racial pioneers in the NFL and MLB, Cooper and Clifton faced hostile crowd shouting racial epithets, prejudiced opponents, and biased officials, but the league integrated more quickly and smoothly than either football or baseball. Black players continued to be added to NBA rosters in steady numbers, usually as small forwards or shooting guards. Most of the first African Americans found their place on NBA teams as role players— there were no black point guards or overpowering offensive players around which a team was structured until the late 1950s.

The success of Robinson as well as other racial pioneers in professional football and basketball marked a significant change in sports after the war. A limited integration of African Americans had taken place in most professional team sports by the early 1950s—hockey would not have its first black player until Willie O'Rhee joined the Boston Bruins in 1958—and some college teams began to recruit more black athletes. Robinson was the most visible racial pioneer because major league baseball was far and away the most popular professional sport in the immediate postwar decades, but other black athletes faced similar challenges, both on and off the field (or the court). While the national press rightly celebrated the accomplishments of Robinson, they generally ignored that most teams refused to hire black athletes. Nor did the press examine the structural and individual racism that continued to pervade sports organizations, preventing true integration. Indeed, integration in sports in the late 1940s and 1950s was much like integration in the rest of society, happening "with all deliberate speed" and often facing "massive resistance." Nevertheless, the limited integration and professional opportunities afforded to black athletes was a very visible illustration of racial change in the United States. When Robinson won the Rookie of the Year award at the end of the 1947 season, his accomplishment signaled the start of a process that would revolutionize both sports and societal attitudes about the abilities of African Americans.

WHAT IS NORMAL? BOOSTER CAMPUSES AND CHEATING SCANDALS

Robinson, Motley, and Cooper stood as symbols of the promise of sport to fulfill what sociologist Gunnar Mydral called the promise of America, even as the players themselves faced racist taunts and sometimes violence. College sports programs, on the other hand, demonstrated many of the more conservative aspects of the association between sport and "the American Way." Universities accepted increasingly commercialized, win-at-all-costs programs, seeing them as a central part of campus life. At the same time, schools and the national media emphasized the "gee whiz" aspects of college sports, promoting campus sports heroes as the best of what the United States had to offer. Fear of communism at home and abroad intensified desires to prove the "normalcy" and stability of society through sports. An emerging Cold War attitude that linked homosexuality to communism also promoted the need for men and boys to participate in sports. Communism and homosexuality were both held to be about weakness, a tendency to succumb to secret enticements and threats. Playing sports was widely held to prevent both "problems" from emerging since it helped boys strengthen their natural toughness and, of course, moral fiber. This idea was critical to creating an illusion that all men in sports were heterosexual.

In college sports, the tension between sport as a major commercial enterprise and sports as a playing field to build citizenship and good moral character ran high, but most chose to ignore the ways that reality undermined ideals. On college campuses, returning soldiers and other students anxious to enjoy postwar stability turned to sporting events as reminders of what Americans had fought for and now deserved to enjoy. The roar of the crowd, tailgating parties at the big game, young men in football uniforms rather than army fatigues, all these promised a return to normal. Within this atmosphere, many colleges and universities—and the state legislatures that financed them— saw sports as a way to make a national name for themselves.

Traditional powerhouses in college football also adapted. As World War II came to a close, many schools, including Princeton University, Cornell University, Ohio State University, the University of Michigan, Texas A&M University, and the University of Wisconsin, announced plans to build new field houses and stadiums. The University of Michigan, for example, added 25,000 seats to its already massive stadium, while fellow Big Ten school Purdue almost quadrupled the size of its stadium. Smaller, urban colleges, especially Catholic schools, often could not afford to field a football team, but poured their money and resources into their basketball programs. The economics of basketball appealed to many athletic directors because the cost of fifteen scholarships was much less than the average of sixty for football teams, and more games could easily be added to the schedule. Other schools, especially Southern state schools, used military veterans to supply their athletic programs with a quick infusion of talent. And some schools developed new systems to make sure these programs had enough money to find and support the best talent.

The war helped to shape postwar college sports. In basketball, for example, men over six foot six were exempt from military service because they were too tall for standard issue uniforms, beds, and other military equipment. Military needs accelerated a trend away from small, quick teams dominated by guards and toward teams dominated by big men. Wartime restrictions on travel also made city arenas, not college gyms, the primary venue for college games. This development continued into the late 1940s, increasing media coverage and the game's popularity among noncollege fans. Military sports programs were equally central to postwar campus athletics. Some schools, including Michigan, Purdue, and Notre Dame, maintained strong football programs throughout the war because they housed officer-training programs for the armed forces. This was true at the service academies as well. Behind the running abilities of the "Touchdown Twins," Glenn Davis, known as "Mr. Outside," and Doc Blanchard, called "Mr. Inside," and the coaching of Red Blaik, West Point dominated college football in the war years. Instructed by his superiors to "to use the West Point football team . . . as an advertisement of the strength of the U.S. Army," Blaik recruited all-American players from other teams and set up a finishing academy for athletes who couldn't meet standards.[26] When West Point played the Naval Academy in the annual Army-Navy game in 1945, the two teams were ranked first and second in the nation. Army won, securing its second consecutive national title, while Blanchard became the first junior to be awarded the Heisman Trophy.

Each branch of the service also developed sports programs that had their own teams in an effort to foster group loyalties and leadership skills. Naval officers, for example, considered sport "controlled conflict" and an excellent simulation of war. The Navy's program fielded military football teams to compete against college teams, and many successful postwar college coaches came out of program. Many postwar stars in football and basketball also spent parts of the war playing sports—football's racial pioneer Buddy Young spent 1945 serving in the merchant marines, starring on the powerful Fleet City Merchant Marine football team in California and then was the MVP of the 1947 Rose Bowl for the University of Illinois.

Norm Van Brocklin, who would later star as quarterback for the Los Angeles Rams, enlisted in the U.S. Navy after high school in 1943. When he earned his discharge in 1946, Van Brocklin took advantage of the GI Bill of Rights to enroll at the University of Oregon, taking the Ducks to the Cotton Bowl in 1948. At many colleges, the GI Bill created an "athletic scholarship" system that was supported by the federal government. The GI Bill, signed into law by President Roosevelt in 1944 just a week after D day, gave war veterans an opportunity for higher education, providing $500 a semester for tuition and a $90 per month stipend for any veteran who served at least ninety days during the war. As a result, veterans flooded the campuses, doubling college registration in the 1940s and forcing schools to build temporary housing facilities.

Young and Van Brocklin's stories were repeated in multiple variations in schools across the country. Sports programs took quick advantage of this flood of mature students. The University of Maryland, for example, hired Paul "Bear" Bryant as their new football coach ten days before his discharge from the Navy. Bryant had been the coach of a very successful preflight football team during the war, and he encouraged his Navy veterans to play for his new college team. Seventeen players accepted Bryant's offer; they were discharged from the service on September 18, enrolled at the university the next day, and played in Maryland's opener on September 27. At the University of Oklahoma, Coach Bud Wilkinson's 1947 team totaled twenty-eight World War II veterans, including at least three Purple Heart winners. As at Maryland, university regents decided to encourage war veterans with football talent in the hope that Wilkinson could "produce some outstanding football teams in which the citizens of the state could take pride."[27]

Following the wartime lead of West Point, Maryland, Oklahoma, and other schools came to be known as "booster campuses," places where sports shaped the identity not just of students but of entire state populations. The University of Kentucky, already a national success in basketball under the direction of Adolph Rupp, also wanted to build a football team that would bring the school similar positive publicity. To this end, president H. L. Donovan added new student fees that were channeled to the athletic department, secured state bonds to expand the football stadium from 20,000 to 38,000 seats, and allowed coaches virtual autonomy in recruiting and retaining players. After promising alumni that he would spare no expense to hire the best football coach in the country, Donovan hired Bear Bryant away from the University of Maryland in 1946. Most significantly, he and the university trustees set up a booster foundation called the University of Kentucky Athletic Association (UKAA), a corporation separate from the university which was designed to funnel money into the sports programs. The creation of the UKAA meant that physical education and varsity sports had nothing in common at Kentucky, while confirming that athletics was business enterprise, with funds separate from university. By 1951, at least 113 football and basketball players were on athletic scholarships at the school, with dozens of walk-ons earning special deals.

Kentucky's approach—treating college sports as a business enterprise designed to boost the profile of the entire state—enjoyed great success on the field and the court. From 1944 to 1952, Rupp's basketball team won more than 90 percent of its games, including nine consecutive Southeastern Conference titles and three NCAA championships. Bryant's football squad went 60–23–5 over an eight-year period and was invited to four major bowl games in the same period, winning three of them. In an enormous upset in 1950, Bryant's no. 7 Kentucky team stunned the top-ranked Oklahoma Sooners in the Sugar Bowl. The defeat ended a thirty-one-game unbeaten streak for Oklahoma, indicating that the Sooners had been as successful as Kentucky in turning football into a veritable state industry. During Wilkinson's tenure as coach at Oklahoma, "football was overtly converted from one of many campus activities . . . to the state institution."[28] His teams won three national championship between 1948 and 1958 and lost only 9 of 117 games. At Maryland, a 1952 educational survey reported that the school ran a "virtual football factory," with 54 percent of all scholarship monies going to the football team. At many of these programs, top-dollar offers to the best recruits was commonplace.

For smaller, nonstate schools, basketball was generally the ticket for creating a national identity. St. Louis University, a Jesuit school that had educated the Catholic elite before the war, was typical of many urban schools, abandoning football as too expensive and investing instead in basketball. The school was helped tremendously by the growing media coverage of the game and by regularly playing Holy Cross College, where future NBA great Bob Cousy attracted considerable national attention and large crowds eager to see him play. Before the war, St. Louis had averaged only a few hundred spectators per game, but by the late 1940s, the Bilikens were a prime attraction in St. Louis, attracting more than 10,000 to every home game. The school's president admitted that "you could not purchase what basketball has done for this school."[29] It was a similar story at LaSalle University in Philadelphia, which won national titles in 1952 and 1954 behind all-American Tom Gola. LaSalle was aided by its participation in Philadelphia's "Big Five" competition. Together, Temple University, the University of Pennsylvania, Villanova University, St. Joseph's College, and LaSalle made the city a hotbed for basketball, with games so popular that radio stations sent announcers on the road with teams for the first time.

It was in New York City, with Madison Square Garden as the mecca, that college basketball reached its zenith of popularity. Under the direction of local promoter and later New York Knicks' owner Ned Irish, the Garden's National Invitational Tournament (NIT) became the sports' premier end-of-the-season championship tournament in the late 1930s. In addition to the NIT, Irish booked twenty-nine college programs into the Garden during the 1945–46 season, averaging crowds that reached 98 percent of capacity. In the following season, the Garden sold out for all but one of its twenty-one college games. The revenues from these games often supported the area's basketball programs and made some into national powerhouses. Nat Holman at City College (CCNY) and Clair Bee at Long Island University (LIU) became widely regarded as two of the country's top coaches. Bee's teams won 95 percent of their games between 1931 and 1951 and featured Player of the Year Sherman White in 1951. In 1950, Holman's Beavers became the first—and only—team to win both the NIT and the NCAA tournament in the same season. After the victories, the media lauded CCNY as a school that combined academic excellence with sporting prowess and a team that demonstrated how hard work and discipline could pay off.

Unfortunately, hard work was not the only aspect of college sports that paid off. The popularity of intercollegiate football and basketball meant that money—much of it from illegitimate sources—poured into both sports. Sports had long struggled to avoid the taint of gambling. The fix of the 1919 World Series by the Chicago White Sox remains the best-known example of players throwing games for money, but associations between players and gamblers is part of the history of sports. What began to change in the late 1940s was the amount of money changing hands and the number of people interested in placing a bet. The invention of the point spread in the mid-1940s made watching—and wagering on—poorly matched teams interesting, since viewers could now root for a team to win by enough points to cover the assigned line on the game. Gamblers bet an estimated $10 million a day on college basketball, and gambling and ticket scalping for the popular West Point–Notre Dame football game, traditionally held in New York's Yankee Stadium, was so widespread that the two schools decided to cancel the annual match-up in 1948.

The seediness of gambling and the wholesome amateur nature of college sports found themselves in sharp conflict by the time City College reigned as champ in 1950. Rumors about players who accepted money to shave points—winning by fewer points than the assigned spread—abounded. Bookies began to complain, since they lost money every time a game was fixed. And in 1951, the lid came off. Three players from the championship CCNY team, all-American Sherman White of LIU—just seventy-seven points from setting the collegiate scoring record—and several other New York City players were arrested for fixing games in the middle of the season. Suddenly, CCNY players no longer looked like role models who symbolized all that was good about American sports. They looked like cheaters.

Many coaches and most of the national press viewed the point-shaving scandal as a New York City problem, brought on by the easy access gamblers had to players, by the money that flowed in and out of Madison Square Garden, and by the bad influence of the big city. Kentucky coach Adolph Rupp, whose teams won national titles in 1948, 1949, and 1951, vowed that "gamblers couldn't get at my boys with 10-foot pole."[30] Despite Rupp's confident assertion, accusations of point shaving spread across college basketball, eventually touching several members of Rupp's own championship teams. Wildcats Ralph Beard and Alex Groza admitted to taking brides from gamblers throughout their careers, including accepting money to lose in the first round of the NIT tournament in 1949. Ultimately, thirty-five players stood accused of accepting a total of over $50,000 to fix games between 1947 and 1951.

Madison Square Garden and the NIT lost stature in college basketball as a result of the scandal, but little else changed. Kentucky canceled its 1952–53 season, but Rupp remained, unrepentant, as coach. Holman, coach at CCNY, similarly accepted none of the blame for the scandal. While he admitted that corrupt admission and recruiting practices might be part of the problem, Holman blamed his players' involvement in point shaving on "a relaxation of the morals in the country . . . boys at loose ends have brought this on."[31] College sport itself was not to blame.

Just as the basketball scandal was moving off the front page in August of 1951, new headlines proclaimed the revelation that West Point Academy cadets had broken the school's honor code by "cribbing"—cheating—on exams. Ninety cadets, including sixty varsity athletes and the coach's son—all-American quarterback Bob Blaik—were dismissed from the academy. As a new war raged in Korea and a pervasive anticommunist sentiment colored every issue on the home front, this seemed the worst of news. Young men who represented all that was decent and virtuous about their country had lacked the moral fiber to resist taking the easy way in a difficult time. Newspaper columnists and politicians used the episode to bemoan the lack of character in American youth and to worry that this episode, coming so closely on the heels of the point-shaving scandals in college basketball, represented a deleterious modification of what was called the American national character. The scandal hit doubly hard because not only was West Point the training grounds for future American military officers, but the Academy football team had become a major powerhouse during World War. II Between 1944 and 1950, Coach Red Blaik's teams compiled a 57-3-4 record and twice won the national title. According to every piece of common wisdom and the testimony of many of who knew them, the dismissed players represented the cream of American manhood. They were winners. Yet they had cheated.

How could this have happen? In part, the fault lay with Academy instructors, who every semester administered identical tests to cadets from two separate formations. The formations attended the same classes on alternate days, so that half the cadets knew they could always "crib" the answers for their upcoming exam. Of course, most cadets chose not to do this. At heart, the 1951 West Point cheating scandal is an example of the pervasiveness of a win-at-all-costs attitude. Named Coach of the Year in 1946, Blaik was a hard-nosed disciplinarian who emphasized rigorous conditioning, constant drilling, and long hours of film study in order to create the kind of precision execution that brought victory. Playing football at the Academy required dedication to the team more than to the school or its honor code. Indeed, several dismissed players argued that their play on the field had brought the Academy national glory and attention and that they should be allowed to attend under different rules. Blaik himself defended the thirty-seven football players dismissed following the scandal, claiming that the players were merely "scapegoats" who had taken the blame for an overly demanding honor system.

Though Blaik created a system that encouraged his players to see themselves as above the system or left them little time to fulfill their nonfootball obligations, he shared no part in the national condemnation that followed the revelations of cheating. Like Adolph Rupp and Nat Holman, Blaik stayed on as coach, as all the blame fell on the players and none on a coach who focused on solely winning. There were a few calls to abolish football at the service academics—perhaps highly competitive sports and military training were not so compatible after all—but Blaik's team rebounded from the dismissals after two poor seasons to again become a formidable team in the mid-1950s. Despite a litany of examples that collegiate sports exhibited a commercialized, win-at-all-costs mentality that cared little for lessons about democracy, the idea that sports turned young men into disciplined, moral American citizens remained persuasive to many Americans.

Coach Bud Wilkinson, who turned the Oklahoma Sooner football program into the country's top team in the 1950s, perhaps best reflects the tension between winning as the "American Way" and the language of character building. The NCAA placed Wilkinson's squad on probation twice in the decade for recruiting violations. These violations stemmed from the desire to create a dominant team for the state, something that Oklahomans deeply wanted. Wilkinson was also competing against coaches such as Bear Bryant, whose assistants regularly "left

$1,000 in $20 bills at the prospect's home."[32] Yet Wilkinson's newsletter to Sooner alumni never mentioned the violations or the punishments, focusing instead on his team's fighting spirit and willingness to work together. Even as he committed himself to doing whatever it took to win, Wilkinson presented the game a wholesome endeavor, as a space where only "dedicated men working together for a common objective" could find success.[33] And once they learned to win on the football field, Wilkinson promised, players would also find success in life because football fostered moral toughness and a competitive spirit. Cutting corners and bending the rules had nothing to do with Oklahoma's success.

2. An Athletic Cold War

*T*he revelations about cheating at West Point and point-shaving scandals in college basketball were only part of the sports news in 1951. The small-city Rochester Royals beat the New York Knicks to take the NBA title. The University of Tennessee Volunteers went undefeated and finished atop the college football polls. And for New Yorkers, especially for New York baseball fans, 1951 was a magical year. The Brooklyn Dodgers held a thirteen-and-a-half-game lead over the New York Giants in August, but, in an incredible stretch run, the Giants made up the difference and the season ended with the two teams tied. When the three-game playoff was decided by Bobby Thompson's famous "shot heard round the world" home run, the Giants had won the National League pennant and the right to face the Yankees in the World Series. Twenty-year-old Willie Mays and nineteen-year-old Mickey Mantle emerged as new stars that season, winning Rookie of the Year honors and sparking their respective teams to the World Series. Mays and Mantle proved just the latest addition to a city studded with baseball stars and bursting with great teams. New York City was the capital of baseball in the late 1940s and throughout most of the 1950s, with the Yankees appearing year after year in the World Series, often playing either the Dodgers or Giants. Fans of the Yankees, who won ten American League pennants between 1947 and 1958, could idolize Mantle, Yogi Berra, or Whitey Ford. For Brooklyn supporters, finally rewarded with a World Series title in 1955, Jackie Robinson, Duke Snider, and Preacher Roe were the heroes. And Mays, Alvin Dark, and Sal Maglie provided the thrills for Giant fans. There were other great players and other good teams, but New York's money—and its emergent status as the world's largest entertainment market—built dynasties and created intense rivalries among the city's five boroughs.

Mantle was perhaps the biggest superstar in a city that was bursting with talent. The Oklahoma-born and raised Mantle played one season alongside DiMaggio, until DiMaggio retired in 1952 and Mantle took his spot in center field. The brawny Mantle averaged thirty-four homers per year from 1952 to 1960, and won back-to-back MVP awards in 1956 and 1957. But Mays, once he returned from a two-year stint serving in the Korean War, was certainly Mantle's equal on the field. His superb homecoming in the 1954 season helped the Giants win the National League pennant and pull off a surprising sweep of the Cleveland Indians in the World Series. Mays had speed, power, and an infectious enthusiasm for the game. But Mantle captured the national imagination because of the swagger and style that backed up his playing abilities and because he was white. The country boy made good on the biggest of stages, Mantle embodied postwar American possibilities and American masculinity. Like Babe Ruth before him, sheer talent seemed to propel Mantle to the pinnacle of his profession, a sharp contrast to the corporate—or factory—environment in which many American men labored. Mantle's power, signified by his many tape-measure home runs and his tough, hard-charging lifestyle, also contributed to his idolization. In an increasingly middle-class society, Mantle stood out as someone who did not have to play by the standard rules or kowtow to corporate bureaucracy.

In the same year that Mays and Mantle broke into the majors and the basketball gambling scandal hit the front pages, sociologists David Riesman and Reuel Denney wrote an article entitled "Football in America." They argued that football, especially college football, stood as a cultural representation of the United States, reflecting American democratic notions of equality, the blurred line between work and play, and the sense that competition was a natural part of the social contract. At a time when the very public troubles of men's college sports led some commentators to question the values of all young Americans, Riesman and Denney held that college football epitomized the United States and its attitudes. Scholar Jacques Barzun disagreed, arguing in 1954 that "whoever wants to know the heart and mind of America had better learn baseball."[1] For good or bad, sports and the people who played them represented something about the character and ethos of the nation. Riesman, Denney, and Barzun were all writing about an issue that preoccupied intellectuals and popular commentators alike in the 1950s—defining the American self, making sense of the American national character. Riesman and Denney had made their reputations as scholars with the 1950 publication of *The Lonely Crowd: A Study of the Changing American Character*, a book whose themes resonated with many Americans. *The Lonely Crowd*, written for an academic audience, proved an enormous bestseller. Riesman argued that American men had become outer-directed, too focused on getting ahead financially to the detriment of an inner moral compass. Somehow the much-valued team players of the 1940s had morphed into get-along and get-ahead company men in the 1950s. Yet, even the most withering social critics continued to believe that sports were part of the solution rather than part of the problem.

This is why sports is always more than statistics, more than winning a pennant or following a winner. During the profound social changes of the 1950s, sports served as both a buffer and a barometer. The natural rhythms of the sporting seasons, the relative stability of the rules, and sports' association with masculine strength and authority softened the effects of a booming marketplace in a rapidly changing consumer society. Fall meant college football season, spring signaled the beginning of baseball. The heroic champions of 1955 invoked the same pride and sense of accomplishment as the champions of 1905. Yet, simultaneously, sports constantly revealed social change and shifting cultural values and sometimes—as in the case of the integration of baseball—was celebrated for doing so. So despite the scandals, despite evidence that sports could corrupt rather than instruct its players and that an overriding emphasis on winning could push institutions, coaches, and players to cheat and lie, sports during the Cold War remained critical to American values. Sports heroes were larger-than-life representations of all that was good about American society. When those same heroes fell, or were corrupted, the fall signified larger problems facing the United States—pride, greed, complacency, lack of will.

Nowhere was this association more pronounced than with Olympic athletes during the Cold War. This chapter will focus on sports as an aspect of international politics and the development of attitudes that privileged traditional gender roles and the nuclear family, before closing with a look at race relations in sports during the 1950s. All of these developments took place and helped to influence a period of profound social change. Though we sometimes think of the 1950s as a stable, almost stagnant decade, American culture was changing rapidly. A country that had spent the 1930s mired in an economic depression now roared with new economic growth. The American gross national product grew almost 250 percent between 1945 and 1960, while per capita income rose 35 percent. Economic expansion, a marriage and baby boom, suburbanization and geographic population shifts, rapid technological advances, and a tense international scene transformed society. All of these development affected the way that Americans watched, played, and thought about sports.

The first section of the chapter focuses on how the meaning of Olympic competitions became conflated with the international rivalry between the United States and the Soviet Union. The Olympics became a critical political platform as well as an athletic competition. The second section explores the role of sports in a middle-class, suburban society that idealized married life, children, and family togetherness. The emergence of bowling as a family-oriented sport, the rise of Little League baseball, Pop Warner football, and Catholic Youth Organization (CYO) leagues and the growing popularity of golf as both a spectator and participant sport demonstrate larger demographic and cultural shifts. Finally, the chapter closes with a look at how racial attitudes—in both the North and the South—affected professional and amateur sports. Robinson's integration of baseball was only the halting first step in a long process. Like the fledging civil rights movement of the 1950s, African Americans' efforts to participate fully in all sports moved in fits and starts, with a few public successes and many less noticed failures.

AN ATHLETIC COLD WAR

With so many European nations still devastated by wartime deprivation and destruction, the American Olympic team dominated the 1948 London Games, winning eighty-four total medals, including ten golds in the track and field events. The media hero of the first postwar Olympics was seventeen-year-old Bob Mathias, who won the decathlon. The Olympics were Mathias's first international competition and only his third decathlon, and his fresh-faced enthusiasm and natural ability made him an instant hero back home. "We sent a boy over to do a man's job and he did it better than any man ever could," said one USOC representative.[2] When asked how he planned to celebrate his victory, Mathias replied, "I'll start shaving, I guess."[3] And though there was no television coverage, Americans could listen on the radio as Harrison "Bones" Dillard won the men's 100-meter dash. In a thrilling race, Dillard and teammate Barney Ewell crossed the finish line together, but judges awarded Dillard the gold medal after studying the photo-finish results, the first time a photo finish was used in the Olympics to decide the winner. Equally significant, though less reported, were the track-and-field victories of Audrey Patterson and Alice Coachman. Patterson finished third in the 200-meter race, making her the first African American woman to ever win a medal in the Olympic Games. Coachman, competing later, won the high jump event with a leap of five feet, six and one-quarter inches, setting a new Olympic record and also becoming the first black woman to win a gold at the Olympics. Patterson and Coachman were among the 385 women competing at the 1948 Games, out of 4,099 total athletes, as female athletes very slowly began to claim a place for themselves in international competitions. The 200-meter dash, long jump, and shot put were added for the London Olympics, bringing the number of women's track-and-field events to nine.

War-torn London remained filled with rubble left by German bombs, and food rationing remained in place. Mathias's decathlon competition exposed the struggles of holding a major international event in England so soon after the end of the war. For the javelin portion of the decathlon, Olympic organizers had to drive cars into the stadium and turn on the headlights to illuminate the foul line for competitors. Athletes were housed in army barracks, and national teams brought their own food to London, contributing the surplus to British hospitals. Indeed, many people had questioned the wisdom of holding the games when much of Europe continued to struggle with starvation and the rebuilding of its battered cities. But the International Olympic Committee believed that the games should continue. In fact, committee members met in London less than two weeks after V-J Day to begin planning for the 1948 Games. In response to critics who claimed that money and national energy could be better spent on rebuilding efforts, the IOC argued that amateur sport had significant benefits in a postwar environment of distrust and would demonstrate the possibilities of international harmony and fair play. Much like Americans who believed sports served as a melting pot that taught fair play and democratic values, the IOC and national Olympic committees placed enormous emphasis on the transformative potential of the Olympics.

This belief had held through more than a decade of difficult times for international sport. The 1936 Olympics, held in Berlin, had been used as a public relations event by Germany's Nazi government, with Jewish athletes excluded from the German team. In addition, Adolph Hitler had sent his army into the demilitarized Rhineland, correctly assuming that the coming Olympics would forestall international criticism. Clearly, the IOC found nothing amiss in Adolph Hitler's use of the game to celebrate Nazi ideology in 1936, bestowing the 1940 Winter Games on Germany. And despite Germany's invasion of Czechoslovakia in March of 1939, the IOC remained determined to hold the Olympics as late as August of that year, finally conceding when Germany invaded Poland on September 1. Both the 1940 and 1944 Olympics were cancelled due to war.

The mounting tensions of the Cold War and the irresistible opportunity to use the Olympics as a political tool would come to challenge the idea that international sports could bring international harmony. When the Olympics opened in London in 1948, international politics were increasingly contentious. In 1945, 38 percent of Americans thought the Soviet Union was "aggressive"; by 1947, 66 percent believed that. Soviet leader Joseph Stalin cautioned Western leaders that there could be no lasting peace with capitalism, while British prime minister Winston Churchill warned of an "iron curtain" falling across Eastern Europe. The Soviet Union began the Berlin blockade in June of 1948, cutting West Berlin off from the West, and the United States responded by starting a vast airlift to keep Berlin supplied with food and fuel. As Cold War tensions increased, a fervent anticommunism within the United States bubbled to the surface. Whitaker Chambers had accused high-level State Department official Alger Hiss of being a Soviet spy, and a government investigation of communists in Hollywood had left many writers and actors blacklisted in the industry. By 1949, fifteen states passed antisubversive laws aimed at preventing possible communists from organizing or even meeting. Nevertheless, the 1948 Games had a very different feel than successive "Cold War Olympics" because the Soviet Union did not field a team. The IOC did not recognize their national organizing committee until after the games had ended.

The Soviet Union, however, knew that it could not ignore the Games in the future. Like the United States, Soviet leaders realized that sports could serve as a powerful international proxy for demonstrations of national superiority—far from promoting harmony, the Olympics would provide the stage for tense physical battles between nation-states. For the Olympic movement, however, there were several significant obstacles to recognizing a Soviet national Olympic committee. Traditionally, each country that participated in the Games had a national Olympic committee that was politically independent from government oversight and financial support. In addition, Olympic athletes were amateurs who did not earn money from sports. Within the centralized, state-controlled Soviet system, neither of these basic tenets of the Olympic movement held. But because IOC members believed that Soviet participation was critical if the Games were to continue to be universal and international, they decided to recognize the state-controlled Soviet Olympic Committee as an independent organization. The state-supported athletes of the Soviet Union (and later, other Eastern bloc countries) would be allowed to participate as amateurs in a brazen disregard for existing rules. For the IOC, inclusion proved more important than amateurism, a decision that would have long-term repercussions on future Olympic contests.

The four years between the 1948 Olympics and the 1952 Games, scheduled for Helsinki, Finland, saw a massive intensification of Cold War rivalries. The Soviet Union exploded its own atomic bomb in 1949, much to the surprise of the United States. That, combined with the fall of China to the communists in the same year, increased international tensions to a fever pitch and helped Senator Joseph McCarthy's claim that there were communists in the State Department seem all too possible. McCarthy's numbers varied—205 communists, or maybe 81 or 57—but his accusation rang true for many citizens who assumed that communists in the Soviet Union and in China must have been aided by traitorous Americans. Then in March of 1951, Ethel and Julius Rosenberg stood trial, accused of stealing atomic secrets and selling them to the Soviets. The trial and their eventual execution in 1953 for espionage and treason came as war raged in Korea. The 1950 McCarran Security Act authorized the government to investigate suspected communists and other subversives and, along with the House Committee on Un-American Activities (HUAC), reshaped American culture, making it dangerous to be different. The world seemed caught in an all-out struggle between communism and capitalism, totalitarianism and democracy.

Sports was part of the struggle. Though sports had been somewhat tarnished by scandal, its position as a wholesome all-American activity remained secure. But the political climate gave its meaning a much harder edge. For the United States and the Soviet Union, the Olympics provided a rare stage upon which they could compete publicly and directly. Avery Brundage, an American businessman and the newly elected president of the IOC, argued in his inaugural speech in 1952 that "if the Games become contests between the hired gladiators of various nations with the idea of building national prestige or proving that one system of government or another is better than another, they will lose all purpose."[4] Brundage was behind the times, for the Cold War had already turned athletes into nationalistic gladiators fighting on behalf of their respective countries. Ironically, it was this animating desire to crush opposing ideological views that made watching the Olympics so fascinating. International brotherhood and harmony are fine ideals, but they do not make for scintillating sports rivalries.

When the American Olympic team arrived in Helsinki, then, they were understood as physical warriors in a very real political fight. "Beat the Russians" had become the paramount goal. Mathias, who set a world record to win his second gold medal in the decathlon, explained that the Soviets were "the real enemy. You just love to beat 'em. You just had to beat 'em. It wasn't like beating some friendly country like Australia."[5] Weightlifting coach Bob Hoffman urged his athletes to "fight for sports leadership, fight for world leadership; fight, if need be, for our lives and those of our loved ones."[6] Much of the press coverage of the Olympics focused on the duels between East and West. "There will be 71 nations in the Olympics at Helsinki. The United States would like to beat all of them, but the only one that counts is Soviet Russia," said *New York Times* sports editor Arthur Daley. "The communist propaganda machine must be silenced. In sports, the Red brothers have reached the put-up-or-shut-up stage. Let's shut them up."[7]

Helsinki was an unlikely meeting place for this Cold War showdown. The smallest city ever to have hosted the Summer Olympic Games, Helsinki was still struggling to recover from World War II: coffee and sugar were still rationed, for example. Americans "won" the Helsinki Games, finishing with 175 total points to the Soviet Union's 141. Though the IOC refused to sanction or even acknowledge the practice, every country kept close track of its cumulative total: gold medals counted for three points, silver for two, and bronze for one. The American men's squad won fourteen gold medals in the track-and-field events, setting seven Olympic records and one world record along the way. Americans swept the medals in four track-and-field events: the decathlon, the shot put competition, the 110-meter hurdles, and the 200-meter dash. While American men dominated the shorter races in track and a majority of the field events, Czech runner Emil Zatopek proved the star of the Games. Zatopek won both the 5,000- and 10,000-meter races in record time and then set a third Olympic record to claim victory in his first marathon.

The nationalistic tone and desire to win went both ways. Joseph Stalin refused to allow the Olympic torch to pass through Soviet territory, afraid perhaps that the torch bearer was a spy for the United States. In addition, Soviet sports officials insisted that all Eastern-bloc athletes be housed in an Olympic village separate from the athletes of other countries. While many countries had come to see the Olympics as a chance to demonstrate social and economic superiority through sport, the IOC continued to struggle with the politics of deciding which countries could attend and who would represent them. The committee had admitted the Soviet Union despite the nation's obvious violation of the amateur code, but now they faced the even more difficult question of ruling on who would represent the divided countries of Germany and China. When the committee decided to allow the People Republic of China and Nationalist China (now Taiwan) to enter as separate teams, Nationalist China withdrew rather than compete against their bitter rival. As luck would have it, the team from the People's Republic of China arrived in Helsinki too late to participate.

Germany and China continued to present problems in preparation for the 1956 Games—East and West Germany ended up competing as one country from 1956 to 1964—but in comparison to other international crises occurring in 1956, they were small potatoes. Major world events occurred between the end of the Winter Games and the November start of the Melbourne Summer Olympics, several that had direct ramifications on the Games. In July, Egyptian president Gamal Abdel Nasser took control of the Suez Canal in a bold bid for national independence. In response, Israel, Britain, and France planned a joint assault on Egypt, with the Israeli army attacking in late October. World opinion and threats from the Soviet Union forced Britain and France to retreat, and an American-negotiated cease-fire finally calmed tensions somewhat. Nevertheless, Egypt, Lebanon, and Iraq withdrew from the Games in political protest when the IOC would not ban France, Great Britain, and Israel for their actions. In Eastern Europe, fervent anti-Communists in Hungary rebelled against the Soviet regime and briefly took over Budapest in early November, installing a liberal government and demanding that the Soviets withdraw from the country. Instead, the Soviet Union responded by sending tanks into the Budapest streets, crushing the brief revolution. To protest Soviet behavior and the bloodshed and repression in Hungary, Spain, Switzerland, and the Netherlands withdrew their teams from Melbourne. The Dutch donated the money that would have been used to send their athletes to a Hungarian relief fund. Finally, the People's Republic of China withdrew two weeks before the Games rather than compete against athletes from Taiwan.

Sixty-seven nations did attend the Games, just two fewer than in 1952, but the number of athletes participating dropped by almost 1,600, from 4,925 to 3,342. In far-away Melbourne, where time-zone differences delayed news back to the United States for up to a day, the Soviet Union emerged as the ultimate winner in total points, with 201 to the United States's 163. In just their second Olympic competition, the Soviets trounced the Americans, taking more of every kind of medal. American men, however, continued to dominate the track-and-field events, winning fifteen of a possible twenty-four gold medals and twenty-seven total. "America had won the big events; Russia had won the big prize," reported *Newsweek*, while *Time* rationalized that the "grim gleaning of points in the final days" had allowed the Soviet Union to creep ahead of the United States.[8] Bobby Morrow, an undergraduate at Abilene Christian College in Texas, took home three golds in the 100- and 200-meter dashes and the 400-meter relay and became the latest media darling back home. *Sports Illustrated* named Morrow its 1956 Sportsman of the Year for his performance. Diver Pat McCormick repeated her 1952 gold-medal performances in both the springboard and platform events, and the men's basketball team won its seventh consecutive gold medal, beating the Soviets in the final. But the most memorable event pitted the Soviet Union against Hungary in the water polo semifinals. With fighting still raging in Budapest, the competition in the pool was fierce and bloody, as both teams tried to settle their differences with fists and elbows. Hungary led 4–0 when star Ervin Zador received a wicked cut under his right eye, pushing the anti-Soviet crowd into a near frenzy. The water tinged red and the spectators hurling abuse, the referee feared a riot and ended the match with less than a minute to go, sending Hungary to the finals and an eventual gold medal.

Cold War fears, international tensions, and high expectations prompted in-depth *Sports Illustrated* coverage before and during the Games: a total of twenty-eight articles in 1956 dealt with the Olympics, a bit more than 10 percent of the magazine's feature articles for the year. As in 1952, most media coverage interpreted the events as more than straightforward athletic competitions. Despite the many Soviet medals, *Newsweek* expanded on John Tunis's old argument that a country's sporting nature reflected its ideological stances, maintaining that there was a "most un-Marxian creative aspect to Olympic victory."[9] The Soviets may have won, the argument went, but only through an ugly, grinding determination and without any of the democratic joy and enthusiasm that characterized American champions. In the Soviet Union, reports held that its team had been successful despite serious efforts at sabotage by United States secret agents. The official Communist paper explained that the CIA had tried to force Soviet athletes to have a good time with young women in Helsinki in a vain effort to break the athletes' concentration. In other words, it was almost impossible to separate sports from politics within the context of the Cold War. Because Olympic sports seemed to be the most dramatic way to demonstrate national superiority, individual athletes became representations of a collective national ego.

The Cold War–inspired desire to crush the Soviet Union in sports created a dilemma for the United States Olympic Committee and the U.S. government. Traditionally, women who competed at the Olympic level received almost no funding or training support. Certainly, there had been a handful of multiple-medal winners, including track-and-field-star Babe Didriksen's dominating performance in the 1932 Olympics; diver Pat McCormick, who won gold medals in 1952 and 1956; and ice skater Tinsley Albright, who won a silver medal in 1952 and a gold in the 1956 Winter Games. Still, Olympic-caliber female talent was very thin. Most American women who competed in sports did so in programs that emphasized cooperation rather than competition. A few women competed in tournaments organized by the newly formed Ladies Professional Golf Association, as amateurs in international tennis, and in AAU-sponsored women's basketball tournaments, but "female" remained an unlikely modifier for "athlete." In a 1950 survey, of the approximately 10,230 professional athletes in the United States, only 540 (or about 5 percent) were women. American professionals did not compete in the Olympics, but the statistic offers some insight into the expectation that athletes would be—and should be—male. All of the rhetoric about the meaning of sports focused on its benefits for men and boys. Few writers even mentioned that sports might help women, and many writers argued that sports would harm the female gender both physically and mentally. Competitive sports, with their emphasis on winning at all costs, seemed especially dangerous, and only an estimated 25 percent of colleges sponsored some form of varsity sport for women in 1951.

Of course, Olympic point tables did not discriminate on the basis of gender. Women's gold medals counted for three points, just as men's did. Yet American women proved no help in maintaining the United States' self-image as the world's strongest country. The Soviet Union and other Eastern-bloc countries simply brought bigger, and better, women's teams to the Games, as did Australia and even South Africa. At the Helsinki Games, the American women's track-and-field team brought only ten athletes, with no one to represent the United States in either the discus or high jump competitions. As a result, the 1952 track team won only one medal, a gold in the 4x100 relay event. In sharp contrast, the Russian women took home ten medals in track and field. In 1956, when the Soviet Union surpassed the United States in the final point totals, the Russian women's team included world-record holders in five of the nine women's track events, and they finished the games with eight medals. Mildred McDaniel's world-record victory in the high jump marked the only time in 1956 that American women heard "The Star Spangled Banner" on the victory stand, though the team bettered its dismal 1952 performance by winning three total medals. Overall, in the four Olympics between 1948 and 1960, American women won six of the thirty-seven gold medals available in track and field. Wilma Rudolph, with a little help from her teammates in the 1960 4x100 relay, would account for half of them.

In swimming, the results were better, but not by much. The women's swimming team won just eight of the twenty-three available gold medals between 1948 and 1960, five of those in 1960 when sixteen-year-old Chris Von Saltza led a formidable squad. The Hungarian women had dominated the 1952 Games, while the Australians, led by multiple-medal winner Dawn Fraser, were top performers in their home waters of Melbourne. Shelly Mann's gold medal in the 100-meter butterfly event in 1956, the first year women swam the butterfly in Olympic competition, was the only American women's swimming gold in the 1952 and 1956 Games. The Soviet Union also quickly took top honors in gymnastics, with the team winning seventeen total medals in 1952 and fourteen in 1956. They swept every event except the balance beam—where they still took silver and bronze—in 1960, a level of dominance unmatched in any other sport. Only in diving, where American women won every gold medal between 1920 and 1956, did the United States truly excel.

The chair of the USOC women's track and field division acknowledged that the USSR spent considerable energy recruiting and training female athletes, giving the Soviets a significant advantage in winning medals. By contrast, the American team depended largely on talented but raw athletes such as sixteen-year-old Rudolph, who in 1956 was competing in her first international event and did not make the finals in the 200-meter event. One solution? Track and field and gymnastics needed "to be glamorized from the girls' point of view," announced the head of the Olympic Development Committee.[10] In a more practical move, the USOC created the Women's Advisory Board in 1958, with representatives from the Amateur Athletic Union, former female Olympic athletes, and sympathetic physical educators, all eager to improve the performance of American women so that the American medal count might rise. The development of women's sports was helped tremendously in 1960 when Doris Duke Cromwell, the heir to the Duke tobacco fortune, donated $500,000 to the USOC to promote women's sports. The Women's Advisory Board and the Division of Girls' and Women's Sports used the money to set up a series of national institutes for training and coaching female athletes. The need to "beat the Russians" helped to overcome the belief that women should play sports for fun and not for competition.

International tensions had eased somewhat by 1960, when Rome hosted the Summer Games. While the People's Republic of China continued to boycott the games, many newly independent African countries participated for the first time. Running barefoot, Ethiopia's Abebe Bikila won the marathon to become the first black African to win an Olympic medal. A record 5,348 athletes from 84 nations competed, staying in the first true Olympic "village," which was built to include parks, recreation areas, and stores as well as cottages for the athletes. The Rome Olympics were the first to be thoroughly covered on broadcast television. Many events were covered live in Europe, and in the United States, CBS paid almost $400,000 to show tape-delayed coverage, flying tapes of the events to New York City daily. Though the Games did not appear during prime time in the United States, television coverage increased the intensity of the rivalry between the United States and the Soviet Union, since now Americans could see the athletes win or lose against the hated Russians.

What viewers saw, however, was disappointing. While many individual American athletes turned in fine performances at the Rome Games, the Soviets steamrolled to national victory, with 218 total points compared to the 160 compiled by the United States. In addition, the men's track team—competing in what *Newsweek* termed the "big events"—failed to live up to its pre-Games hype as the best team ever assembled. UCLA student president and *Sports Illustrated* 1958 Athlete of the Year

Rafer Johnson narrowly won the decathlon, and Don Bragg and Otis Davis set world records in the pole vault and 400-meter race respectively, but Ray Norton, unbeaten for two years in the 100- and 200-meter dash, symbolized the team's struggle, finishing sixth in both races.

The men's basketball team featured three future NBA Hall of Famers, Jerry Lucas, Oscar Robertson, and Jerry West, and won the Olympic tournament handily, defeating the Soviet Union in the finals. Their victory helped to erase the bad memories of an American loss to a Soviet amateur team in a sanctioned tournament in Chile in 1959. The U.S. amateur team, made up of members of the Air Force, lost 62–37 to the Soviets, delighting the Latin American crowd and leading to local headlines such as "Russia Ate the U.S. and Washed Them Down with Coca-Cola." As one *Sports Illustrated* writer explained, "when the people who actually invented the sport, people generally regarded as a brash and cocky lot anyway, are humiliated by those with whom they are in competition on so many other grounds, this is not just fun and games."[11] In other words, the American Olympic team had something to prove once they arrived in Rome.

Three American boxers won gold in the ring, including Cassius Clay (later Muhammad Ali), who was so excited that he refused to take off his medal for two days. The United States' smallest weightlifter, bantamweight Charles Vinci, won a second consecutive gold medal, while Tommy Kono, who had taken home gold medals in 1952 and 1956, continued to shine, securing a silver in the middleweight class. It was the end of an era for American weightlifters, however. Though the Americans had been at the top of the world standings after World War II, the Soviet team had begun using steroids by 1954 and quickly surpassed the United States team. The Cold War stoked the already intense competitive urges of world-class athletes to a fever pitch and encouraged some governments to develop systematic programs to improve and achieve better results. One American lifter explained that if his doctor "had told me to eat grass, I would have done so to get strong."[12] Winning mattered that much. By the time American lifters began to experiment in earnest with drugs in the early 1960s, an Eastern-bloc drug program had already achieved impressive results, and those nations had come to dominate the strength events.

The most surprising winner at the Rome Olympics was female sprinter Wilma Rudolph, who won gold medals in the 100-meter, 200-meter, and 400-meter relay events. The first American woman to win three gold medals in a single Olympics, Rudolph ran effortlessly, seeming to float to her victories. Notwithstanding her gender, Rudolph was an unlikely

American hero. Born in rural Tennessee the twentieth of twenty-two children, at four Rudolph was stricken with scarlet fever. The disease left her unable to walk without braces until she was eight. Yet she became a star in high school, dominating the junior division of the AAU championships. After her experience at the Melbourne Olympics, she returned home to finish high school and improve her running skills, but she got pregnant and dropped out of competition for a year. She returned to the track, however, as a freshman at the historically black Tennessee State University. Nearly the entire women's track-and-field team in 1960 was drawn from historically black colleges and universities, where female athletes had been more likely to be encouraged to be competitive.

Rudolph was also the first African American woman to be celebrated as an athletic Cold War hero—one of the American gladiators against the "evil empire" despite her gender. She used her Olympic success to argue for civil rights in the South, including demanding that her victory parade in Clarksville, Tennessee, be integrated. She also met President John F. Kennedy in the White House and won the 1961 Sullivan Award, given annually to the top amateur American athlete. And though some sportswriters made her sound much like a pet when they called her a "black gazelle," Rudolph received generally very positive press, with stories presenting her as both a lady and a "good American."[13] Her graceful demeanor and the importance of her victories in an Olympics where the men's track-and-field team failed to meet expectations allowed Rudolph to be feminine and athletic without contradiction.

Some Soviet and American athletes had become friends, or at least friendly, by the 1960 Games. Male and female athletes from the two countries flirted and taught each other dance steps in the Olympic Village, for example, and Rafer Johnson and his Soviet rival compared notes after the decathlon. But most Americans continued to view the Olympics solely through the lens of the Cold War. They worried that the mounting Soviet victories meant that the United States was physically weaker, both in the fitness of its citizens and in its ability to defend itself. Despite all sorts of counterevidence, the Olympic medal tally seemed to represent the respective strength and commitment of the two nations. "We're never going to win as long as our youth is more interested in hot rods, television and fun," complained Tip Goes, the head of the U.S. Rowing Federation.[14] Like Goes, many worried that economic prosperity and the lures of television were making American culture soft and ruining the nation's competitive character. In 1956, President Dwight Eisenhower created the President's Council on Youth Fitness in response to widely publicized reports that American children performed much worse than Europeans on physical-fitness tests. After the Rome Olympics, President John F. Kennedy expanded the scope of the program on physical fitness, eager to encourage all Americans—not simply youth—to remain physically active because "our growing softness, our increasing lack of physical fitness, is a menace to our security."[15] Sports and fitness were a patriotic duty, since the United States need to prove on a world stage that a free society produced better athletes—stronger, more talented, more eager to win—than a communist society.

SUBURBAN FAMILIES AND NEW ATTITUDES ABOUT SPORTS

The fear of "going soft" because of material success linked Cold War attitudes about sports to fears about the impact of a postwar economic growth on American culture. *Newsweek* columnist John Lardner joked that American athletes faltered in any race longer than 1,500 meters because "800 meters is, after all, the outside limit of a commuter's run for the train."[16] By the mid-1950s, almost 60 percent of families earned enough to be labeled middle class, compared to only 31 percent during the 1920s. While many justly celebrated these developments, some critics worried that a middle-class emphasis on materialism meant the nation would grow "flabby" and "unfit." Riesman in *The Lonely Crowd* and others who bemoaned the flaws of middle-class society shared a similar fear: that Americans would become too focused on financial success—getting ahead and "keeping up with the Joneses." As a result, the nation would lose its soul, its energy, and the individualistic strivings that had made it the world's most powerful country. Ironically, economic achievements held the possibility of physical and mental decline. One Chicago priest conflated the physical and the spiritual in a diatribe against materialism, exhorting his parishioners to stay strong. He thought it was "intriguing and amusing that with all of suburbia out there and all the dads out there coaching in the little league two years in a row, the hungry kids from Monterey, Mexico have won the Little League World Series."[17]

The priest's use of the Little League World Series to make his point demonstrates just how central sports had become to the American image. Picture a ten-year-old white boy in a blue "Tigers" T-shirt, a baseball cap crooked on his head and a too-big mitt on his hand, his dad in Bermuda shorts and a golf shirt smiling proudly in the background. This, as much as any, is a defining image of the 1950s, a symbol of the suburban innocence and economic possibility of the decade.

And though the 1950s were never as conformist, or as white and middle class, as they are now remembered, Cold War fears and a strong focus on family life certainly marked the period. A 1955 study found that a vast majority of Americans believed that they had sacrificed nothing by marrying and raising a family. Fewer than 10 percent thought that an unmarried person could be happy. Marriage became the defining event of adulthood and the essential ingredient for a happy and productive life. Over 96 percent of women and 94 percent of men who came of age during and after World War II married, and the median age for marriage dropped to twenty for women and twenty-two for men. This was a massive reversal of the trends of the early twentieth century, when marriage rates had steadily dropped and marital age had steadily risen. Most of these young couples had children. The national fertility rate rose 50 percent from 1940 to 1957, and the absolute number of children per family rose from an average of 2.4 children in the 1930s to 3.2. A national magazine proudly described a co-ed volleyball game played in a suburban backyard in which five of the women were pregnant. Fertility was hip.

In this context of family togetherness, postwar team spectator sports faced a great deal of new competition. Television was both a blessing and a curse for professional and college sports. Though fans could now watch their favorite sports on TV, they could also watch many other programs, spending time in front of the TV when they might once have gone to the ballpark, arena, or stadium. In 1948, about 3 percent of American homes had televisions. Just eight years later, an astonishing 81 percent did. Families, many now with their own sets, could choose from *I Love Lucy*, Edward Murrow's documentaries on *See It Now*, *The Jack Benny Show*, or former radio comedian Milton Berle on *Texaco Star Theatre*. The Rochester Royals, for example, beat the New York Knicks for the 1951 NBA title, but, despite their success, the Royals struggled to attract spectators to Edgerton Park Sports Arena. Royals owner Lester Harrison blamed television for the team's loss of fans. "Milton Berle put us out of business on Tuesday," Harrison argued. "And then on Saturday with Sid Caesar and Imogene Coca—they put us out of business. That's why we didn't draw. The people stayed home and watched—had beer parties and watched the games there."[18] The appeal of television decimated audiences for Hollywood movies, all but destroyed minor-league baseball, and contributed to a serious slump in professional-sports attendance.

The emphasis on the nuclear family in the 1950s also affected attitudes toward sports. The baby boom and its results—families of three, four, and five children—made Pop Warner football and Little League baseball into major family activities and made family-oriented leisure activities a staple of American life. This was particularly true in the suburbs, which were growing fifteen times faster than any other part of the country. The same GI Bill that helped to reshape college sports allowed World War II veterans and their families to buy homes with no money down and low-interest loans. Housing developments such as William Levitt's "Levittowns" used prefabricated walls and frames assembled on-site to build up to thirty houses per day, all in an effort to keep up with the overwhelming demand from families eager to own their own home outside the noise and grime of the city.

Perhaps the most common reason given for moving to the suburbs was that it was a better place to bring up children, a reason closely connected to opportunities for physical play in a safe environment. These new suburbs were neighborhoods especially developed for families, designed to include parks, schools, swimming pools, tennis courts, and athletic fields. Families spent hours outside, barbequing in the backyard, playing tag in the street, biking to the pool, working on the car in the driveway. The very landscape of the suburbs made playing sports a central part of American family life.

Like many boys of his generation, President George W. Bush played Little League baseball, remembering the experience as one of the best of his childhood. His father wrote that he was "so proud" of George because "he is out for Little League, so eager. He tries so very hard. He has good fast hands and even seems to be able to hit a little."[19] Playing ball was a way for boys to make their fathers proud, a critical bonding experience between them, and a part of being an American boy in the middle of the century. Little League was a game, but, like many sports, it quickly came to represent something more. At the beginning of each season, Bush and all the other Little Leaguers pledged to trust God, promised that they loved their country and would respect its laws, and resolved to "play fair and strive to win." The game, it was believed, taught democracy through action. Of course, the leagues were not just for boys. Each team was run by adults—almost always men—who coached and yelled during the games and then organized postgame outings for ice cream and hot dogs.

Little League was part of the 1950s general celebration of boys, part of a culture that offered television viewers the Nelson sons growing up on *Ozzie and Harriet*, "the Beav" on *Leave It to Beaver*, a widowed father and his boys male bonding on *My Three Sons*. Popular culture promoted an image in which fathers "knew best" and led their sons to manhood by playing catch in the backyard and patiently teaching them the rules of football. Some girls played sports—softball and half-court basketball in the Midwest or field hockey and tennis in Eastern prep schools—but sports in the suburbs largely belonged to boys. Little League had been invented in Williamsport, Pennsylvania, in 1938, but it was not until 1947 that the organization expanded outside of Pennsylvania and started the Little League World Series. In 1949, there were 307 leagues in the United States. Just nine years later, there were over 4,000. New houses, new ballparks, and new teams emerged simultaneously, and Little League quickly became nearly synonymous with the suburbs. In 1953, the seventh annual Little League World Series was televised for the first time, with rookie announcer Jim McKay, who would later become the voice of the Olympics, doing the play-by-play for CBS. Birmingham, Alabama's all-star team defeated Schenectady, New York, in the finals, a clear sign of the league's national reach and the game's far remove from unorganized sandlot play. And of course, Birmingham's white-only team also reminded anyone paying attention that Jackie Robinson's integration of Major League Baseball did not automatically solve all the racial problems in sports.

Baseball was not the only organized game available for boys. They could play football in the Pop Warner League and basketball and other sports in the CYO, the B'nai Brith leagues, or the YMCA. Named after famous college coach Glenn "Pop" Warner, the Pop Warner Football League started in 1927 in Philadelphia as a program to keep young men off the streets. Like Little League, its real expansion came after World War II as young families moved to the suburbs. The league held its first national postseason "bowl games" in 1954, now catering mostly to young boys between eight and fifteen, with teams from as far away as Southern California. CYO leagues, run by the Catholic Church but open to non-Catholics, sponsored flag football, basketball, baseball, and boxing. In Chicago, CYO flag football and basketball programs ran end-of-the-season tournaments complete with trophies for the winners. As in Little League, each CYO player pledged to "be loyal to my God, to my Church, and to my country" and to be a "good citizen now and always."[20] No matter how much fun playing sports was, the need to remind youngsters of their Cold War responsibilities was never far from the surface.

Suburbia also meant consumption—cars, washing machines, televisions, lawn furniture—and sports and sports equipment were an important aspect of this. A survey from 1953 found that Americans spent more than $18 billion per year on leisure and recreation activities, including participant sports, spectator sports, camping, hunting, boating, and travel. This figure did not include the cost of television sets, on which families could watch *Friday Night at the Fights* or wrestling, roller derby, baseball, and college football. Bowling balls, whether in black, solid colors, or psychedelic swirls, proved a popular consumer item, and entrepreneurs built bowling lanes at a rate of 4,000 per year in the 1950s. Bowling became the number one participant sport in the United States. An estimated 22 million people bowled regularly, spending approximately ten times more than Major League Baseball collected in gate receipts. Seventeen million bowlers played on teams that belonged to a league, playing to win rather than only to socialize.

One key to bowling's popularity was a change in image. In the 1930s and 1940s, fans frequented bowling *alleys*, playing in industrial or factory leagues or as a part of a night of drinking and socializing. The American Bowling Congress (ABC) sponsored regular tournaments. Andrew Varipapa and Ned Day, America's best-known bowlers in the 1940s, toured the country giving demonstrations and made promotional films, but bowling nevertheless carried a slightly seedy reputation, much like pool. By the time Varipapa won back-to-back All-Star/U.S. Open bowling tournaments in 1946 and 1947, the game's image was already beginning to shift. For one, owners started calling their establishments bowling *lanes* rather than alleys, trying to dispel the sport's low-class image. Technological advances also helped tremendously. The Brunswick Corporation introduced the automatic pinsetter in 1956, eliminating the need for the "pinboys" who had a reputation for abusing the customers. Brunswick's competitor AMF introduced the electric hand dryer and the "AMF Pindicator," designed to help bowlers locate which of their pins had fallen. These two corporations became two of Wall Street's most spectacular growth companies in the decade. By January 1958, about 67,000 bowling lanes, at a cost of between $90,000 to $1,500,000 each, had been approved by the American Bowling Congress, and bowling had blossomed into a $350,000,000 sports industry.

The game's newfound success expressed both gender and class expectations of the decade. A lengthy 1956 article about bowling in the *New York Times* explained that the game had "gone chic" and had appeal because players could "slip into a cocktail dress or dinner jacket . . . listen to an orchestra, be fitted for bowling shoes, bowl a few games, then leave without tipping the pinboy as most boys have been traded in for new, non-cursing pin-setting machines."[21] Of course, bowling remained hugely popular among blue-collar families, but, with a few modifications, the sport now also appealed to middle-class couples eager for respectability.

An official of the American Bowling Congress claimed that women had made the difference in the sport's popularity, arguing "the number one reason for the bowling boom . . . is that Mama has accepted it as a wholesome recreation, not only for her husband but for herself and her whole family."[22] "Mama" accepted it in part because bowling lane owners used the decade's commitment to "family togetherness" to promote the sport. Some owners installed closed-circuit television so that mothers could bowl and watch their children playing in the designated nursery. The ABC emphasized the sport's inherent equality in an effort to appeal to women, presenting it as a space where "anyone who bowls can be equal to anyone else who bowls," regardless of gender. Lanes sponsored weekly family nights as well as afternoon sessions designed specifically for women. Many also joined new women's leagues. By 1958, there were about six million female bowlers, compared to approximately 82,000 in 1940. More than one million women participated in the Women's International Bowling Congress, which sponsored competitive tournaments and offered limited prize money. A new fashion industry also emerged to create "bowling attire" for women, further marking the lanes as a place where women could be physical without worrying that they would seem unfeminine.

To be sure, bowling succeeded because it worked within existing gender norms, not because the sport challenged them. Women might bowl, but even at the lanes, their primary identities remained wives and mothers. The president of the Brunswick Corporation explained it most clearly when he noted that "the housewife used to find it difficult to enjoy bowling. Now it's just what Mama wants." Coverage of the "first family of bowling" is instructive. Laverne and Don Carter, both bowling champions in the 1950s, met and married on the tour. Don was named bowler of the year four times in the 1950s and twice more in the 1960s. Laverne had a reputation as a hard-charging, aggressive bowler, though neither she nor any other woman could beat all-time great Marion Ladewig, but Laverne toned down her image in order to appeal to a wider audience. Though Laverne played regularly and enjoyed competition, she made sure to explain that "bowling isn't actually my life. My family is."[23] One six-page story featured several action photographs of Don at the lanes, while Laverne was shown surrounded by her children, braiding her daughter's hair, and discussing favorite recipes. Bowling was Don's career but LaVerne's pastime, a diversion from her real job as wife and mother.

Sports in the decade were also a part of workplace culture. With employees working shorter hours, there was more time than ever for leisure activities, and many companies added additional programs for workers. Work-sponsored sports was not a new development in the 1950s. Industrial teams had become popular in the 1920s and 1930s, particularly among blue-collar and factory workers. Some companies also sponsored higher-quality teams—such as the Fort Wayne Zollner Pistons or the women's basketball team run by Hanes Hosiery in the 1940s and early 1950s—in the hopes of attracting local and national publicity. These teams formed a semiprofessional option for good athletes. The top college basketball player in 1946, Bob Kurland, chose to play for the Phillips Petroleum Company rather than for an NBA team. Players such as Kurland and Hanes Hosiery star Eunice Fuchs worked for the company. As Fuchs explained, female players especially "just jumped at a job. And to play basketball and work was the treat of all treats."[24] Most blue-collar workers, of course, simply joined organizations such as the "Hawthorn Club" of the Western Electric Company in Chicago, which offered recreation competition for both men and women.

By the early 1950s, the kind of companies sponsoring sports programs had expanded far beyond the blue-collar level. Increasingly, white-collar firms felt that offering its salaried employees recreational opportunities was a key way to build loyalty among workers and simultaneously cut down on absenteeism, accidents, and complaints. These programs featured much more than bowling leagues, though given bowling's popularity in the 1950s, it was generally a company option. Companies spent about $1.5 billion a year on employee recreation by 1962. The Lockheed Corporation provided its employees with bowling, softball, basketball, and tennis leagues as organized sports, with 120 bowling teams competing in 7 separate leagues. The Eastman Kodak Corporation in Rochester, New York, built a multimillion-dollar recreation center that could hold up to 7,000 employees at a time. Instead of building a recreation center, the Minnesota Mining and Manufacturing Company (3M) simply bought a 366-acre park for its 11,000 employees, which included a golf course, ski run, field archery range, skating rink, riding trails, camping areas, and even park rangers. Though 3M was perhaps the most extreme example, American companies owned 125 golf courses by the late 1950s.[25]

Companies purchased golf courses because, increasingly, it was a game their employees wanted to play. The number of public golf courses also exploded in the 1950s. Universities established golf teams, improving the talent level in professional golf and exposing a new audience to the game. Even President Eisenhower used the White House lawn as a putting green. As more people played golf recreationally, professional golf, under the auspices of the men's Professional Golf Association (PGA) and the Ladies Professional Golf Association (LPGA), gained wider audiences. Texan Ben Hogan dominated professional men's golf in the late 1940s. Hogan had emerged as a force in 1940 and had won six Tour victories in a row in 1942. Wartime restrictions forced the cancellation of most tournaments between 1943 to 1945, but after the war, Hogan returned with a flourish, winning the PGA Championship along with twelve other tournaments in 1946. Before a near-fatal car accident that fractured his pelvis in 1949, he also won the 1948 PGA Championship and the U.S. Open. Hogan proved as great a human-interest story as a golfer. His stunning comeback in 1950—he won the U.S. Open just weeks after returning to the tour—sparked new interest in the sport. A 1952 *Life* magazine contest offered Americans the chance to play a round of golf against Hogan to celebrate the second-annual National Golf Day. Of the more than 87,000 contestants, 15,000 used USGA-assigned handicaps to "beat" Hogan's score of the same day. In addition to winning three of golf's four major events in 1953, Hogan was also one of golf's first stars to master the consumer angle of the sport, promoting Hogan-approved golf clubs and clothing, and writing a classic of golf instruction, *Five Lessons*, in 1957.

Female golfers moved toward professionalism and mass appeal more slowly than men. Golf, along with tennis, was considered a more genteel, upper-class sport that women could play without overtly challenging gender norms, but openly playing for money removed the fiction that tournament play was "just for fun" for women. It made golf a career instead of a game. The best-known female golfer of the postwar period was Babe Didricksen Zaharias, who had won two gold medals in track and field at the 1932 Olympics. A tremendous athlete, Zaharias struggled to make a living from sports after her Olympic success, playing semiprofessional basketball, challenging men to competitions, and even appearing in a vaudeville show. Her athletic skills, competitive drive, and roughhewn manners made Zaharias an easy target in the press, and she struggled against constant accusations that she was unladylike.

Partly in response, she married professional wrestler George Zaharias and turned to golf as a way to change her image and make money from sports. Sportswriter Paul Gallico, who had previously ridiculed Zaharias for her appearance, wrote approvingly of the changes she had made, explaining to eager readers that Babe had given him a peek at her silk-and-lace undergarments and then "opened her handbag and let me peer at the usual female equipment of lipstick and compact, eye shadow and lace handkerchief."[26] In her new guise as a "lady," Zaharias won fourteen tournaments in a row in 1946 and 1947, as well as the U.S. Women's Open in 1948, 1950, and 1954. She proved a big draw at tournaments, with spectators eager to see how a former Olympic champion would fare on the links. Along with stars such as Patty Berg and Louise Suggs, Zaharias decided that the women's tour could succeed on a professional level, since many of the golfers were eager to benefit financially from their sport. In 1950, Berg, Suggs, Zaharias, and ten other golfers founded the Ladies Professional Golf Association, finally moving top-level women's golf away from its amateur status.

Hogan's inspiring comeback success and Zaharias's flashy personality helped to turn the golf tour into a popular spectator sport. Television also helped; despite the openness of the course, golf benefited from television coverage, with cameras easily able to capture the flair of the tee shot and the drama of the putting green. The game had arrived. By 1956, over 25 percent of *Sports Illustrated*'s regular "department" coverage concerned golf. Only horse racing, which garnered about 16 percent of the department coverage, even came close to competing in terms of sheer number of articles. Three years later, the magazine published 124 feature articles on golf, compared to 116 on baseball, making golf the most covered sport in *Sports Illustrated*.

And then came Arnold Palmer. Hogan was a superb player and shrewd marketer, but Palmer was something new: a golf superstar with mass appeal. Palmer never won as many tournaments or as many major events as Hogan, but he captured the public imagination in a way that no golfer had before. A golf pro's kid from Pennsylvania, Palmer's style and charisma completed golf's transition from an upper-crust game played at exclusive country clubs to one enjoyed by suburban hackers and average Joes. Palmer played golf like the guy next door, if the guy next door were hugely talented, that is. Blonde and tanned, he chain-smoked between the holes, swung with his shirt untucked and his hair flopping in his eyes, and played an aggressive, gritty game, going for big shots in a way that brought him a following called "Arnie's Army." Like any good businessmen, he capitalized on his success, creating clothing and golf-shoe lines and even an Arnold Palmer bug repellent and endorsing cigarettes, Heinz ketchup, and, of course, golf clubs.

Sports Illustrated wrote that "with his golf credo—'Hit it hard'—that horrifies traditionalists, his boyish enthusiasm, his athletic good looks and irrepressible will to win," Palmer had become golf's new super-star.[27] Palmer appealed to many precisely because he was a powerfully built white man, a "man's man" with "the build of a football halfback." Much like Mantle, he provided a comfortable hero for many men, who may have *admired* the skills and determination of Robinson or Mays, but wanted *to be* like Arnie, strong, aggressive, and in control. Palmer won the U.S. Amateur Tournament in 1954 and then turned pro, winning his first tour victory in 1955. Four years later, at age twenty-eight, Palmer won his first Masters and finished the year number one on the PGA Tour money list with just over $40,000 in winnings. This was the same year that the PGA changed the format of most of the tour's tournaments from match play to medal play in order to keep major stars playing longer for television cameras. Palmer's greatest victories came in 1960, first at the Masters, where he carded birdies on the final two holes to beat Ken Venturi by one stroke. Then, two months later at the U.S. Open, Palmer overcame a seven-stroke deficit with a final round 65 to win by two over a young Jack Nicklaus. Combined, these two exciting victories made Palmer *Sports Illustrated*'s "Sportsman of the Year" for 1960. The magazine wrote of "women swooning [and] men sighing" when Palmer played and called him "the King." He became golf's first millionaire.

GROWING RACIAL INTEGRATION

The popularity of golf signaled the decade's celebration of a white, middle-class, suburban ethos. Few sports were less integrated. A black man did not win a major PGA-sanctioned tournament until Charlie Sifford's victory at the *1967* Hartford Open. Within this atmosphere, the 1950s were a mixed blessing for black athletes and for black Americans. African Americans benefited financially from the economic boom of the decade. The median income among black families rose 69 percent between 1947 and 1952. By that same year, nearly 40 percent of African Americans held jobs defined as white-collar, skilled, or semi-skilled, almost double the proportion in 1940. The armed services began to integrate their troops in 1949, meaning that black and white soldiers fought in the same units for the first time during the Korean War. Culturally, blacks made extraordinary contributions. Ralph Ellison's *Invisible Man* was published in 1952; James Baldwin's *Go Tell It on the Mountain* in 1953. The rhythms of Dizzy Gillespie, Coleman

Hawkins, and Charlie Parker changed the direction of jazz. Rhythm and blues, renamed roll-and-rock, began to capture the fancy of American teenagers. Chubby Checker and Fats Domino emerged as early stars, though many r&b songs reached the top of the charts when covered by white artists. In sports, new stars arrived to take their places on a national stage: Willie Mays and Cubs shortstop Ernie Banks in baseball, Wilma Rudolph and Rafer Johnson in Olympic track, Dick "Night Train" Lane and Jim Brown in football, Bill Russell in basketball, and Althea Gibson in women's tennis.

But black men continued to be lynched in the South, including fifteen-year-old Chicago native Emmet Till in 1955, killed for whistling at a white woman. The primary Southern response to the 1954 *Brown v. the Board of Education* decision reversing the prevailing separate-but-equal doctrine was outright defiance and rapid organizing to prevent integration. In early 1956, five Southern legislatures passed more than forty-two laws reinforcing Jim Crow policies in schools. In Georgia, for example, a new law made it a felony to spend tax monies on schools attended by both black and white children. In the North, official redlining policies and de facto housing segregation meant that many African Americans remained trapped in urban slums, unable to partake in the rush to home ownership in newly built suburbs. Many of the newly built bowling lanes closed their doors to blacks, and the American Bowling Congress prohibited African Americans from playing in their tournaments until 1950.

Although sports was celebrated for its critical role in social integration, many problems remained. The visibility of Robinson and his Dodger teammates Roy Campanella and Don Newcombe along with the national attention paid to Mays contributed to the persistent idea that sports were a promising avenue of upward mobility for African Americans. A few teams realized that African Americans were a relatively untapped talent pool, but most preferred to hire only token black players or no black players at all. Rather than sign players immediately out of high school or college, many major-league clubs continued to use the rapidly failing but still segregated Negro Leagues as a natural farm team for top African American players. Both Chicago Cubs star Banks and Milwaukee Braves slugger Hank Aaron got their starts in the Negro Leagues. The Cubs signed Banks after seeing him play for the Kansas City Monarchs in 1950. Aaron played for the Indianapolis Clowns before joining the Braves.

Banks, famous for his "let's play two" enthusiasm, was the Cubs' first black major leaguer, joining the team in 1953. The Yankees waited even longer to integrate. Elston Howard joined the team in 1955, eight years after Robinson was named Rookie of the Year for the Dodgers. Howard, who like Robinson was chosen for his demeanor and personality as well as his abilities, faced not-so-subtle racism from both general manager George Weiss and team manager Casey Stengel. Howard was named to the American League All-Star team nine times over the course of his career, despite serving largely as a utility player—rotating between catcher, left field, and first base—for the Yankees until 1961. In addition, over the next six years the Yankees promoted only two other blacks to their big-league club, this in a city with a significant black population where both the Dodgers and Giants had led the way in integration. The Boston Red Sox and their owner Gene Yawkey waited until 1959 to add even one black player to their major-league team, a full twelve years after the game had first been integrated. And this in a city where first Chuck Cooper and then all-time great Bill Russell played on the hard court.

For individual players, MLB could seem a cold and forbidding place in the 1950s. The league made almost no effort to shield players from the effects of racism. The experience of minor-league baseball could be hellish for some black players, especially those who were the only African American on a small-town team in the South or the West. St. Louis Cardinals center fielder Curt Flood remembered feeling "too young for the ordeal," and would "break into tears as soon as he reached the safety" of his room.[28] Spring training was no picnic either. In addition to trying to make the team or hold onto their positions, African American players faced the harsh segregation of the South in Florida. As late as 1961, twelve of the thirteen teams that trained in Florida housed their black players in separate and inferior housing. While their white teammates stayed in a whites-only hotel, Milwaukee Braves superstar Hank Aaron and his black teammates Charlie White and Billy Bruton boarded with a local woman named Lulu Gibson. During another preseason, Aaron shared a boardinghouse with black players of visiting teams and noted that "sometimes the place is so crowded that they have two guys sleeping in the hall."[29]

While their white teammates often brought their families to enjoy Florida's spring weather and beaches, black players almost never did, in part because Jim Crow laws generally restricted blacks from using the state's theme parks, golf courses, parks, and even beaches. Cincinnati Reds star Frank Robinson had a miserable time every spring: "no movies, no bowling, nothing. It was watch our step every time we went on the street."[30] Not until 1961, pushed by growing NAACP activism in

Southern spring-training towns, did major-league clubs begin to challenge local laws and customs about housing and to desegregate the seating, ticket windows, and restrooms at their Florida ballparks. Far from being the leader in the struggle for integration, MLB followed the lead of a new group of black activists who had been inspired by the Montgomery bus boycotts in 1955 and the lunch counter sit-ins that began to sweep across the South in 1960. As the general manager of the Kansas City Athletics, which had only one African American player, explained, baseball was not interested in "spearheading any political movement."[31]

The growing number of Latin American ballplayers coped with similar challenges. In 1948, only one Latino ballplayer played regularly in the major leagues. By 1965, there were forty-eight players, including some of the biggest stars in the game: Juan Marichal and Orlando Cepeda of the San Francisco Giants, Tony Olivia of the Minnesota Twins, and, especially, Roberto Clemente of the Pittsburgh Pirates. Nevertheless, Latin American players faced racial stereotyping on their clubs. In their explanations of how best to manage Latino players, for example, managers Billy Martin and Buck Canel made the players sound like pets. Martin explained that Latinos needed to be handled "gently but firmly. If they respect and like you, they will do anything for you," while Canel added that managers needed to "give them a pat on the back once and a while. A physical pat . . . that touch of your hand makes a Latin feel alright."[32] In addition to these sorts of patronizing attitudes, Latin American players, especially Afro-Latin players, sometimes confronted more overt forms of racial discrimination. In 1964, for example, San Francisco Giant manager Alvin Dark blamed his team's bad play on minority players. "We have trouble because we have so many Negro and Spanish-speaking ballplayers on this team," said Dark. "They are just not able to perform up to the white ballplayers when it comes to mental alertness."[33]

The combination of racial prejudice and language barriers made Latin American athletes what Clemente called a "minority within a minority," even as they began to succeed on the field of play. Clemente, who broke in with the Pirates in 1955, became increasingly outspoken over the course of his eighteen-year career. Like African American ballplayers, a dark-skinned Clemente faced segregation and overt prejudice during spring training. His open displays of anger at this treatment contributed to a career-long reputation as a hothead. A sensitive but supremely self-confident athlete, Clemente also bristled when sportswriters belittled his talent and his competence in English with stereotypes. "I no play so gut yet. Me like hot weather, veree hot. I no run fast cold weather," was how one sportswriter reported a conversation with Clemente.[34] An enormous hero in his home of Puerto Rico, he gradually won over fans in Pittsburgh with his sterling play, though he was dogged throughout his career by accusations that he lacked the gumption to play hurt. Still, between 1964 and 1967, Clemente won three batting titles and the National League Most Valuable Player award. His arm from right field was legendary, and he led the league in outfielder assists five times. In 1971, after his play led the Pirates to a World Series championship against the Baltimore Orioles, he reminded sportswriters that too many of them assumed "Latins were inferior to the American people. Now they know they can't be sarcastic about Latins, which is something I have fought for all my life."[35]

In the NFL, the number of African American players dropped from nineteen to seventeen in 1951, and six teams had no black players at all. The practice of "stacking" limited their playing time; the majority played running back, defensive back, or end, meaning that blacks often competed with each other for a starting job at those positions. New black stars emerged in the 1950s, including two defensive backs, New York Giant Emlen Tunnell and Detroit Lion Dick "Night Train" Lane, who transformed the position with their combination of size, speed, and, in Lane's case, ferocious tackling. In Lane's 1952 rookie season, he intercepted fourteen passes in just a twelve-game regular season, a record that still stands. Tunnell became the first African American elected to the Pro Football Hall of Fame and the first black assistant coach in the league. Despite their abilities, an informal quota remained on the number of African American players on any one team. When superstar running back Jim Brown joined the Browns in 1957, he explained that black players knew that "each team would have six, perhaps eight, blacks on a roster. Never seven though: it was always an even number, so none of the white guys would have to share a room with a black."[36] Casual racism remained the prevailing order in the NFL.

College sports, which had a much longer history of team integration—at least outside the South—were also affected by the racial attitudes of the 1950s. Many teams struggled to balance the desire for national attention with the dignity of their African American players. In college football, three of the four best-known postseason bowl games were held in cities in the Deep South. In the 1930s and early 1940s, most Northern colleges either had no black players on the team or agreed to play without them in order to attend the bowl game. In 1940 and 1941, for example, Boston College benched their starting halfback so that the team could accept invitations to play in the Cotton and Sugar Bowls. But after World War II, schools began to protest rather than to acquiesce to Southern norms, forcing bowl committees to modify their stance to recruit the best teams. The Cotton Bowl invited Penn State, which had two black players, to participate in the 1948 game, and the Sun Bowl, after the embarrassment of an integrated team turning down their invitation in 1951, changed its policies in 1952. Seating at both bowls remained segregated by race, but the teams themselves could be integrated. In a typical statement that again points out the cultural importance of sports, one newspaper claimed that the Cotton Bowl's 1948 decision carried "more significance then does a Supreme Court decision against Jim Crowism or . . . a Federal Fair Employment Practices Act."[37]

Although the state of Florida had laws prohibiting public colleges from hosting integrated teams, in 1953 the Orange Bowl signed an agreement with the Midwestern-based Big Seven (now the Big Twelve) Conference that promised an annual match-up between the champions of the Big Seven and the Atlantic Coast Conference (ACC). By the mid-1950s, a majority of the Big Seven schools had at least one black player, and the first integrated Orange Bowl came in 1955 when the University of Nebraska played Duke University. Despite this development, Florida state schools, including the University of Florida and Florida State University, continued to be prohibited from playing against integrated teams until the late 1960s.

The Sugar Bowl in Louisiana proved most resistant, especially after the 1954 *Brown v. Board of Education* decision when many Southern whites felt their way of life was under attack. In New Orleans, allowing integrated visitor seating in 1955—primarily so that black band members could sit with the band—turned out to be a major concession. After committee members invited the University of Pittsburgh, which had one African American player, to the 1956 game, Georgia governor Marvin Griffin urged the school's board of regents to prohibit Georgia Tech from playing, warning that "the South stands at Armageddon. . . . We cannot make the slightest concession to the enemy in this dark and lamentable hour of struggle. There is no more difference in compromising the integrity of race on the playing field than in doing so in the classroom."[38] Only after a mob of Tech students rioted and burned Griffin in effigy did the regents decide to let Tech play. In Louisiana, the state legislature passed a new law prohibiting interracial games. Though the Supreme Court struck down the law in 1959, an integrated team did not play again in the Sugar Bowl until Syracuse University in 1965.

The disparate decisions of two Southern schools demonstrate the racial tensions of the South in the 1950s. North Texas State College in Denton, Texas, decided to abide by new federal laws and integrate its campus in 1956. Much like Branch Rickey, the North Texas football coach realized that black players were an untapped source of talent and decided to integrate the team as well. In part by encouraging white players to see the two African American recruits not as symbols of desegregation but as a step toward winning the conference title, the coaches set a tone of grudging acceptance. The starting quarterback explained that "you might not necessarily like somebody [and] therefore you discriminate against them off the field. But as a quarterback, I'm only interested if you can get me yardage or catch the ball. I don't care what color you are."[39] The team accepted its new players on the field, but ignored them off of it, though the entire team faced spectators' wrath during the season. Opposing fans shouted "nigger lover" at white players and chanted "kill the niggers" to the two African American athletes. Despite the struggles, the school continued to recruit African Americans, including Pittsburgh Steeler "Mean" Joe Greene, holding a monopoly among southern schools on black football players until 1966.

It was a different world in Mississippi, where the flagship university was the University of Mississippi, or Ole Miss. In 1948, the same year as what came to be called the Dixiecrat Revolt—where a majority of Southern delegates walked out of the Democratic Convention and nominated their own candidate for president—the school adopted new symbols for its sports teams. The adoption of the rebel flag and Rebel Colonel as its mascots and *Dixie* as its school song helped to link Ole Miss to its Confederate past and offered powerful symbols of the school's values. The fact that the football team became a Southeastern Conference (SEC) powerhouse in the same years, invited to nine major bowls games between 1953 and 1964 and winning five, only helped to cement the connection. In 1956, when Jim Crow customs were further threatened by new federal laws, the school's band began to wear Confederate uniforms and call itself the "Band of the South,"[40] while the school's basketball team walked out of an All-American Basketball Tournament in Kentucky because there were black players on opposing teams. By the time James Meredith attempted to integrate the university in 1962, the symbols of the school's sports teams had become a potent aspect of Ole Miss identity, adding fuel to the opposition to black students.

While Southern schools used sports to support segregation, three college basketball players—Bill Russell, Oscar Robertson, and Wilt

Chamberlain—rewrote expectations about black athletes playing for white teams in the North. African Americans had long played for Northern teams, but in very limited numbers and often in role positions, rarely as their team's star. Russell, who played for the University of San Francisco Dons, shattered those ideas, leading his team to fifty-five consecutive wins and back-to-back national championships in 1955 and 1956. Russell so dominated the game from his center position that the NCAA changed the width of the foul lane from six feet to twelve. The seven-foot-one-inch Chamberlain, a Philadelphia schoolboy legend, earned coverage for his basketball abilities in *Sports Illustrated*, *Time*, *Newsweek*, *Look*, and *Life* magazines before he even went to college. Chamberlain chose the University of Kansas in 1955, proving so dominant that he sometimes faced triple and even quadruple coverage and forced the NCAA to change its rules about offensive goal-tending and to briefly ban dunking. Robertson had been a high school star in Indiana, leading his all-black Crispus Attucks team to consecutive state titles, the first time an all-black team had won. Robertson also became the first African American to be named college basketball's Player of the Year three times, earning the award by averaging 33.8 points (without the benefit of the three-point shot) and 15.2 rebounds per game between 1958 and 1960. Despite taking the Cincinnati-Bearcats to the Final Four in his junior and senior seasons, Robertson was not welcome at the restaurants and movie theaters near the school and, like Chamberlain in the Midwest, struggled with the racial attitudes of some of his fellow students. Nevertheless, from 1955 to 1960, these three young stars reshaped the expectations of college basketball fans and created new opportunities for young black players. The trio demolished unwritten but long-standing quotas that limited the number of black athletes on college basketball teams.

Although both professional and amateur sports did not always welcome African Americans, sports nevertheless remained critically important in the black community during the 1950s. Sports stars were heroes and held up as shining examples of racial advancement. Jackie Robinson was the subject of comic books celebrating his achievements—Robinson may have been a baseball player, but like Martin Luther King Jr., he was also seen as an important activist for the race. Two other African American athletes also demonstrated the possibilities of using sports as a platform for racial change. Tennis star Althea Gibson and boxing great Sugar Ray Robinson served different functions—Gibson was a racial pioneer in a largely white sport, Robinson became a brash model of black attitude and style.

Gibson, a shy, but fiercely competitive New Yorker, was barred by custom from United States Tennis League (USLTA) tournaments until 1950. The five-foot-ten-inch Gibson instead honed her game on the all-black American Tennis Association circuit, winning her first tournament in 1945 at the age of eighteen and then taking ten straight women's singles titles between 1947 through 1956. Former women's champion Alice Marble proved instrumental in pushing the USLTA to invite Gibson to participate, writing a public letter to the association's magazine that chided them for ignoring her obvious abilities. Gibson was invited to the U.S. Open in 1950, the first African American of either sex to play in the tournament. When she played at Wimbledon in 1951, the white press covered her on-the-court abilities, but they also felt obliged to reassure their readers that she took a bath every afternoon. As a black woman, Gibson faced gender-based challenges similar to Zaharias, challenges intensified by common assumptions about black women. Even the black press, which usually heaped praise on African American stars, was discomfited by Gibson's athleticism and aggressive manner on the court. Gibson became a dominant player in 1956, after a year-long goodwill tour through Southeast Asia sponsored by the U.S. State Department. Her time as a representative of the best of American democracy honed her game and she won the French and Italian Open tournaments, followed in 1957 by victories at Wimbledon and the U.S. Open.

These victories marked the first time a black player had won either tournament, and for her accomplishments Gibson was named Female Athlete of the Year by the Associated Press. *Sports Illustrated* lauded her as "the Negro girl who made good in the big-time tennis." Like Zaharias, Gibson worked on her personal style and public image, noting that she "began to understand that you could walk out on the court like a lady, all dressed up in immaculate white, be polite to everybody and still play like a tiger and beat the liver and lights out of the ball."[41] She repeated at Wimbledon and the U.S. Open in 1958, then retired at the top of her game.

Sugar Ray Robinson was a different kind of hero, the most famous black boxing icon in the fifties. Like Mantle and Palmer for white fans, Sugar Ray embodied a particular hip style that made him hugely popular among African Americans, especially black men. He had stunning abilities in the ring, where he won forty-eight consecutive bouts between 1946 and 1951 as the champion of the welterweight class. In 1951, he moved up to challenge larger men in the middleweight division, ultimately winning the middleweight belt five times. Contests between Robinson and Jake LaMotta provided particularly good theater, as the men met six times in the ring between 1942 and 1951. Robinson won five of the six meetings, the last one called the "St. Valentine's Day Massacre" because LaMotta was so dominated by Robinson's speed and power. Late in his career, Robinson mixed it up in four vicious fights with Gene Fullmer and Carmen Basilio, first losing the title to each man, then winning it back in a rematch. An incredible puncher, Robinson won 174 fights over the course of his long career and laid claim to the title of "pound for pound, the best."

Although he was not a heavyweight, Robinson took the mantle of greatness from Joe Louis, combining it with a flamboyance and flair that Louis rarely dared. Robinson wore expensive suits, owned a nightclub in Harlem, and was often surrounded by a huge entourage that included a masseur, a voice coach, and many beautiful women. Robinson was particularly proud of his choice in cars. "When people think they recognize a celebrity, they hesitate a moment," he said. "But whey they saw me in that car, they didn't have to hesitate. They knew. They was only one like it—Sugar Ray's pink Cadillac."[42] He was so cocky that most of his fellow boxers hated him, especially since he was generally able to back up his boasts in the ring. For many, Robinson embodied black pride and black strength, an African American who could do as he pleased and say what he wanted. If Jackie Robinson was generally termed a "credit to his race," Sugar Ray signaled instead a new kind of black masculine power that thumbed its nose at mainstream white styles. His combination of attitude, flashy style, and boxing abilities prefigured another African American boxing star, Muhammad Ali, and paved the way for black athletes in all sports to express their individual personalities.

*I*n a stunning development, the Boston Braves won the 1948 National League pennant by six and one-half games, their first pennant since 1914. Manager Billy Southworth's team depended so heavily on workhorse pitchers Warren Spahn and Johnny Sain that the prevailing refrain in the city became "Spahn, Sain, and pray for rain." That championship was the team's high point in Boston. Though the team was an original member of the National League, organized in 1876, it had long been second in the hearts of Boston baseball fans behind the American League Red Sox. Ballpark attendance had reached one million only three times in the franchise's history, and, after a spike during the 1948 season, gate receipts dropped steadily when the team returned to the middle of the National League standings in 1949. In 1952, Hank Aaron's debut year, the future home-run king's franchise sold only 282,000 tickets. As the number-two team in Boston, the Braves could compete neither against the Red Sox nor against the appeal of new television stars such as Milton Berle or Lucille Ball. Spahn and Sain were great pitchers on a second-rate team; Berle and Ball were great comedians on a first-rate invention. The public had little trouble in deciding which to watch.

As a result, Braves owner Lou Perini hated both Boston audiences and the medium of television and was keen to move his club to a new locale where he could have total control. In many cities, baseball fans were starved for a team to call their own, and they seemed more likely to attend games, even with Lucille Ball on TV. Major League Baseball was largely concentrated on the East Coast and in the Midwest in the early 1950s. In addition to the Braves and Red Sox in Boston, St. Louis, Philadelphia, and Chicago each had two teams, while New York City had three. The league's stability—no franchise had moved since 1903—gave it credibility, but it meant that baseball owners left many potential markets untapped. There were no "big league" cities in California, indeed none south or west of St. Louis. This was an increasingly untenable situation. The combination of geographic migration to the South and the West and emergent television markets created new opportunities for team owners to make money and new demands from cities eager to have a team to call their own.

Because Perini controlled the minor league franchise in Milwaukee as a part of the Boston farm system, he had exclusive territorial rights to the area and he secured permission from his fellow owners to transfer the team there. When the announcement came that MLB owners had approved the move of the Braves to Milwaukee, a local booster predicted the team would be "the greatest psychological lift Milwaukee ever had," and would show that "the community can be as great as its citizens want it to be."[1] Over 12,000 exultant fans crowded into the train station to welcome the Braves to Milwaukee and the city held a parade through the downtown area to celebrate. Civic boosters adopted a new slogan—"Let's be big league all the way"—that built on the new status many felt the Braves conferred on Milwaukee.[2] Like the chancellors at the University of Kentucky and the University of Oklahoma who saw sports as the ticket to national recognition for the state, Milwaukee officials believed that sports teams brought status and prestige, and they were willing to do almost anything in order to attract a franchise. Professional sports teams served much the same cultural function as college football and basketball teams did for their universities and states. A "major-league" sports team made the city in which it played "major league." Fans of teams that moved, however, brutally discovered that professional sports was a business and that though they might speak of "our Brooklyn Dodgers" or "our Philadelphia A's," these teams ultimately belonged only to their owners.

The Braves won the National League pennant in 1957 and 1958, beating the Yankees four games to three to take the 1957 World Series. Aaron, Spahn, third baseman Eddie Mathews, and pitcher Lew Burdette paced the 1957 club, which attracted a major-league record 2.2 million fans to the ballpark. In part this was because Perini banned the telecast of all Braves games in the state of Wisconsin, meaning that local fans did not see their team on TV until the Braves made the World Series. For Milwaukee residents, beating the "Big Apple" on a national stage was particularly sweet, curing what *Time* magazine called "a civic inferiority complex."[3] Though only two of the Braves players had been born in Wisconsin and none were from Milwaukee, the victories seemed proof that the city stood equal to New York City in stature. Despite the victories, Milwaukee did not stay "major league" for long. Attendance gradually dropped after 1957, but the real problem was that other cities—other media markets—wanted the Braves. In 1962, Perini sold the club to new investors who promptly began to negotiate with city officials from Atlanta. By the beginning of 1964, the new owners had agreed to a sweetheart deal that would take the Braves to Atlanta.

Milwaukee fans were at once furious and heartbroken. Though the Braves had only been in the city for ten years, residents believed that they owned the rights to the team. But in reality, they were just a rented media market. In Milwaukee, the team had earned $400,000 in local broadcast rights once Perini grudgingly allowed Braves games to be shown in Wisconsin. In Atlanta, the Braves' first television contract was for $2.5 million. The lure of money had brought the Braves from Boston, but now that same appeal would pull them to another city. Neither could Milwaukee compete with the wide-open advertising market that Atlanta offered. No other major baseball team played within seven states, so the Braves could market themselves as the team of the South. When a Milwaukee city official moaned that "television money is clearly at the bottom of everything," he was right on target.[4]

Television spurred the relocation of existing teams, the rapid expansion of professional leagues, and the development of new leagues to challenge the monopoly of the existing order. Everyone, it seemed, wanted to benefit from the money and exposure that television promised. As a result, television had the curious effect of exposing sports as a multi-million-dollar industry bent on maximizing its profits while simultaneously fueling the much more personal connection between sports and self-identity. Milwaukee city officials who longed for a big-league team put together a business deal that benefited Perini and hurt their city financially. But seeing Milwaukee written in script across slugger

Hank Aaron's chest and having other Americans make the association between team and city when they tuned into a baseball game made the cost of acquiring the Braves seem inconsequential. The same proved true in Atlanta, where mayor Iven Allen aggressively recruited sports teams with favorable financial terms and proudly noted that the city built Atlanta–Fulton County Stadium "on ground we didn't own with money we didn't have for clubs we had not yet signed." Like the people of Milwaukee, he believed the Braves would vastly improve his city— and his region—for the better, making them "a symbol of Southern zest and drive, a major league state, in a major league region."[5] Acquiring a team was a business deal, but it held the promise of much more.

Television changed the relationship between spectators and sports in many ways. Most fundamentally, it made sports more accessible to the average American, expanding the audiences for sports. Instead of going to the ballpark, the ballpark could come to spectators. Televised sports were both more personal and more spectacular than what had come before. Sports on TV were an entertainment and an escape, a sort of long-running masculine soap opera that featured ups and downs and favorite characters. This had been true before television, of course, as fans closely followed the fortunes of their favorite team or player, agonizing with a loss and rejoicing after a win. Newspaper coverage sometimes offered the "behind-the-scenes" story, and sharp fans could read fatigue or determination in players' eyes while at the stadium. Indeed, the fact that sports seasons—and the careers of individual players—are dramatic and absorbing is part of what made them such good television. Television enhanced these qualities, featuring storylines that emphasized the dramatic, the ridiculous, or the inspirational, anything that made audiences watch. Winning and losing still mattered, but sports also needed to be entertaining. TV also made the experience of watching sports more mediated. Viewers now saw their favorite games as interpreted by the camera and the show's producer. Just as the written press had long done, television announcers imposed meaning onto games, creating a narrative structure that made the actions in sports more intelligible and more culturally relevant. The difference was that television interpreted the events as they were happening, imposing a single viewpoint for all its viewers. More fans now shared the same experience and heard the same interpretation.

The 1950s and early 1960s were a time of transition. The first section of this chapter explores the relocation of existing baseball teams to new cities and then the expansion of MLB in the early 1960s, developments spurred by both population shifts and new television markets.

The second section looks at the development of television from the early 1940s through the creation of *The Wide World of Sports* in 1961. This section focuses on the tremendous impact that television had on boxing and professional and college football. The third section spotlights the most successful twentieth-century challenge to an existing league by examining the American Football League (AFL) and its quest for respectability. The AFL and NFL eventually merged, greatly expanding the visibility and reach of professional football. One result of the merger was the annual Super Bowl contest. First held in 1967, the Super Bowl would become the ultimate expression of the power of television to engage the sporting imagination.

TEAM MOVEMENT

The move of the Braves to Atlanta and the general expansion of professional sports leagues into the West and South in the 1950s and 1960s reflected larger demographic developments. In 1940, Houston, Texas, did not rank among the twenty largest cities in the country. By 1960, this once sleepy Southern port town was the nation's seventh largest city. The same changes occurred on the West Coast. The city of Los Angeles had about 1.5 million residents in 1940. Twenty years later, there were approximately 2.5 million. In general, the decades after World War II saw a tremendous shift of population from the Northeast into growth cities in the West and South. In addition to Houston and Los Angeles, Atlanta, Phoenix, Dallas, Seattle, and San Diego boomed. The transitions and moves in Major League Baseball in the 1950s and 1960s simply mirrored larger demographic and geographic shifts in the American population.

The Braves were just the first team to move to greener pastures—a green that had nothing to do with the field and everything to do with financial benefits. Record crowds attended Braves games, watching in a new stadium financed by public funds. The stadium had been built, for approximately $6.6 million, before city officials knew that they had secured a team. The following year, Bill Veeck's St. Louis Browns finally earned league permission to move, accepting Baltimore's offer of a publicly financed stadium and changing their team name to the Orioles. The Browns had struggled for years as the second team in St. Louis, briefly emerging from their cellar-dwelling status during World War II, but they averaged only 250,000 spectators per year. Veeck, an innovator in many areas, had been the first owner to realize the potential of other markets, but fellow-owners had been reluctant to allow the

Browns to move. But in 1953, after the Browns lost 100 games and drew only 3,174 fans to their final game, Veeck sold the team to a group of Baltimore investors and St. Louis's sad-sack second team was gone. Though the team again lost 100 games the following year, almost 16,000 Baltimore fans attended each home game. By the mid-1960s, the Orioles had become an American League powerhouse.

Teams kept moving. In 1955, the Philadelphia Athletes accepted a proposal to move to Kansas City. Attendance in Philadelphia was so poor that the league office pushed for change; the team's puny gate receipts were having a negative impact on visiting teams. As a result, owners Roy and Earle Mack sold the team to Arnold Johnson, who ran the New York Yankees' minor-league team in Missouri, for nearly $3.4 million. Johnson then sold his minor-league stadium to Kansas City, whose officials agreed to rebuild it to meet major-league standards and then to lease it back to Johnson.[6] Kansas City's close ties to the powerful Yankee organization helped the city gain its "major-league" status, despite offers from San Francisco and Minneapolis to finance new stadiums for the team. However, Kansas City was already losing ground to emerging cities further west and south, and the Athletics would move on to Oakland, California, in 1968.

The Athletes, Braves, and Browns all moved into cities eager to support a team. But none of the three cities—Kansas City, Milwaukee, and Baltimore—had benefited from the massive postwar population migration to the South and West. This set the stage for further relocation, since the state of California had gained 2 million new residents during World War II, drawn in part by jobs in defense plants and near military bases. Its population continued to boom in the 1950s. Lakewood, California, a suburb of Los Angeles that was home to gold-medal diver Pat McCormick, was the fastest growing housing development in the country, selling a hundred homes in one hour in 1950. Within three years, Lakewood had grown from farmland into a town of 90,000 people. Yet while both Los Angeles and San Francisco hosted NFL franchises, the only professional baseball in California came in the Triple A Pacific Coast League. Joe DiMaggio got his start with the San Francisco Seals in 1933, and many other big-league stars passed through the league. But it was not the major leagues. The Pacific League had no hold on the national imagination.

In 1957, the Brooklyn Dodgers and New York Giants shocked New Yorkers by announcing their decisions to move to the West Coast. The National League's greatest rivalry was headed to California. The Dodgers and Giants were not traditional cellar dwellers, unlike the first teams to relocate. Certainly the Yankees were the "first team" of New York, but both the Dodgers and Giants had fanatical supporters and a solid record of postseason success. Both teams benefited from being in the country's largest entertainment market and enjoyed lucrative television and radio contracts. Indeed, the borough of Brooklyn would have been the fifth largest city in the United States if it had not been part of New York City. But their stadiums were old and in declining neighborhoods, and city officials in Los Angeles and San Francisco, keen to claim the "big-league" status they were sure they deserved, promised sweetheart deals to Dodger owner Walter O'Malley and Giant owner Horace Stoneham. The money-making potential of the California market was too much too ignore.

Giant and Dodger fans were outraged. Dodger fans, led by local businessman Henry Modell, formed a "Keep the Dodgers in Brooklyn Committee" that organized protest rallies and lobbied government officials. When it was clear that the Dodgers would leave the borough, Modell tried to place a "hex" on the team in its new location by sticking hatpins into a doll dressed in a Dodger uniform. As Bill Veeck, former owner of the recently moved St. Louis Browns, explained, Brooklyn supporters "never doubted for a moment that their beloved Bums were as much a part of their heritage as Prospect Park. They discovered that they were wrong. The Dodgers were only a piece of merchandise that passed from hand to hand."[7] To compound the misery, three-time league MVP and fan-favorite Roy Campanella was paralyzed in a January 1958 car accident, ending his career.

Stoneham and O'Malley had seen what moving to Milwaukee had done for the Braves. The dramatic rise in gate receipts and broadcasting revenues had propelled an also-ran club to the top of the league, allowing its owners to sign and keep better talent. If a move had helped the Braves, what might it do for already successful teams? Stoneham and O'Malley were also worried about their gate receipts because Dodger and Giant attendance had been steadily declining throughout the 1950s. Attendance at the Polo Grounds, for example, had fallen from 1.2 million in 1954 to less than 633,000 in 1956. After the move had been announced, Stoneham was asked if he felt any remorse when he thought about the children of long-time Giant supporters. He replied that he felt "bad about the kids, but I haven't seen many of their fathers lately."[8] Fans continued to identify with the teams but, increasingly, did not make it to the ballpark. Some of them had left the city, part of a larger relocation to the suburbs of Long Island and New Jersey. Neither area made driving to the game simple, and many fans found it easier to watch their favorite team on TV or listen to radio broadcasts of the games. With attendance dwindling, if one team left the city, the other seemed almost bound to follow, since the Dodgers and Giants remained each other's best draw at the ballpark.

Thus, suburbanization, an expanding car culture, and declining urban neighborhoods all played a role in the move. O'Malley had been negotiating with city officials for several years for a new stadium to replace Brooklyn's Ebbets Field. He wanted it to be built in a different neighborhood, with more parking—Ebbets Field had parking for just 700 cars—and better access to freeways. And he wanted New York City to pay for it. When negotiations for the stadium stalled, O'Malley turned to Los Angeles. O'Malley had wisely convinced Stoneham to join him on the West Coast, enlisting the mayor of San Francisco in his efforts. The joint decision made it easier for other owners to approve the move since the long West Coast trip that teams would have to make included two teams instead of just one. Fearing that the Polo Grounds would be condemned to make way for public housing, Stoneham flirted with city officials in Minneapolis, who had built a new suburban stadium for their minor-league club, but in the end decided to follow the Dodgers. To convince the Giants to move, San Francisco city council members voted to build the Giants a municipal stadium. Candlestick Park, which quickly earned a reputation as one of the coldest, windiest, and most difficult parks in which to play, opened in 1960. So strong were the gusts of wind that during the 1961 All-Star game held at Candlestick, Giant pitcher Stu Miller lost his balance in the wind and fell over.

O'Malley wanted Los Angeles to build him a stadium as well, but instead the city sold O'Malley a 300-acre site in Chavez Ravine and pledged to spend approximately $5 million for public improvements to the area. O'Malley then built the $15.5 million Dodger Stadium, the last baseball stadium constructed with franchise capital. The stadium held 56,000 fans, compared to 35,000 at Ebbets Field, had 24,000 parking spaces for car-happy Los Angeles fans, and the latest technological advances of the day, including an electronic scoreboard. The delay in constructing Dodger Stadium makes it clear that O'Malley moved his team for the possibility of increased television revenues more than any stated problems with Ebbets Field. Dodger Stadium did not open until 1962, and while the stadium was being built, the Dodgers spent their first four seasons in Los Angeles using Memorial Coliseum, which was best configured for football games, as their home ballpark. It hardly mattered. Money from the broadcasting agreement made the franchise the league's second most profitable club, trailing only the Yankees.

Major League Baseball orchestrated the 1958 schedule well. The Giants opened the season on April 15 against the Dodgers, shutting them out 8–0, with rookie first baseman Orlando Cepada hitting the first major-league home run on the West Coast. While West Coast fans celebrated, back east *New York Times* sportswriter Arthur Daley called opening day "a moment of poignant heartbreak . . . baseball's first manifestation of transcontinental grief."[9] The Giants then traveled south for the following series, and the Dodgers took the first game 6–5 before 78,672 fans at the Coliseum. It was the start of a new season and a new era. Within six years, five MLB teams had moved to new locales, shattering the league's stability and devastating long-term fans in the cities they had left. But with the Dodgers and Giants in California, league officials proclaimed that the game was now truly national in scope.

For rapidly growing cities without teams and the businessmen anxious to own a profitable franchise that could reap the bonanza of television dollars, however, this claim rang false. Overall, the U.S. population had grown from approximately 76 million in 1900 to over 179 million in 1960, yet baseball still had only sixteen teams. Relocation would not be enough to satisfy emerging cities yearning to be "major league." As a result, businessmen, led by Branch Rickey and New York lawyer William Shea, announced the formation of a rival league that would place teams in New York, Denver, Toronto, Houston, Minneapolis, Dallas, Atlanta, and Buffalo by 1961. Many of these men had worked for years to try to bring baseball to their home cities. In Houston, George Kirksey spent nine years trying to bring in baseball, attempting to buy, in rapid succession, the St. Louis Cardinals, Cleveland Indians, Cincinnati Reds, Chicago White Sox, Chicago Cubs, and Kansas City Athletics, in order to relocate them to Texas. "The only thing I learned," he later said, "was that big league baseball was a citadel and that we would have to take it by storm."[10]

Rival leagues were rarely a profitable enterprise, and the new Continental League existed largely to take MLB "by storm" and force it to admit more teams. The ploy worked. Worried about possible congressional action against baseball's antitrust exemption if they did not act, the American League reluctantly admitted two new teams in 1961, while the National League added two in 1962. The Continental League then disbanded without ever playing a game, secure in the promise that four of its franchises would be added to the majors. One clear sign that media markets were a driving force in the placement of teams was the addition of the Los Angeles Angels to the American League and the New York Mets to the National. Of the other potential cities slotted for

Continental League teams, only Houston and Minneapolis gained teams, with Minnesota's new franchise actually a move of Clark Griffith's Washington Senators to the upper Midwest. Washington, D.C., then earned the fourth new team as a replacement.

In addition to paying O'Malley a $550,000 fee for invading his territory, the Angels rented space in Dodger Stadium from the Dodger owner until 1966, when the city of Anaheim built the team its own ballpark. The franchise then changed its name to the California Angels, displaying the beginning of a move away from a city-based identity and toward a more regional identity for teams. The Houston franchise played for their first three years in the heat and humidity of Colt Stadium as the Colt .45s. In 1965, the team relocated to the Astrodome, the so-called Eighth Wonder of the World, and changed its name to the Astros. Roy Hofheinz Jr., the former mayor of Houston and principal owner of the team, pushed through a general obligation bond bill for $22 million at an interest rate of less than 4 percent to build the Astrodome. He also convinced the Texas Highway Department that a fourteen-lane highway bordering the site should be pushed to completion five years ahead of schedule. Ultimately, the new stadium cost local taxpayers $45 million to build. Hofheinz promised Houston taxpayers that the domed stadium would produced 250,000 extra customers a year, arguing that "if you were assured comfort and convenience such as this, and a guarantee against rainouts, even on the miserable day, what would you do? You'd go to the ballgame, just as sure as there's a pig in Texas."[11] Perhaps he was right. Despite poor showings by the Astros, who never finished better than eighth in their first four years in the Dome, the team drew at least one million fans every year until the mid-1970s. The Astrodome—and its new surface, Astroturf—would transform the way Americans watched sports, becoming the model for the many domed stadiums to come.

For the most part, the expansion teams struggled terribly in their early years. No team was as inept as the Mets. The Mets set a modern record for futility in 1962, finishing with 120 losses. Playing in the largest city in the United States, the team drew only 922,530 fans to the ramshackle Polo Grounds for their first season, with many of the spectators presumably fans of the opposing teams. Shea Stadium, named for the lawyer who helped to bring National League baseball back to New York, opened in October 1964. Another publicly owned stadium, Shea cost $28.5 million, with $4.5 million paid in overtime to the building crew so that the ballpark would be ready for the 1964 season.

The Angels finished eighth in their first season, climbed to a surprising third in 1962, but then sank again to the bottom of the American League standings. The expansion Senators fared worst, losing at least 100 games in each of their first four seasons. With Red Sox great Ted Williams at the helm, the team finally reached the .500 mark in 1969, their ninth season. Still, constant mediocrity depressed ballpark attendance and the Orioles cut into the Senators's broadcasting area. As a result, owner Robert Short found a multi-million-dollar up-front payment for television and radio broadcast rights from Dallas very appealing and moved the team to Texas in 1972.

To accommodate the two new teams in each league, MLB moved from a 154-game regular season to 162 games. This change led to controversy in its very first season, when Yankee outfielder Roger Maris mounted a challenge to Babe Ruth's single-season home run record. Maris out-slugged his more famous teammate, Mickey Mantle, and broke Ruth's record in the final game of the season, but the often negative attention he faced during the season was intense. "As a ballplayer, I would be delighted to do it again," Maris explained. "As an individual, I doubt if I could possibly go through it again."[12] Even baseball officials belittled the ballplayer. As Maris pounded his way ever closer to the record, baseball commissioner Ford Frick declared that if Maris needed more than 154 games to break the record, an asterisk would be placed next to his name in the record books. Even as the league expanded to new coasts and added new teams, change came hard to such a traditional, hidebound sport.

The move to the West Coast, and the increased revenues from broadcasting rights and ticket monies, kept the Dodgers and Giants near the top of the National League standings. Though the Dodgers finished seventh in their first season in Los Angeles, the franchise rebounded to win the World Series in 1959 and 1963. With a pitching staff that included Don Drysdale and Sandy Koufax, the Dodgers provided their new fans with sparkling pitching after the team moved into its new stadium. Drysdale won twenty-five games and the league's Cy Young Award in 1962, but it was Koufax who quickly emerged as the ace of the staff, if not the best pitcher in the major leagues. The overpowering left-hander finished with the lowest ERA in the National League in 1962, then went 25–5 with 1.88 ERA and 306 strikeouts in 1963. Drysdale, however, more thoroughly exploited the possibility of his crossover appeal into other forms of entertainment. Helped by his Los Angeles locale, he appeared regularly in television commercials and guest-starred on television programs such as *You Bet Your Life*, *The Donna Reed Show*, and, late in his career, *The Brady Bunch*.

The Giants and Dodgers continued their fierce rivalry on the West Coast. In 1962, both teams won 102 games and finished the season tied. Just as in 1951, the Dodgers lost a three-game playoff series, and the Giants moved on to the World Series. In fact, with the notable exception of the Dodgers' representing a new city, little seemed different at the top of professional baseball. Between 1958 and 1966, either the Yankees and Dodgers played in every World Series, with the two teams meeting in 1963. In that series, Koufax, who struck out 306 batters in 311 innings during the regular season, dominated the Yankees, winning the first and fourth games of the Series. With Koufax, Drysdale and Johnny Podres on the mound, the Dodgers swept the Series in four games. Expansion and rising fees for television contracts did little to change the traditional leaders of the sport.

IT'S A WHOLE NEW BALLGAME

Despite its position in the 1950s as the most popular sport in the United States, baseball struggled with the small screen. The structure of the game held out the promise of effective television: the repeated match-ups between pitcher and batter allowed broadcasters to develop narrative storylines within the game; the ends of innings created natural breaks for commercials; and the rich history of the league gave even the most insignificant midseason game a link to a storied past. These advantages were not enough to overcome some serious limitations. For one, the limited number of game cameras in the first years of televised baseball made it difficult for many TV viewers to follow the action. The ball was small and sometimes difficult to pick up on a black-and-white screen. The subtle nuances and wide-open nature of baseball action were also difficult to capture on camera. Unlike boxing, which took place in an enclosed space, or football, where plays were often limited to a small part of the field, baseball players spread out over a lot of ground. There were not enough cameras to contend simultaneously with infielders and outfielders, the batter and the third-base coach, the pitcher and the catcher, robbing television viewers of the opportunity to see the whole field and understand the complex relationship between the game's component parts.

Though baseball did not make particularly good television, franchise owners benefited tremendously from the new medium's dollars. The league signed a five-year contract with NBC and Gillette in 1957 that brought revenues of $3 million per year for the broadcasting rights to the World Series and $250,000 for the All-Star Game. For the regular season, each owner signed his own contract, with no effort to make sure teams benefited equally from television's revenues. Baseball owners rejected any suggestion that called for signing a contract that would reward each team equally, calling the idea socialistic, un-American, even communistic. Local broadcast revenues in 1950 reached $3.4 million and then nearly tripled in ten years, jumping to $9.4 million by 1960.

Professional and major men's college sports had been shaped by money-making opportunities for owners and schools for decades. But the amount of money TV offered for the rights to sports altered the relationship between sports and financial gain. Television networks generate a majority of their profits from advertising revenues. Finding a consistent fit between advertising revenue and audiences quickly led networks to prefer programs that appeared at the same time each week and whose storylines featured familiar settings and characters in slightly varied situations. Each week built on the previous week's episode and the resulting fan loyalty to a series became a commodity that networks could sell to advertisers. Sports fit beautifully within this emerging pattern. Baseball, basketball, and football had regular seasons and, like sitcoms, featured familiar settings and characters with whom viewers could identify. Even boxing and other individual sports that lacked a regular season nevertheless featured standard, repeating elements on which viewers could depend. For a sport to be a successful television show, it only had to generate enough viewers to create a desire for advertisers to reach them. Sports had the added bonus of delivering "special events" that held exceptional appeal—the World Series, for example—but nevertheless contained features that felt familiar to viewers. Networks could charge advertisers extra for these, certain that they would attract larger than average audiences.

Sports were a crucial part of early television programming. A baseball game in May 1939 between Columbia University and Princeton University was the first sporting event to appear on TV. It was a local broadcast in which one camera, stationed along the third base line, tried to follow the action. In December of the same year, approximately 500 households in New York City and visitors to the RCA Pavilion at the World Fair watched the NFL's Philadelphia Eagles play the Brooklyn Dodgers. Other sports programs followed during the war years—especially boxing matches and baseball games—but only a tiny audience saw them. Still, sports became a staple of the emerging medium, an easy way for producers to fill programming time. As much as 30 percent of the prime-time schedule was devoted to sports programming during the 1940s. Boxing was particularly popular. In 1946, for example, NBC televised the Joe Louis–Billy Conn heavyweight fight at Yankee Stadium to an estimated audience of 150,000. Most of the TV-watching audiences were gathered around ten-inch sets in local bars. Almost no one had a television set in their home. Approximately thirty people watched each set tuned to the fight, many who were seeing their very first television program.

Though television become a sort of semi-holy entertainment shrine and a staple of the family living room by the mid-1950s, in its early years the medium drew viewers out of the home and into the neighborhood tavern. These viewers were mostly men, and in this way, television reinforced older patterns that associated sports with masculine bar culture—drinking, smoking, gambling, and carousing. Getting together to watch the fight or the big game quickly became a staple of masculine social life. This was an environment that could be far removed from the civic virtues so often attributed to sports in the period, but television simultaneously encouraged the association between sports as virtue and sports as vice.

Advertisers soon signed on to sponsor sports programs. The Gillette Razor Company realized as early as 1944 that televised sports might be a cheap and effective way to promote its brand, sponsoring the *Gillette Cavalcade of Sports* on NBC, first to local audiences in New York City and then nationally after the war. The show aired for fourteen years, the longest continuous run of any of the many boxing shows that would emerge in the late 1940s. The close association between Gillette and sports would help the company's market share of shaving products rise from 16 percent in the 1930s to more than 60 percent in the late 1950s. In 1945, the Boston Red Sox and Rhode Island's Narragansett Beer signed an agreement giving the brewery sponsorship rights to telecasts of Red Sox games. Narragansett paid nothing for the privilege, in part because neither the brewery nor the Red Sox management had any idea if there was money to be made in the infant medium. Other local breweries quickly followed suit. In St. Louis, Griesedieck Beer hosted a sports program featuring Harry Caray at the microphone. In Detroit, the Goebel Brewery began to sponsor telecasts of Tiger baseball games in 1947.

These early associations between consumer products and sporting events had an immediate impact. Televised sports were a medium for renting an audience to advertisers eager to sell their products. Of course, some companies had long sought to associate themselves with sports, and individual athletic heroes made good money promoting consumer goods off the field: football star Red Grange earned $10,000 in 1925 for endorsing cigarettes with the slogan "I don't smoke but my best friend smokes." TV, however, added something new to the relationship between sports and consumption. With televised sports, companies got more than a static advertisement featuring one star; they could also reach a far wider audience. TV exploded the sports marketplace, creating new narratives of adventure and excitement around which companies could pitch their products.

Watching sports on television also reinforced dominant gender relations. For one, television endorsed the already powerful association between sports and masculinity, since female athletes were almost entirely absent from television. The language of television announcers followed the patterns set down in print media, linking sports to toughness and male virility and celebrating athletes as American heroes. The connection between product and audience was mutually reinforcing. Between commercials, a largely male audience watched other men play. (NBC aired a fifteen-minute primetime show called *Sportswoman of the Week* in 1948, but the show attracted few viewers and was quickly canceled.) As the advertisements for beer, razor blades, and cigarettes made clear, advertisers also assumed that viewers would be men. This very fact would ultimately push most sports coverage out of regular primetime hours, as TV executives and advertisers realized that sitcoms and dramas would attract a more mixed audience and that women were important consumers to target.

When Gillette and Narragansett Beer began to associate their products with sports on television in the early 1940s, there were only about 6,000 sets in use. Just five years later, when the Yankees played the Giants in the World Series, more than 12 million sets had been sold in the United States. The cost of sponsorship rights rose significantly as well. For the 1947 World Series, which was the first one televised, Gillette paid $65,000 to attach the company's name to the broadcast and $175,000 for the radio rights. TV was a novelty and the company assumed that most people would listen to, rather than see, the games. Nevertheless, by 1948, every major-league club except the Pittsburgh Pirates had some sort of local broadcasting contract and televised a certain number of games. Though owners agonized over the impact of television on gate receipts, they also came to realize the potential financial windfall that television offered. "The majors seems unable to resist the lush profits that the expansion of television promises to yield," noted one New York critic.[13] In 1951, Gillette lost sole sponsorship of the World Series and the cost of television rights for the event rose to $925,000. In 1953, baseball commissioner Happy Chandler agreed to a "Game of the Week" sponsored by Falstaff Brewery and aired on ABC. With former pitching star and good-ol'-boy Dizzy Dean at the microphone, the game soon garnered a 51 share on Saturday afternoons, despite an owner-imposed MLB blackout in cities with teams. By the late 1950s, both CBS and NBC carried at least one weekly national game, and local stations showed local games. Under this system, approximately 800 games appeared annually in 1958.[14]

This kind of coverage had a devastating impact on minor-league teams. After the war, the number of minor leagues had risen from twelve to forty-two, and small cities across the country found themselves the hosts of baseball teams. However, if given a choice between watching major-league baseball on TV and going to the park to see the minor leaguers, most choose the first option. As early as the beginning of the 1948 season, the *Sporting News* ran a front-page story asking "Is TV Killing the Minors?" The magazine reported that minor league clubs in Newark and Jersey City simply could not compete when Giant and Dodger games appeared on television. The New York area was a harbinger of things to come. A 1950 study reported that more than 50 percent of fans in cities with a minor-league team would prefer to watch a major-league team on television than go to the ballpark. They also seemed to prefer Milton Berle and Lucille Ball to their hometown clubs, meaning that attendance at the minor leagues plunged from 49 million fans in 1949 to just 15.5 million by 1957.

The new amounts of money that television offered had a major impact on both professional and amateur sports. But TV affected the sports landscape in other ways as well. It helped to transform professional football into one of the most popular spectator sports in the United States. It brought boxing into homes and taverns five nights a week for most of the 1950s. Boxing and the more theatrical semi-sport of professional wrestling were hugely popular among early TV producers since there was no need to hire a cast or build a set and the confined space of the ring made it easy to see the action despite the limitations of early cameras. The structure of boxing—a three-minute round followed by a one-minute intermission—also pleased advertisers since it provided plenty of time for them to promote their product. Boxing fans could watch the small screen nightly during the week. In April of 1953, for example, truly avid boxing fans could tune into the DuMont Channel on Mondays at 9 P.M., ABC on Tuesdays at 9 P.M., CBS on Wednesdays at 10 P.M., ABC on Thursday at 9 P.M., NBC on Fridays at

10 P.M., and ABC again on Saturdays at 9 P.M.. NBC's *Gillette Cavalcade of Sports* ran for fourteen years on Friday nights, at first featuring bouts from New York City but in later years traveling across the country to cover top fighters. ABC started its coverage in 1949 with a different angle, featuring unranked and unknown young boxers on *Tomorrow's Boxing Champions*. The plethora of choices did not last, but even as late as 1960, two primetime boxing shows remained on ABC. Production costs for boxing were low and ratings high throughout most of the 1950s, though, significantly, the programs failed to attract female viewers in any significant numbers.

All the best boxers of the era appeared on the small screen, sandwiched between the advertisements for beer, grooming products, cigarettes, and cars. Viewers might tune in and see the great Sugar Ray Robinson face off in epic fights against Jake LaMotta, Gene Fullmer, or crowd-favorite Rocky Graziano. They also saw Rocky Marciano bull his way through the heavyweight division. The son of Italian immigrants and a high school dropout, Marciano was deemed too short and too small to be successful heavyweight, but a powerful right hand and the ability to withstand punishment brought him triumph in the ring. His televised performances helped him become one of American most popular athletes. "A guy with a bankroll has got something, right? Well, a guy with a good body, he's got something, too" he said. "I always wanted to have more strength than the average guy. It makes you feel proud."[15] Marciano was the poor white boy made good, an athlete whose background allowed announcers to create a narrative about the power of sports to redeem. He rose to fame at a moment when immigrant and working-class experiences were gradually disappearing from TV sitcoms, as the white, middle-class families of *Father Knows Best* and *My Three Sons* displaced the working-class couples of the *Honeymooners*. In this environment, boxing became a critical space for demonstrations of working-class masculinity, a site where viewers could still see different class values in action. There were no gray flannel suits in boxing, at least not in the ring.

Marciano earned a shot at the heavyweight title by beating aging former champion Joe Louis in what would be Louis's final fight. Viewers then cheered as Marciano overcame a first-round knockdown to win the heavyweight title in thirteen rounds against Jersey Joe Walcott in 1952, finishing the fight with a devastating right to Walcott's jaw. The tradition of the rematch helped to make boxing an easy promotion for television producers; audiences would be likely to tune in to the televised rematch between the same two fighters in 1953. In that bout,

Marciano knocked Walcott out in the first round, too quick to be good television, but satisfying nevertheless for his growing number of fans.

Marciano again defended his title in bloody back-to-back matches with Ezzard Charles in 1954. In the second, Marciano, bleeding from a split nostril and a cut on his forehead, went on the attack and knocked out Charles in the eighth round. This kind of nonstop action made for engaging TV, drawing the kind of audiences that Gillette and other boxing sponsors desired. It did not hurt his popularity that Marciano was a white man defending the heavyweight title against mostly black challengers. Walcott, Charles, and Archie Moore, who Marciano knocked out in his final title defense, were all African Americans. Marciano was also ideal for an audience that preferred the knock-out punch to strategic boxing; forty-three of his fights ended with his opponent lying prone on the ring floor. In any case, Marciano proved a sure bet for advertisers eager to promote a winner, finishing his professional career with a perfect 49–0 record.

Of course, given the overwhelming number of programs, viewers also saw many boxers who, without a television audience, might never have had careers. In this respect, television fundamentally changed the process of advancement in boxing. The medium's constant need for fighters eliminated the long-standing club system, where boxers had learned how to fight in front of small audiences before getting the opportunity to compete on a major level. The demand for fresh blood—sometimes literally, given the brutality of action in the ring—meant that young fighters appeared before large audiences much earlier in their careers, making them much more likely to be sluggers rather than boxers.

This trend was exacerbated by seeing boxing on television rather than in person. The camera, and the home audience, preferred wild, fast-moving bouts. Watching from the local bar or from the living room recliner made it difficult to realize how much violence was happening in the ring, in part because the images on a black-and-white TV failed to capture the bruises left by body punches or the cuts caused by blows to the face. TV audiences wanted action that they could see; the roundhouse right and the uppercut seemed much more dramatic than a jab or left cross. Boxing ultimately suffered from both overexposure and a devastating fixing scandal that brought investigation from Congress. The 1960s had its share of great fighters, but most of the publicity centered on the heavyweight division. The days of middleweight and featherweight boxers capturing the public imagination were largely over.

The NFL used TV much more successfully over the long haul, though this was not obvious even as late as 1959. Six percent of *Sport Illustrated*'s feature stories covered boxing that year; less than 2 percent of the stories concerned the NFL. (Baseball and golf led the way with approximately 12 percent each.) Twenty year later, however, professional football was the topic of almost 10 percent of the stories, and boxing had fallen to 3 percent. (Baseball coverage remained steady at 12 percent.) Though print media continued to privilege baseball, football made great television. For many viewers, football made more sense on the small screen than at the stadium. While live games sometimes seemed a confusing jumble of well-padded bodies, television could isolate the ball carrier and make it possible for even the casual fan to follow most plays. The structure of football—the minidrama of each first down attempt and the natural break between each play—simultaneously kept viewers' attention riveted to the screen and created space to speculate about what might happen next. Every play was a separate story around which announcers could weave a cohesive narrative. For college football, with its venerable traditions of Saturday tailgating parties, team sweaters, and cheerleaders (though a majority were men until the late 1950s), the action on the field was just part of the spectacle. For amateur football, television enhanced an already popular product. But professional football had fewer rituals in the 1950s and was less connected to a lasting tradition of "sis-boom-bah" spirit. For the NFL, television's clarity helped tremendously.

As early as 1940, the Mutual Broadcasting Co. paid $2,500 for rights to telecast the NFL Championship game. In 1950, Los Angeles became the first NFL team to have all of its games—both home and away—televised. The team paid heavily for their decision to broadcast home games, as its attendance dropped almost by half in 1950 despite winning the Western Conference title. The following season, team management blacked out home games in Los Angeles, a policy adopted leaguewide by 1952. The NFL Championship Game was televised coast-to-coast for the first time in 1951 when the DuMont Network paid $75,000 for the rights to the game. Three years later, one poll estimated that 37 percent of homes with televisions were watching the NFL on Sundays. The NFL had become a popular enough product that in 1956 CBS paid for the rights to broadcast certain regular-season games to selected television markets across the nation. Still, throughout the 1950s, NFL teams signed their own local broadcasting agreements in the same manner as MLB. As in baseball, revenues varied widely. The large-market New York Giants collected $158,000, while

Chicago's "second team," the Cardinals, earned only $15,000 for television rights. Despite the disparities, football owners proved much more willing to work together and to delegate authority to Bert Bell in the commissioner's office. By the mid-1950s, Bell had begun discussions among owners that would eventually recreate the NFL as a single economic cartel that negotiated television contracts as a group.

Television made NFL stars much more a part of the national consciousness. Quarterbacks Johnny Unitas of the Baltimore Colts and Bobby Layne of the Detroit Lions thrived on the attention. Along with players such as receiver Frank Gifford of the big-market New York Giants, who was named the NFL's Player of the Year in 1956 for what *Sports Illustrated* called his "dazzling bursts of ball carrying," and Cleveland Browns running back Jim Brown, their talents and personality gradually transformed the game into a serious contender for the country's favorite spectator sport. Unitas joined the Colts as a free agent in 1956 after being cut by his hometown team, the Pittsburgh Steelers. He threw touchdown passes in forty-seven consecutive games, but was best known for his leadership abilities and toughness, especially when the game was on the line. Baltimore teammate John Mackey once explained that it was "like being in the huddle with God."[16] Unitas's confident style fit well into the traditional crew-cut, clean-living model of sports hero. Indeed, with the help of television, he helped to define it. His on-the-field success—four NFL championships and one Super Bowl—and off-the-field laconic demeanor made Unitas a standard bearer for a style of leadership based more on action than words. Layne, on the other hand, may have been the first "bad boy" national hero of the league, as well known for his late-night carousing as his last-minute touchdown drives and ability to perform under pressure. Playing without a facemask, Layne led the Lions to three NFL titles in the 1950s, earning him widespread national coverage for his often colorful quotations delivered in a deep Texas drawl.

Unitas and the Colts made history in the 1958 championship game against the New York Giants. The first "sudden-death" championship in the NFL had an estimated 30 million fans watching their TV sets and is widely credited for transforming the NFL into a major consumer product. In addition to Unitas, the game featured several of the league's top stars, including Gifford and Colt receiver and difference maker Raymond Berry. It was a see-saw affair, and in what *Sports Illustrated* called "thirteen plays to glory," Unitas marched the Colts eighty yards in overtime, with fullback Alan Ameche scoring from one yard out to make the final score 23 to 17. Other games had been as exciting, but the combination of a championship game, overtime heroics, and television cameras made this one a perfect launching point for future NFL growth. And, of course, given the association between team and city, Baltimore residents reveled in being "winners" and in beating New York. For the day, Baltimore, despite a declining job base and emerging inner-city troubles, was king of American cities.

The small screen was also perfectly suited to the rhythms and pageantry of the college game. College football had been a perennial source of interest since the late nineteenth century, certainly the number-two team sport in the United States in terms of fan support after baseball. Booster clubs and alumni associations, slush funds for players, and an almost obsessive desire to gain national recognition certainly predated the advent of television. The universities of Oklahoma, Maryland, and Kentucky, to name just three "booster campuses," had realized in 1946 that pouring money into sports programs could enhance their schools' national reputation. However, when college football began to appear regularly on television and schools began to appreciate the financial benefits of the medium, boosterism and the impulse to cheat became even more pronounced. As early as 1949, CBS had paid $100,000 for the broadcasting rights to the Rose Bowl, a clear indicator of the enormous appeal of the game to its viewers.

Ironically, then, television played a significant role in the consolidation of authority over college sports into the NCAA's hands. The new medium emerged during a contentious time for college sports. The combination of point-shaving scandals in college basketball, cheating at the U.S. Military Academy, transcript tampering at William and Mary College, and widespread distrust and disagreement among schools about scholarships for athletes made many in college athletics fear that outside intervention was imminent. Amidst those developments, the University of Pennsylvania and the University of Notre Dame signed independent broadcasting contracts with ABC and the DuMont Network. Many other schools followed suit, inking contracts that offered their games on a regional or local level. These individual television contracts raised the stakes and led many schools to believe that the money gained from broadcasting rights might lead to an even more unequal playing field in the college game.

In addition, the NCAA emphasized the possibility of declining attendance at games to its member schools. Television Committee Chair Thomas J. Hamilton of the University of Pittsburgh struck the general tone when he explained that "with the drop in attendance, all of us are faced with a decline in revenue. As television has swept from one area to another, and with networks extending throughout all areas and able to carry games from one section to another, we feel the problem is truly national and needs collective action."[17] The idea of playing in front of half-empty stadiums—and losing gate revenues—was enough to convince many schools that firm regulation was needed. Combined, these fears forced many schools to accept a stronger oversight organization and to give more power to the NCAA to regulate their behavior.

Walter Byers became executive director of the organization in 1951. Just thirty years old, he had been a sports reporter and had worked for the Big Ten conference before joining the NCAA. Byers helped to create regulations that permitted limited scholarships for athletes, forced all schools that belonged to affiliated conferences to join NCAA, and developed harsher punishments for schools that disregarded NCAA rules. Byers also negotiated the first television contract for the 381 member schools in 1952. The contract granted NBC the rights to televise NCAA football games for $1.14 million. The newly empowered NCAA cracked down on unlimited contracts between a single school and the networks, forcing Pennsylvania and Notre Dame to give up their contracts. Member schools agreed that twelve Saturday afternoon dates would be made available for "sponsored network telecasts." To make sure that no school gained an advantage by appearing too often, the twelve games had to originate from different areas of the country and each school could only appear nationally once a season. This meant viewers saw one college football game once a week, though local stations could sometimes add an extra game of "regional interest." Unlike professional boxing, the NCAA made sure their product was not overexposed.

Though some larger schools groused about the terms, the NCAA's broadcasting plan was successful. Attendance at college football games rose in 1954 and the NCAA negotiated progressively larger contracts with network TV for rights to broadcast Saturday games. NBC carried college games for most of the 1950s, with the annual fee rising to $2.2 million by 1959. In 1960, ABC, then the third network in terms of prestige and money, made a surprise play for the NCAA football contract, upping the price to approximately $3.1 million. With bidding fierce, CBS increased the price to $5.1 million just two years later.

The combination of television revenues and the NCAA decision to permit schools to award scholarships based on athletic ability led to another fundamental change in college football—the formation of the Ivy League. These Northeastern schools had long played each other on an informal basis, but in 1952, Ivy League presidents announced that all the colleges would now play each other at least once every five years and, more significantly, would abide by the same rules. Then in 1954, the "Ivy Group" announced the adoption of a yearly round-robin schedule in football to start in 1956. Ivy schools had invented the game in the late nineteenth century and had dominated on the field through much of the early twentieth. Columbia University, never a powerhouse in sports, had won the 1934 Rose Bowl, while Princeton halfback Dick Kazmaier took home the Heisman trophy in 1951. The formation of the Ivy League effectively spelled the end of this long tradition of national success. Under the new agreement, teams agreed to cut back in recruiting, eliminate spring practices in football, and forego awarding athletic scholarships. Pennsylvania, which had created its football schedule to include games against the University of Michigan and other big-time schools before the decision, went 3–5–1 in 1953 and then lost eighteen straight games in 1954 and 1955. Unlike other schools and other conferences, the Ivy League backed away from the possibilities that the potent combination of television and athletic scholarships held.

On-the-field developments in college football helped to make the game more exciting for viewers. In 1953, college football reinstituted single-platoon football after eight years, meaning that athletes played both offensive and defensive positions. Substitutes could enter the game only once each quarter. However, having made this decision, officials then liberalized the policy every year, gradually allowing more and more substitution within the game in order to give coaches greater leeway in creating complex formations. By 1959, single players could freely substitute at any time. With the readoption of two-platoon football in 1965, the number of athletes per team exploded since players now tended to play only offense or defense. By the early 1970s, several top schools carried 200 football players, with up to 120 on scholarship. And in response to the new rules, college coaches invented three new offensive formations—the I-formation by John McKay at the University of Southern California; the veer by Bill Yeoman at the University of Houston; and the wishbone by Darrell Royal at the University of Texas. All of these made offenses more potent and college football more exciting to watch.

Changes wrought by television gradually changed the power balance in Division I football. Despite the efforts on the part of the NCAA to limit television appearances and maintain competitive balance, fewer schools achieved top rankings by the late 1950s than had in the

1930s and 1940s. The days of Santa Clara College finishing the season ranked in the top ten or Lafayette College being invited to the Sugar Bowl were over. Television also transformed the meaning of going to a postseason bowl game. The number of bowls rose dramatically. They remained an economic boon mostly for Southern towns, but with the advent of televised coverage of the games, they also offered larger pay-outs for participating teams and an excellent opportunity for national recruiting. Alabama coach Bear Bryant admitted that television was so vital to his program that "we will schedule ourselves to fit the medium. I'll play at midnight if that's what TV wants."[18]

College football appeared only on Saturday afternoons, of course, but situation comedies and dramas gradually pushed other regular-season sporting events out of primetime in the 1950s. Nevertheless, sports departments grew in importance within television networks. There were other changes as well. Throughout much of the 1950s, advertisers such as Gillette had often sponsored the entire cost of a sports program, supplying the money with which networks then paid professional leagues or the NCAA. As contract prices escalated in the early 1960s, however, this was no longer possible. Televised sports were now too expensive for individual advertisers to pay for the sponsorship of major events by themselves. Instead, networks sold advertising spots to multiple companies who remained eager to associate their product with the positive values of sports.

The competition to win the right to cover major sporting events became a race for dominance among the networks. Much the same as cities clamored for teams to confirm their major-league status, ABC, NBC, and CBS came to see the coverage of sporting events as a hallmark of institutional superiority. Television coverage had significantly increased the visibility of sports, making them a central feature of American entertainment. This visibility, in turn, made it more vital that networks cover them.

Starting in the early 1960s, ABC, the youngest and smallest of the three major networks and perennially third in the ratings, became the leading network for sports coverage. Under the leadership of Edgar Scherick and Roone Arledge, the network transformed how sports would be packaged and sold to viewers. ABC acquired the Gillette Razor Company's enormous advertising budget in 1959 by agreeing to broadcast boxing despite the sport's declining ratings. The money allowed ABC to bid on—and win—the NCAA football contract for the 1960 season. Though college football was already a ratings success, Arledge was even more determined to get "the audience involved emotionally." He believed that "if they didn't give a damn about the game, they might still enjoy the program," meaning that the pageantry surrounding the games and the human-interest stories within them became as important as the action on the field.[19] For sports to be "good TV," Arledge believed he needed to reach not just the devoted fan, but the casual viewer, someone who might not care—at least at the start—about the game's outcome. Arledge and his producers emphasized the human angle of a game. They pioneered the use of hand-held cameras to get shots of praying fans in the stands as the team prepared for a goal line stand and field microphones to pick up a tackle's thud and crunch. They trained their cameras on cheerleaders and band members, screaming coaches and players ecstatic after a score, and they used blimps and cranes to get wide angle shots of the stadium or the college town. Sports, Arledge understood, made excellent theater, especially if the on-the-field action were supplemented with dramatic flourishes from the crowd and the sidelines.

Other technological advances further changed the sport. CBS pioneered the use of sports instant replay at the annual Army-Navy football game in 1963. (The same technique had been used in the news division several weeks earlier to replay Jack Ruby's shooting of Lee Harvey Oswald.) Instant replay became crucial to how viewers saw the game. Suddenly a runner's moves could be broken down frame-by-frame in close-up, with each cut and acceleration analyzed and admired. Fans could watch a pass settle gently into a receiver's arms and see his feet dance along the sidelines as he struggled to stay in bounds. Instant replay made football beautiful. It also created a nation of better-informed second guessers, with TV viewers now able to argue endlessly about whether the referee made the correct call.

In addition to his work on college football, Arledge created a new kind of sports program. The *Wide World of Sports*, started in 1961, was developed in part because ABC did not own the rights to MLB broadcasts and struggled to fill its weekend hours during the summer. The show would ultimately help to reshape the relationship between sports and television. Arledge scouted a huge range of possible sports for the show, from the familiar but never televised spring football game at the University of Notre Dame to the oddities of Western rodeo and Mexican cliff diving. Most critical to the show's early success, he negotiated with the AAU for the right to broadcast amateur track-and-field events, providing the *Wide World of Sports* with a steady stream of events well known to viewers from the Olympics. Arledge and host Jim McKay ranged far and wide to bring TV audiences what McKay called a "new and exciting global concept of sports," though the key to the first season was a track meet between the United States and the Soviet Union in Moscow. Cold War rivalries made for good ratings and encouraged advertisers to spend their money for sports on the show.

The *Wide World of Sports* is perhaps best-remembered for its slogan: "the thrill of victory, the agony of defeat." The key to the show's long-term success—it was on the air from 1961 to 1991—was its emphasis on the personal, combined with an attitude that treated all events, no matter how mundane or bizarre, as seriously as more familiar sports. It treated sports as both news and entertainment.

The contract between the AAU and ABC contributed, ironically, to the AAU's demise as the major governing body in American track and field. Television money exacerbated a long-term, serious fight between the AAU and the NCAA over control of the sport. In 1962, college and high school track coaches voted to form the United States Track and Field Federation to represent the interests of track athletes and coaches, eroding the power of the AAU. Bill Bowerman, the track-and-field coach at the University of Oregon and one of the leaders of the effort to break with the AAU, explained that "track meets are run on college facilities by college coaches. . . . Do you know of any track in this country owned and operated by the AAU?"[20] The new federation would be followed by wrestling, gymnastics, and basketball federations. The NCAA argued it represented the majority of American athletes but only had a minimal voice in AAU affairs and endorsed the creation of new federations in other sports as well. When representation meant television money, the stakes over who would wield power grew, and the AAU and NCAA continued to snipe over the sanctioning of track meets throughout the 1960s and 1970s. By the early 1970s, one New York City lawyer claimed that the fighting had grown so bitter that NCAA and AAU officials "make the Teamsters look like undernourished doves."[21]

AFRICAN AMERICAN ATHLETES MAKE THE MOST OF TELEVISION

The combination of rapid league expansion and the appeal of television sometimes worked to considerable advantage for African American athletes. Like the Brooklyn Dodgers in 1947, team owners and college coaches tried to balance their desire to acquire the best talent and win games with suppositions about which players the audiences would want to see. As leagues added new teams and the stakes of winning grew higher with television revenues, some teams grew more willing to add black—and, in baseball, Latino—athletes who might push their clubs to championships. Champions were a better product. They attracted bigger audiences, and bigger audiences brought more revenue. While gate receipts had long made this pattern clear, television contracts made fielding the best possible team even more necessary. Some teams, including almost all Southern colleges, the NFL's Washington Redskins, and MLB's Boston Red Sox, continued to field an all-white, or almost all-white, product, but others gradually began to recruit the best talent, not the best white talent. This put sports in the vanguard of the world of entertainment. In the almost lily-white environment of primetime TV, sports regularly presented African American men (and, in the example of Wilma Rudolph, women) as heroes and stars.

For African Americans, televised sports offered a visibility almost completely unavailable on primetime sitcoms and dramas. When TV producers used black actors or featured black themes, the results provoked controversy. *Beulah*, which ran from 1950 to 1953, concerned an overweight "mammy" who worked happily caring for a white family. *Amos and Andy*, adapted from a long-running radio program, debuted in 1951 despite bitter protest from the NAACP and included almost every possible cultural stereotype of African American behavior during its three-year run. Sophisticated singer Nat "King" Cole had his own variety program for one season in 1956, but within an atmosphere of deepening racial unrest, the show could not attract sponsors and was cancelled at the end of the year. Advertisers were sensitive to the views of white Southerners, seeing them as a large market that would not buy products too closely associated with African Americans. Though entertainers such as Ella Fitzgerald, Pearl Bailey, and Count Basie sometimes appeared on variety shows in the late 1950s, not until Bill Cosby appeared in *I Spy* in 1965 did primetime feature an African American hero and not until Diahann Carroll starred as *Julia* in 1970 did a black actor earn the title role in a sitcom. Black faces were so rare that *Jet* magazine, whose readership was largely African American, offered a regular feature that listed black performers who would be appearing on television during the upcoming week.

Only in sports could television viewers regularly see blacks on television. When college football's All-America team made their yearly appearance on the popular *Ed Sullivan Show*, the black players were generally the only African Americans to appear on the hour-long variety program. Black fighters turned up regularly on the many primetime boxing programs, though boxing promoters preferred to televise white boxers. Young Floyd Patterson, who would become heavyweight champion in 1956, spent his early career struggling both to earn a title shot and to get television coverage. Still, with television, New York—and then San Francisco—residents could thrill to the talents of Willie Mays without ever going to the ballpark. Even the most casual of boxing fans, those who would never have attended a fight in person, could enjoy Sugar Ray Robinson's boxing ability and grace in the ring when they saw him on TV.

As the NFL became increasingly popular Sunday afternoon viewing, Jim Brown's astonishing running skills electrified a generation of television spectators. Brown was drafted by the Cleveland Browns out of Syracuse University in 1957, arriving in the league just as it had begun to capture the imagination of American TV viewers. At Syracuse, Brown had been a multisport athlete, named an All-American in football and lacrosse and lettering in basketball. Once a pro, the 6'2", 230-pound athlete dominated the game from his fullback position, rushing for an average of 104 yards per game over his nine-year career. He scored 126 total touchdowns, led the NFL in scoring for eight of his nine seasons, and ran for more than 1,000 yards in a season seven times. He also never missed a game. There had been other great black players in the NFL, including Brown's predecessor Marion Motley, but Brown was the league's first major African American superstar, a player who had to be nominated in any discussion about which player was the league's best. In 1963, he ran for a then-record 1,863 rushing yards over the course of a fourteen-game season. The following season, his 1,446 yards helped lead Cleveland to the NFL title. When Brown led the Cleveland Browns to a win over the hapless—and determinedly all-white—Washington Redskins, television viewers in the District of Columbia could appreciate columnist Shirley Povich's comment that "Jim Brown, born ineligible to play for the Washington Redskins, integrated their end zone three times yesterday."[22] Brown, the NFL, and television emerged as powerful forces at the same time, making Brown one of the best-known sports figures in the United States.

Visibility did not eliminate racism. Chicago Cubs fans who lived in the all-white suburb of Cicero could argue that African American shortstop Ernie Banks was the best player on the team and remain determined to keep him out of their neighborhood. Cassius Clay was called the "Louisville Lip." Black superstars such as Aaron, Mays, and Brown had few endorsement deals, as advertisers proved wary of using African American athletes to pitch their products. After outfielder Frank Robinson won the American League Triple Crown and MVP award in 1966, he was asked to make only one television appearance and two $500 speaking engagements. In comparison, when Red Sox outfielder Carl Yastrzemski won the MVP the following year, he estimated that it made him more than $200,000 over a three-year period. Robinson's agent explained to him that advertisers "don't want you and there's nothing I can do about it."[23] Robinson was not alone. In one small sample during the fall of 1966, the Equal Opportunity Commission found that black athletes appeared in only 5 percent of the 351 commercials associated with New York sporting events. Still, televised sports offered African Americans a rare visibility in the late 1950s and 1960s, a visibility that would be matched only by coverage of the civil rights struggle in the South.

THE AFL, THE SUPER BOWL, AND MONDAY NIGHT FOOTBALL

The formation of the American Football League in 1960 demonstrated the importance of television to sports, the considerable demographic shifts in the population since World War II, and the increasing amount of money to be made from investing in sports. The addition of eight AFL teams to the professional football landscape challenged the NFL, but it also increased public recognition and the popularity of the sport. In 1963, the Cleveland Browns, playing seven home games and one exhibition, came within 8,000 fans of equaling the number of spectators attending the sixty-five Cleveland Indian home games, and they did take home higher gate receipts. A survey taken in 1965 found that, for the first time, more Americans chose professional football (41 percent) as their favorite sport than baseball (38 percent). By 1969, when the AFL New York Jets defeated the Baltimore Colts in the third Super Bowl, professional football had been completely transformed from its origins as a hardscrabble, working-class minor sport into a serious contender for the title of "America's national game."

Like MLB, the NFL had not kept pace with the country's expansion in the Sunbelt and the West. When the AFL began, the San Francisco 49ers and Los Angeles Rams were the only two NFL teams west of the Mississippi. No team was farther south than the Washington Redskins, despite the region's acknowledged devotion to football. As broadcasting rights for the sport steadily increased in the 1950s, wealthy businessmen, including Southerners Lamar Hunt and Bud Adams, tried to break into the NFL's owners' circle, but they were consistently rebuffed. Existing NFL owners resisted all efforts to expand the league, fearing that overexposure might hurt their profits. In response, Hunt gathered businessmen interested in owning teams and announced the formation of a rival league, with franchises in Dallas, Houston, Denver, Buffalo, Boston, Oakland, New York, and Los Angeles. AFL franchises were located in a careful mix of new cities and major media markets that already had NFL teams, a formula designed to appeal to television executives.

The AFL struggled financially as owners lost an estimated $3 million in the first year. Competing with the Giants, the New York Titans, for example, averaged just 19,000 spectators per game and team owners lost $450,000. The NFL had responded to the AFL by adding two new teams in Dallas and Minneapolis, with the expansion Cowboys competing directly with Hunt's AFL Texans (the Texans would move to Kansas City after the 1962 season and become the Chiefs). AFL owners had deep pockets, however, and signaled immediately that they intended to compete with the NFL. Adams's new club, the Houston Oilers, successfully challenged the NFL's Rams for the rights to Heisman Trophy running back Billy Cannon. The Oilers paid Cannon $100,000, $50,000 more than Los Angeles had offered, in a move that gave the fledging league some credibility. Houston used Cannon's legs and George Blanda's arm to go 10–4 during the AFL's first regular season and then to defeat the Los Angeles Chargers 24–16 in the championship game before 32,183 fans. The Oilers and the Chargers met again in the second title game, though the Chargers had decamped to San Diego, abandoning the crowded Los Angeles market to the NFL's Rams.

Despite some superior players and exciting games—including the longest game in professional football history in 1962 between the Oilers and Dallas Texans—the league's finances remained shaky until 1964. Then the AFL agreed to a $36 million contract with NBC that gave the network the rights to league games for five years. NBC's offer came after CBS offered the NFL $14 million for two years. Because professional ratings had risen nearly 50 percent from 1961 to 1963, both networks believed that the contracts were a sound investment. In addition, the recently invented technique of instant replay promised that football would make even better television. The competition between the rival leagues had proven beneficial to both, raising the level of interest in the game. That same year, the New York Jets joined the MLB-expansion Mets in the recently finished Shea Stadium and drew a AFL-record 60,300 fans to a game against the soon-to-be league-champion Buffalo Bills. After the season, Jets management, banking on the potential of the NBC contract, signed University of Alabama quarterback Joe Namath to a record $427,000 contract. Namath was brash and stylish off the field, and the AFL Rookie of the Year on it, throwing for 2,200 yards and 18 touchdowns in 1965. By the end of the year, the league had become stable enough to admit its first expansion team, the Miami Dolphins.

Television coverage and television money brought the AFL respect. That, combined with an escalating salary war and the hard-nosed style of the new AFL commissioner Al Davis, who favored raiding NFL rosters for players, forced an alliance between the two leagues in 1966. The AFL and NFL agreed to hold a championship game between the winners of each league starting in 1966 and to hold a joint draft of college players. The leagues would then merge in 1970.

Pete Rozelle, the commissioner of the NFL, was the smooth operator who made it all happen. Rozelle, perhaps better than any other person associated with sports in the early 1960s except Roone Arledge, understood the enormous money-making potential of television. Like Arledge, Rozelle appreciated the spectacle of football: the halftime marching bands, the screaming fans, the cheerleaders. Rozelle's special talent, however, came in realizing the power of consolidation and the need for competitive balance between the league's teams. He created a new business model for the game, ultimately making the NFL far more financially valuable than other American sports. Rozelle did his job so well that Pittsburgh Steeler owner Art Rooney called him "a gift from the hand of Providence."[24]

Rozelle had been a compromise candidate for commissioner in 1959 after the powerful Bert Bell died suddenly of a heart attack. Only thirty-three, Rozelle nevertheless proved a key stabilizing factor in a league facing rapid change, most crucially convincing long-time rival owners to share television revenues between large-market television "haves" and smaller-market "have-nots." For this to be effective, Rozelle first had to lobby Congress to change the federal law that prohibited league teams from negotiating as a single entity. While both the NCAA and the AFL already engaged in the practice, it was technically illegal under antimonopoly laws and NFL owners were worried about lawsuits. Rozelle persuaded Washington lawmakers to grant the league—and by extension, all leagues—an exemption to the Sherman Antitrust Act that would allow the NFL to bargain with TV networks as a single cartel. As a result, small-market teams such as the Green Bay Packers earned over $300,000 as their cut of the NFL contract with NBC in 1962, allowing them to remain competitive with larger-market teams. The contract was the first to cover all regular-season games and all teams as a package. When the AFL and NFL began their merger in 1966, Rozelle used the sport's rapidly growing appeal to negotiate a single contract for all the teams, guaranteeing a leaguewide equilibrium that made every game potentially exciting to watch.

Rozelle's legal maneuvers and negotiating abilities also remade the ranks of ownership. A majority of AFL owners were fabulously wealthy businessmen who saw professional football as both a potential money-maker and as a status symbol of success. As Rankin Smith, who paid $9 million for the right to run the expansion Atlanta Falcons in 1965, explained, "I don't know anything about football, but doesn't every male adult want to own his own team?"[25] These were not old-style football men who made their money from their teams. This was also true in the NFL, as the lure of television revenues and improved stadium deals brought in a new kind of owner. By 1963, only five of the fourteen franchise owners were either original owners or the sons of the original owners. Art Rooney and Tim Mara, father of New York Giants owner Jack Mara, had been bookmakers who invested their winnings in their clubs. Rooney had launched his team with a $200,000 winning streak at the Saratoga race track. The Chicago Bears owner-coach George Halas had been given the team as a gift. The new breed of owner made their money differently and spent much more to acquire their teams. The new owner of the Philadelphia Eagles, Jerry Wolman, was a multimillionaire building contractor who pledged $5.5 million to take over the franchise. The expansion Minnesota Vikings were run by Bill Boyer, owner of a large car agency, while the equally new Dallas Cowboys had the backing of Texas wheeler-dealer Clint Murchison. Detroit Lions owner Bill Ford was part of the automobile-making family and had recently purchased the franchise for $4.5 million, while the bigger-market Los Angeles Rams had been bought in 1962 for $7.1 million. In this way, expansion and television revenues began to gradually change both the type of owner and the financial value of the franchises themselves.

Television had become so important to the league that one of the most memorable games in professional football's history meant little to the season's standings. In November 1968, the game between the Oakland Raiders and New York Jets ran long, and NBC made the decision to switch to its scheduled programming, a special showing of the children's movie *Heidi*. When the game went off the air with just over a minute remaining, the Jets were comfortably ahead, but the Raiders struck back with two touchdowns in forty-two seconds and ended up victorious. Switchboards at TV stations across the country lit up with callers, including more than 10,000 in New York City, protesting the decision to pull the game. What came to be called the "Heidi game" reveals both the impact of television on professional football and how important professional football had become to Americans.

The merger between the two professional football leagues ultimately created the most watched, most talked about sporting event on television, the Super Bowl. AFL architect Lamar Hunt earned credit for the name, inspired by his daughter's high-bouncing super ball. The first game attracted approximately 61,000 fans to the Los Angeles Coliseum to see the AFL upstarts, represented by Hunt's Kansas City Chiefs, square off against the more established NFL and its champion, the Green Bay Packers. Tickets prices topped out at twelve dollars, and the University of Arizona marching band provided halftime entertainment. The Coliseum held 100,000, so the game was a bit short of a sellout, but an estimated 60 million viewers watched the game on television. Viewer interest was high; 79 percent of the televisions on at the time showed the game, a level that has never again been equaled. Perhaps this was because two networks, NBC and CBS, carried the game, with CBS taking a forty-three share and NBC a thirty-six share. The networks sold one-minute commercials for between $75,000 and $85,000.

Like many of the Super Bowls that would follow, the first was not the most entertaining game of the season. The Chiefs proved no match for Green Bay quarterback and game MVP Bart Starr, wide receiver Max McGee, and safety Willie Wood, who carried the Packers to an emphatic 35–10 victory. Starr passed for 250 yards and went ten for thirteen on third-down conversions, while McGee had the best game of his career, with two touchdowns and 138 yards receiving. Wood's forty-yard interception came early in the third quarter when the Packers led only 14–10 and broke the game open for Green Bay. But despite the lack of drama, the Super Bowl quickly developed into the most hyped and anticipated game of the year, a vivid demonstration of how effectively professional football had used television to transform a second-string sport into the nation's top spectator sport.

By the early 1970s, nothing equaled the Super Bowl in hype, but Arledge tried. He and Commissioner Rozelle agreed to a new concept in which ABC would televise one game a week in primetime. Neither man had much to lose. Rozelle, always looking for new angles to promote football, feared that professional football had reached its maximum audience on Sunday afternoons; ABC and Arledge trailed the other major networks in primetime rating. In return for a $8.5 million contract, Rozelle promised ABC quality match-ups for the evening games and *Monday Night Football* was born with an opening contest that featured "Broadway Joe" Namath and the New York Jets.

By itself, football in primetime would not have been revolutionary television. But Arledge turned the game itself into a spectacle. He committed two production crews to the game, one for live coverage, the other for technical effects such as instant replay. Nine cameras followed the action, including action in the stands and the sidelines. Arledge also believed that "the time has passed for sports announcers who just put captions on the pictures," and so created a new kind of announcing crew for *Monday Night Football*. He encouraged commentators Howard Cosell, Don Meredith, and Frank Gifford (who replaced Keith Jackson after the first season) to think of themselves as part of the show, so "that people would be interested regardless of the game or the score."[26] Just as with *Wide World of Sports*, the emphasis was on human drama and the spectacle of the game, with Arledge packaging football to audiences who might not otherwise be interested in sports.

FIGURE 1. Boston Red Sox outfielder Ted Williams (left) and shortstop Johnny Pesky were among the more than five hundred major league baseball players who served in the military during World War II. With so many top players on active duty, the level of play on the field dropped and, to continue to draw crowds, baseball officials depended heavily on the patriotic image of players in uniform. Source: AP Photo, 04/24/1943.

FIGURE 2. When Minneapolis Laker center George Mikan (no. 99) scored a record forty-eight points at Madison Square Garden in 1949, professional basketball barely registered on a national level; most players favored the two-handed set shot and games were low-scoring events often marred by fistfights on the court. The seven-foot Mikan's scoring abilities turned the Lakers into perennial contenders for the NBA title and made him the league's first superstar big man. Source: Bettmann/Corbis Photo, 02/22/1949.

FIGURE 3. College basketball enjoyed an enormous national following in 1950 when coach Nat Holman's (center) City College of New York team won both the National Invitational Tournament and the NCAA title and were feted as all-American role models. In the middle of the following season, however, three CCNY players were arrested on charges of point shaving and throwing games. Ultimately, thirty-five players across the country were implicated in the scandal. Source: AP Photo, 3/28/1950.

FIGURE 4. In 1952, the United States Olympics Committee provided almost no training or financial support for female athletes, reflecting a general lack of opportunity for women in sports. These winners of the individual track-and-field events at the U.S. Olympic Trials stood little chance against better-trained teams from the Soviet Union and other eastern bloc countries. In the "beat the Russians" atmosphere of the Cold War, this would eventually compel the United States to improve opportunities for women in Olympic sports. Source: AP Photo, 7/5/1952.

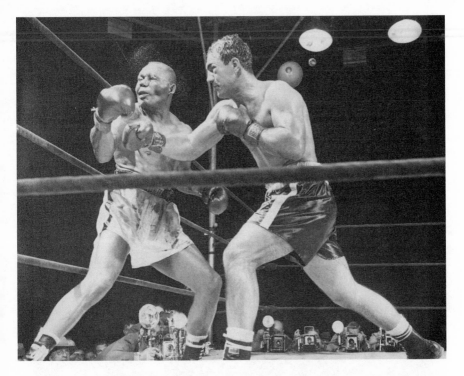

FIGURE 5. The powerful fists of Rocky Marciano knocked out champion Joe Walcott in the thirteenth round of this 1952 title fight. Marciano's reputation as a winner—he retired with a perfect 49–0 record—and the appeal of his working-class toughness made him a natural on the new medium of television. In the mid-1950s, boxing fans could find a fight in primetime nearly every night of the week. Source: Bettmann/CORBIS/ Herb Scharfman, 9/23/1952.

FIGURE 6. In 1957, Althea Gibson became the first African American ever to win titles at Wimbledon and the United States Open tennis tournaments. Like other racial pioneers, such as MLB's Jackie Robinson and the NFL's Marion Motley, Gibson overcame persistent racial discrimination to rise to the top of her sport. In addition, her on-court aggressiveness led many spectators, both black and white, to question her femininity. Source: AP Photo, 7/3/1958.

FIGURE 7. The Brooklyn Dodgers' owner Walter O'Malley's announcement that he was moving his successful and much-beloved club to Los Angeles led to widespread protest by fans. Though Dodger infielders Pee Wee Reese (left) and Don Zimmer chipped in to bring attention to a spring training T-shirt campaign, the "Keep the Dodgers in Brooklyn" crusade failed. Together with the New York Giants, the Dodgers moved to California before the start of the 1958 season. Source: Bettman/CORBIS, 3/4/1957.

FIGURE 8. After learning that he had won college football's Heisman Trophy, Navy quarterback Roger Staubach nevertheless kept his attention focused on the annual Army–Navy game. He guided the Midshipmen to their fifth consecutive victory against the Cadets in 1963, a game postponed a week to honor the memory of slain President John F. Kennedy. Staubach served on active duty during the Vietnam War before joining the NFL's Dallas Cowboys in 1969, making him a role model for conservative Americans unsettled by the changes of the 1960s. Source: Bettman/CORBIS, 11/26/1963.

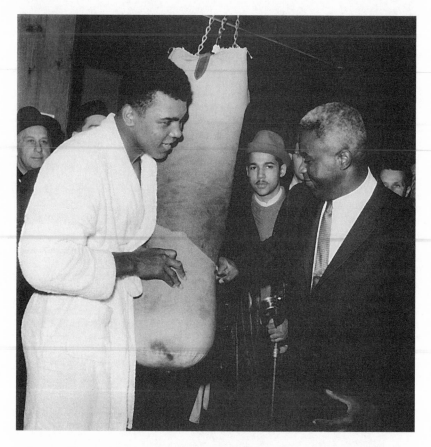

FIGURE 9. Heavyweight champion Muhammad Ali was still known as Cassius Clay when former Brooklyn Dodger star Jackie Robinson visited his training camp in 1963. Robinson and Ali both spoke out against the racial discrimination facing African Americans in the United States. Robinson lent his voice and fame to Martin Luther King Jr.'s nonviolent civil rights movement, while Ali joined the Nation of Islam and became a forceful advocate for black power and antiwar movements. Source: AP, 3/13/1963.

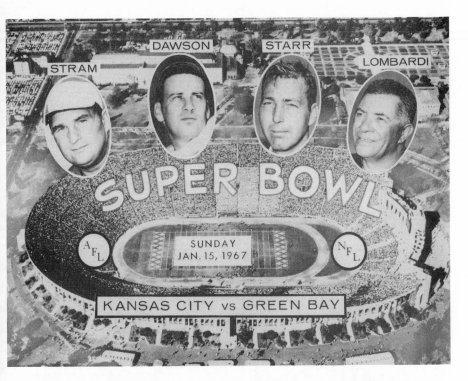

FIGURE 10. When the upstart American Football League Kansas City Chiefs faced off against the powerhouse NFL Green Bay Packers in 1967, the atmosphere and the publicity for the game was underwhelming: the game did not sell out, and the University of Arizona marching band provided the halftime entertainment. By the time the AFL and NFL merged into one league in 1970, however, the Super Bowl had become the country's most watched annual sporting event, a television spectacle without rival. Source: Bettman/ CORBIS, 1/10/1967.

FIGURE 11. Together, sprinters Tommie Smith and John Carlos became the defining symbol of the black power movement when they raised their black-gloved fists during the playing of the national anthem at the 1968 Olympics. Both athletes had been part of a movement of African American athletes that pushed for a boycott of the Games to protest racism in the United States and South Africa. Smith, the gold medal winner, and Carlos, the bronze medal winner, were suspended from the team for their actions and sent home. Source: Bettman/CORBIS, 1968.

FIGURE 12. When the top-ranked Nebraska Cornhuskers and the no. 2 Oklahoma Sooners met for conference bragging rights in 1971, it was a "Game of the Century" that largely lived up to its pregame hype. Nebraska won 35–31, part of an undefeated season that brought the school its second straight national title. For many Nebraska residents, Cornhusker college football did not just represent the university; it was also a source of pride and tradition for the entire state. Source: Bettman/CORBIS, 11/25/1971.

FIGURE 13. The "Battle of the Sexes" tennis match between Billie Jean King and fifty-five-year-old Bobby Riggs was as much media circus as sporting event, with King attended by bare-chested "gladiators" and carried into the event on a feathered cart. King had won the French Open, the U.S. Open, and Wimbledon in 1972, but it was her straight-set victory over Riggs that proved to a national audience that female athletes could attract large audiences and win on a national stage under extreme pressure. Source: Bettman/CORBIS, 1973.

FIGURE 14. Steve Prefontaine (left) and Frank Shorter helped to ignite a passion for long-distance running among middle-class Americans in the 1970s. Before he died in a car accident at twenty-four, Prefontaine had such potential and charisma that he had made the cover of *Sports Illustrated* at eighteen. Shorter ran to victory—and to national acclaim—in the 1972 Olympics marathon and then helped to transform the New York City Marathon into a major event with thousands of competitors. Source: Bettman/ CORBIS, 6/8/1974.

FIGURE 15. Nolan Ryan tossed his fifth no-hitter in September 1981 for the Houston Astros, a high point in a difficult season for Major League Baseball. Faced with threats from the owners to undermine free agency, Ryan and other players went on strike for fifty days in the middle of the season. The strike, which ended when the owners ran out of insurance money, alienated fans from the game and forced MLB to create an odd "split season" format in order to salvage the season. Source: AP Photo, 9/26/1981.

FIGURE 16. In 1984, Coach Pat Summitt and her players gleefully celebrated the first-ever Olympic gold medal for American women's basketball. Summitt, who played for the 1976 silver-medalist Olympic team, became the coach at the University of Tennessee and turned the Lady Volunteers into one of the top programs in the country, winning five national titles between 1987 and 1998. Source: Bettman/CORBIS, 8/7/1984.

FIGURE 17. After diver Greg Louganis won his first gold medal at the 1984 Los Angeles Olympics, one national magazine called him the "classiest act" of the Games and suggested that he was the physical embodiment of a Greek god. In 1995, when Louganis announced that he was HIV positive, media coverage changed dramatically. Because Louganis had previously come out as a gay man, his admission received much more negative scrutiny than that of the Los Angeles Lakers' star Magic Johnson, who announced that he was HIV positive in 1991. Source: Bettman/CORBIS, 8/8/1984.

FIGURE 18. Wearing a signature pair of Nike Air Jordans, Michael Jordan of the Chicago Bulls soared to win the 1988 slam-dunk competition, beating Dominique Wilkins of the Atlanta Hawks on the final dunk. Jordan's otherworldly on-the-court skills and his off-the-court consumer appeal transformed the NBA from a marginal professional league into an international success story. Jordan, who led the Bulls to six NBA titles, became the most famous man in the world. Source: AP Photo/John Swart, 2/6/1988.

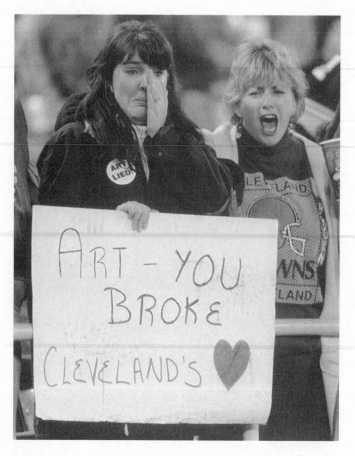

FIGURE 19. Owner Art Modell of the Cleveland Browns broke fans' hearts in 1995 when he accepted a lucrative offer to move the team to Baltimore. Modell and other NFL owners were engaged in what NFL commissioner Pete Rozelle called "franchise free agency," lured by city officials who promised new stadiums and massive tax breaks in order to be known as "big-league" cities. Baltimore fans had cried similar tears in 1984 when the Colts left for a better deal in Indianapolis. Source: AP Photo/Gene J. Puskar, 11/14/1995.

FIGURE 20. After Brandi Chastain launched the winning goal kick past Chinese goalie Gao Hong in the 1999 Women's World Cup finals, her postgoal celebration created a media firestorm of discussion about the state of women's sports and the image of the female athlete. The United States's victory in the World Cup, combined with the rise of other powerful female athletes such as tennis superstars Venus and Serena Williams, demonstrated an enormous shift in attitudes about how female athletes should look and act since the passage of Title IX legislation in 1972. Source: AP Photo/*The San Francisco Examiner*, Lacey Atkins, 7/11/1999.

FIGURE 21. Skateboarder Tony Hawk became a superstar for the under-twenty set, thrilling crowds with his tricks on the board and helping to create a major buzz around extreme sports. Like other superstars in more established sports, Hawk diversified, using his image to sell skateboards, clothes, and the wildly popular "Tony Hawk's Pro Skater" video game. Source: Getty Image, 6/4/2002.

4. Making Sense of the Sixties

January 1, 1964: The top-ranked University of Texas Longhorns faced the number two Midshipmen of the United States Naval Academy in college football's Cotton Bowl. Navy's star quarterback Roger Staubach threw for 228 yards, but the Longhorns dominated from the start, winning the contest 28 to 6 and finishing their season a perfect 11–0. On the same day, coach Bear Bryant's Alabama team kicked four field goals to hold off Ole Miss 12 to 7 in the Sugar Bowl, while the Nebraska Cornhuskers narrowly overcame the Auburn Tigers in the Orange Bowl, and Illinois beat the University of Washington in the Rose Bowl. It should come as no surprise that the Alabama, Ole Miss, Texas, and Auburn squads had no African American players. In fact, Ole Miss earned a spot in the Sugar Bowl because bowl officials decided against offering a bid to an integrated Pittsburgh Panthers, who demanded that their two African American players be allowed the same training privileges as white players. Even the Navy squad represented a school that admitted only fifty-one African Americans in the twenty years between 1945 and 1964; the football team itself had remained all white until Darryl Hill integrated the unit in 1962.

Less than two months after the all-white Texas team claimed the national championship, former Olympic gold medalist Cassius Clay challenged menacing heavyweight champion Sonny Liston in Miami. Despite Clay's exhortation to "save your money and don't bet on Sonny!" the twenty-two-year-old fighter was given little chance to win by most fight prognosticators.[1] But in a stunning upset, Liston remained in his corner when the bell rang for the seventh round and Clay became the new heavyweight champion by technical knock-out. At the time of the fight, the young fighter had been meeting secretly with representatives from the Black Muslims, and, just months later, Clay renounced what he called his "slave name" and became Muhammad Ali. He had flirted with the Nation of Islam as early as 1961, believing that the religious group offered good answers to the complex questions inherent in being a black man in the United States. But the announcement of his conversion proved more stunning than his defeat of Liston. With a mantra of "I don't have to be what you want me to be, I'm free to be who I want," Ali proclaimed his freedom from white standards and demanded to be taken seriously as a militant black man.[2]

Thus, the United States simultaneously boasted a national championship team from a university that refused to allow African Americans to play on its football team and a heavyweight champion who belonged to a militant religious sect that denounced the white race as evil. Staubach, Navy's quarterback and the year's Heisman Trophy winner, would do four years of duty in Vietnam; Ali would be jailed for refusing to enlist. These were the extremes, but evocative moments and figures regularly combined with real protests in the 1960s, allowing people of every inclination to find a hero. Sports and social change were on a collision course, especially around the issue of racial justice.

Despite the many remaining segregated collegiate football teams, black athletes had made significant progress in integrating sports. With Willie Mays, Hank Aaron, and Frank Robinson among the best of baseball, Jim Brown the brightest star in the NFL, Arthur Ashe the first black player named to the Davis Cup team, and Bill Russell and Wilt Chamberlain the superstars of the NBA, the color barriers that had been so entrenched just twenty years before seemed to be crumbling. Prior to the movement for racial justice in the 1960s, sports officials could pat themselves on the back and call themselves innovators for their willingness to allow African Americans to play alongside whites. Indeed, on the surface, sports sometimes seemed the only "level playing field" in American society, a place where merit and skill outranked the color of a person's skin. Liberal Americans pointed to several teams—the Los Angeles Dodgers, the Cleveland Browns, the Boston Celtics, the UCLA Bruins—as sites of interracial harmony and as potential models for the rest of society.

But the language and activism of the struggle for racial justice gradually permeated the world of sports, sparking revolts within sports about the treatment of black athletes. Access to opportunity was no longer enough. For first time, large numbers of black athletes began to question how they were treated in sports and began to demand equality. Larry Doby, the first African American player in the American League, had walked away when opposing players spat tobacco in his face; Jackie Robinson remained quiet even as opponents had heckled him with racial slurs. Both men, and the athletes who followed in the 1950s, understood that questioning the system or fighting back too openly could potentially end their careers and impede future opportunities for African Americans. The same sort of politics of respectability that led civil rights activists to wear suits and Sunday dresses when they sat in at lunch counters propelled pioneer black athletes. Most black athletes were willing to swallow their grievances for the opportunity to compete. By 1968, however, Doby, for one, was no longer silent and no longer grateful. Sports, he argued, treated African Americans like cattle, a commodity to be used and then discarded. While baseball had moved Doby "to the front of the bus," it only allowed him to stay there while he was productive. Then, he said, "it told me to get off at the back door."[3]

In turn, sporting events and black athletes provided the civil rights movement with visible role models and spokespeople for social change. In the 1960s, sports and politics became increasingly difficult to separate. The desire to succeed and the will to win remained as potent as ever for athletes, but the social unrest of the 1960s meant that, for some, new layers of meaning emerged. Many athletes challenged traditional ideas during the decade. Sometimes this manifested itself as active protest against injustices within sports and in the larger society. At other times, it appeared in new clothing styles and hair lengths or as a rebellion against coaching authority. Though most black athletes were neither civil rights activists nor black power enthusiasts, sports became the most visible arena in which the cultural tenets of black power were expressed. Sports were important symbolically, but they were also a major industry that provided African Americans with the opportunity for economic advancement and a chance to make a national impact.

By the late 1960s and into the 1970s, some African American athletes were right to wonder whether they could be "just athletes" in an atmosphere that identified them as the physical personification of racial pride. Yet for Americans worried or appalled by the seemingly radical direction of the 1960s—the strident protests against the Vietnam War, for example, or the rise of drug use that accompanied the counterculture—sports also proved a source of comfort. Ali's conversion to the Nation of Islam, a proposed boycott of the 1968 Olympics, and growing black militancy on college teams were only part of the story. Conservatives who bemoaned the unraveling of American society by hippies and beatniks could look to the hard-nosed, crew-cut-wearing Green Bay Packer coach Vince Lombardi as a role model, someone who embodied traditional masculine values and extolled the virtues of self-discipline and hard work. Ohio State University coach Woody Hayes seemed a citadel of stability, as did players such as the Naval Academy's Roger Staubach and Green Bay Packer quarterback Bart Starr. Even in a decade of profound social change, sports continued to function as a site of conservatism.

This chapter looks first at the mid-1960s and the ways that minority athletes began to slowly apply the language and the lessons of the civil rights movement to their own lives. A few athletes joined the movement itself, lending their images to Southern struggles for the right to vote and the right to access to public accommodations. This section concludes with a discussion of Ali's boxing career and public pronouncements. Ali was the most important athlete of the decade, a lightning rod for controversy, and a man who changed the way athletes—both black and white—were perceived. The chapter's second section looks at sports in 1968, a year of massive upheaval in society. Even as Southern college programs gradually allowed African Americans to join their teams—often several years after black students had integrated the classroom—other black athletes began to revolt against perceptions of inequality within collegiate sports. College sports—and then the Olympics—became a highly visible site of civil rights activism and black power rhetoric. Not all athletes endorsed revolutionary activism. The third section looks at the conservative heroes of the 1960s, as sports continued to promote a tough, clean-cut version of masculinity. This chapter closes with a look at the NBA and its rival league, the American Basketball Association (ABA). The racial composition of professional basketball changed dramatically in the 1960s, but the most lasting effect of this transformation was stylistic rather than political. Pro basketball made afros cool and dunks an expression of black power.

MUHAMMAD ALI: ICON OF BLACK POWER AND
ANTIWAR SENTIMENT

Heavyweight boxer Muhammad Ali emerged as the most flamboyant, most quotable, most controversial athlete of the decade. Called the "Louisville Lip" in his first years as a professional because of his colorful boasts, Ali would become a spokesman and icon for racial pride and self-determination for a generation of African Americans. Actor and activist Harry Belafonte claimed that "out of the womb of oppression he was our phoenix. He was the spirit of all our young. He was our manhood."[4] Like heavyweight champion Joe Louis before him, Ali embodied the dreams of a community. Unlike Louis and other great black athletes, however, Ali both defied white behavioral norms and spoke out vehemently about the need for social change.

Before Ali, civil rights organizations did more to change racial inequality in sports than athletes did for the movement. Only a few well-known black athletes took an active part in the civil rights campaigns of the early 1960s, most notably Jackie Robinson. Robinson had retired from baseball after the 1956 season, but he remained an enormously important figure within the black community. Using his influence, he raised money for Martin Luther King's Southern Christian Leadership Conference (SCLC) voter registration drives, the sit-ins organized by the Student Nonviolent Coordinating Committee (SNCC), and the Freedom Summer campaign. Robinson also lent his image to the movement. Along with heavyweight boxer Floyd Patterson, for example, Robinson went to Birmingham, Alabama, in 1963 as part of the campaign to end segregation in that city.

But Robinson was unusual. Most African American athletes were symbols of social change rather than activists. Groups fighting for racial justice, including the NAACP and the Congress of Racial Equality (CORE), tried to mobilize African Americans to pressure sports owners to hire black players and, later in the decade, black coaches and black league officials. These were workplace issues, and civil rights activists used their power as consumers, especially boycotts and pickets, to try to influence league policies. Most significantly, the Southern civil rights movement gave athletes a language for making sense of the problems they faced. Players themselves gradually began to apply the lessons and tactics of the civil rights movement to their own environment. Rather than blame a specific coach or manager, a few athletes began to argue that racism was endemic within the structure of sports and that it was their duty to speak out about the problems they faced.

When the African American players on the Boston Celtics were denied admission to several bars and restaurants during a 1962 exhibition tour of Indiana and Kentucky, Bill Russell, K. C. Jones, and Satch Sanders boycotted a game in Lexington, Kentucky, to protest. African American stars threatened to boycott the 1965 Pro Bowl because they faced serious discrimination in the host city of New Orleans. Art Powell, a receiver for the New York Titans in the American Football League, claimed that if the players agreed to stay in New Orleans, it would "imply that we accept such treatment for ourselves and our people."[5]

These sports-based boycotts seem inconsequential compared to the determined efforts to gain the vote and end Jim Crow practices in the South. But protests within the world of sports emerged from the same frustrations and demanded the same full rights of citizenship as the sit-ins to desegregate lunch counters and "freedom rides" to integrate Southern bus terminals. Most athletes spent far too many hours in the gym or on the practice field to be wholeheartedly a part of a movement for social justice. Individual success and team victories remained their priority. As part of a team, many athletes also faced pressure to conform from coaches and teammates. But the language and actions of advocates for racial justice began to permeate the world of sports.

Ali's personality alone marked him as a fresh voice in the push for civil rights and racial justice. His inventive rhyming schemes, prefight predictions of when he would knock out each opponent, and boasts that he was "the greatest" had already marked him as different from previous black champions before he met Liston in 1964. Unlike Louis, for example, the "Louisville Lip" was not seen as a "credit to his race" by the white press corps, many of whom hated him for his arrogance and his free spirit. But Ali seemed blithely unconcerned about what people, especially white people, thought of him. His approach worked. The combination of the force of Ali's personality and the enormous coverage afforded by television created a new kind of sports celebrity. No athlete used television better, although no athlete was more reviled by the white press.

By rejecting Christianity and joining a black militant religious sect opposed to racial integration, Ali defied the way that great black athletes presented themselves to the world. In the emergent spirit of the sixties, Ali promised to be both true to himself and a new, more outspoken role model for the black community. When criticized for not being a positive role model like Louis and Sugar Ray Robinson, Ali replied that the fighters had made little difference since "they're gone now, and the black man's condition is just the same, ain't it? We're still catching hell."[6] Rather than turn to the Christian-led Southern civil rights move-ment, with its nonviolent approach to social change, Ali looked to the urban ghettos of the North and the fierce rhetoric of Malcolm X. The Nation of Islam was a religious and political group led by Elijah Muhammad, but it was most closely identified in the public's mind with Malcolm X and his exhortations to fight racism "by any means necessary." An American invention, the religion joined ideas about black nationalism with tenets of the Islamic faith. It offered dispos-sessed African Americans a religious identity that simultaneously val-ued their blackness and demanded self-improvement and community development. With Malcolm X as the most public early spokesman, the Nation of Islam emerged as a small but powerful alternative to King's leadership, and the group eventually provided the ideological founda-tion for the concepts of "black pride," "black power," and "black con-sciousness" that emerged in late 1960s and 1970s.

After taking the championship belt from Liston in 1964, Ali defended his title eight times over the following two years. These were difficult times. Freedom Summer, a voter registration campaign that brought hundreds of idealistic Northerners to Mississippi to work with the state's African Americans, began in June 1964. But just days into the project, three young civil rights workers disappeared in the rural countryside; their bodies were found in a mass grave in August. The civil rights movement experienced a great moment of triumph when President Johnson promised the nation that "we shall overcome" racial discrimination and then pushed through the 1965 Voting Rights Act, but the nonviolent movement was beginning to lose steam. A racially based riot in Watts, California, in August, 1965 left thirty-four dead and started a succession of "long, hot summers" in American cities, as some poor and minority urban residents, fed up with police brutality, substandard housing, and massive unemployment, turned to violence. Within this atmosphere of racial discontent, Ali infused each of his bouts with overt political meaning, presenting himself as fighting for the liberation of black Americans and, increasingly, black people worldwide, when he stepped into ring. Ali knocked out Liston in a rematch in 1965 and then toyed with his opponents, calling other black fighters "Uncle Toms" and ridiculing white fighters. In the process, Ali transformed himself into the standard bearer for racial mil-itancy and became perhaps the most visible proponent for what came to be called black power.

The idea of black power emerged as a concept within the civil rights movement in late 1965 but was always somewhat fuzzy in its practical application. Sometimes it was used to express the need for political power; at other times it seemed a rejection of the goals of racial integration and cultural assimilation. In their influential 1967 book, *Black Power: The Politics of Liberation in America*, Stokely Carmichael and Charles Hamilton argued that black power was not reverse racism but a move toward self-determination and self-identity by blacks. For many white Americans, the slogan was both frightening and divisive. For many African Americans, black power stood for the development of pride and self-esteem, a celebration of black culture in the face of white oppression. In this respect, though athletes generally made poor civil rights activists, they proved to be compelling symbols of black pride and assertions of black culture. Every time Ali knocked out an opponent, every time he spun a rhyme, every time he demanded that writers call him Ali rather than Clay, he was black power personified.

Though Ali was already a militant advocate for black power by late 1966, it was his fervent opposition to the Vietnam War that made him the most famous athlete of the 1960s. Ali's life changed forever on April 1, 1967, when the government ordered him to report for induction into the Army. Just one month before his championship bout with Liston in 1964, Ali had failed the Armed Forces Qualifying exam and been classified 4-F, mentally unfit for military service. Retested three months later under supervision to make sure that he had not failed the exam intentionally, Ali again scored too low to be admitted into service. Given Ali's intense verbal abilities, natural wit, and his self-discipline in the ring, his failure to achieve a passing score speaks to the inferiority of the generally segregated educational opportunities afforded to African Americans in the 1950s and 1960s.

In 1964, the manpower needs for the war in Vietnam remained light. But Congress approved the Gulf of Tonkin Resolution in August after North Vietnamese torpedo boats allegedly attacked U.S. destroyers, opening the door for massive American involvement in Vietnam. President Johnson sent the first significant number of troops overseas in March 1965, with approximately 120,000 American soldiers serving in Vietnam by the end of the year. That number would grow to over 485,600 by the end of 1967. As American involvement in the war deepened and manpower needs increased, the Johnson administration searched for ways to enhance troop strength that would not affect an increasingly resistant student population, establishing what came to be called Robert McNamara's Project 100,000. Project 100,000 was presented as an opportunity for disadvantaged young men who needed the marketable skills the armed services could offer but had failed the qualifying exam. As part of the project, the Department of Defense lowered the minimum admissible test score from thirty to fifteen, meaning that Ali's status suddenly changed from 4-F to 1-A.

In the days immediately after he received his draft notice, Ali, like many young men, worried about its implications on his life, asking over and over again, "Why me, why me?" By the end of that first day, he would famously assert that "I ain't got no quarrel with them Vietcong." His view then quickly became more nuanced. Drawing on ideas promoted by black power leaders such as Carmichael, who maintained that black men were serving a country that refused them civil rights, Ali made a connection between civil rights struggles in the American South and the war overseas. "Why," he asked, "should they ask me and other so-called Negroes to put on a uniform and go 10,000 miles from home and drop bombs on brown people in Vietnam while so-called Negro people in Louisville are treated like dogs and denied simple human rights?"[7]

Citing his religious opposition to the Vietnam War, Ali refused military duty at an induction center in Houston. As he explained to the press, "I am a member of the Black Muslims and we don't go to war unless they're declared by Allah himself." To make certain of Ali's intentions, the induction officer called the heavyweight champion twice, once asking Cassius Clay to step forward, then calling on Muhammad Ali. Ali's opposition to the war had little chance of prevailing. Until 1966, the law held that deferments were available only to individuals who opposed all wars based on a belief in a Supreme Being. The most successful conscientious objector applicants were from traditional "peace churches": the Quakers, Mennonites, and Brethren denominations. Obviously, anyone associated with a recognized Christian church had much easier time gaining objector status than did the members of the Nation of Islam. The religion's separatist beliefs and their merger of religion and politics made earning C.O. exemption extremely unlikely. Still, Ali was not alone in claiming objector status. The numbers of young men citing religious or moral objections to the war as reason not to serve rose from 18,000 in 1964 to 61,000 by 1971. Prosecutions also rose, and, during the height of the war, draft cases such as Ali's accounted for a tenth of all cases appearing in federal courts, though less than 2 percent of the men accused were convicted.

Nevertheless, when Ali made his decision to defy the draft, the Vietnam War remained relatively popular among the American public and the antiwar movement was quite small. The first draft cards had been burned in a 1965 demonstration in New York City, but not until late in 1967 did significant numbers of students and other Americans begin to actively protest against the war. A national demonstration in Washington, D.C., in October 1967 attracted over 100,000 people to the Lincoln Memorial. Then in January 1968, the North Vietnamese army launched the Tet Offensive, attacking more than one hundred cities and military installations and the United States Embassy in Saigon. Most of the attacks were quickly repelled, but in the imperial capital of Hue City the fighting raged for three weeks. The United States and South Vietnamese had greatly underestimated the strength of the enemy and Tet revealed to many Americans that the war was not close to the resolution promised by President Johnson. Some began to ask whether victory in South Vietnam was worth the price in American lives. In this context, Ali's stance electrified many students, especially within the African American community, pushing some to reconsider their position on the war.

For Ali personally, his decision had dramatic consequences. Just days after his refusal to be inducted, and long before standing trial for draft evasion, Ali's heavyweight title was revoked by the New York State Athletic Commission and his boxing license was withdrawn because his stance violated the "best interests of boxing." On June 20, 1967, a Texas jury took just twenty minutes to find the twenty-five-year-old boxer guilty of draft evasion. The judge then sentenced Ali to the maximum penalty of five years in prison and a $10,000 fine.

Most of the white press and many other Americans approved wholeheartedly of the decision. Instead of the proud American who had won a gold medal in the 1960 Olympics, Ali now represented for some all that was wrong with American society. Ali was "as sorry a spectacle as those unwashed punks who picket and demonstrate against the war," said respected columnist Red Smith.[8] Ali seemed unpatriotic and ungrateful for the opportunities that sports had offered him, a cocky loudmouth and dangerous black power advocate. He was also frightening. As heavyweight champion of the world, Ali commanded attention, and his combination of moral principle and athletic ability made him a powerful symbol of dissidence and opposition to the federal government.

Unable to box, but out of prison while his lawyers appealed the decision, Ali hit the college lecture circuit, traveling around the country to discuss his case and the place of black people in the United States. He applied the same sort of self-discipline he displayed in the ring to developing his public speeches, working for months to hone them. While the white press ridiculed him, his forthright stance against government policies in Vietnam and his willingness to sacrifice his career for his beliefs made him a hero for many African Americans and for college students opposed to the war. In *Soul on Ice*, Black Panther leader Eldridge Cleaver called Ali "the first 'free' black champion ever to confront white America . . . a genuine revolutionary, the black Fidel Castro of boxing."[9]

After three and a half years of exile from boxing, Ali won a lawsuit against the Boxing Commission that had denied him a license to fight before his conviction for draft evasion. In making his case, his lawyers documented numerous instances in which boxing authorities had licensed men convicted of rape and theft. Ali reentered the ring in a bout against Jerry Quarry in October 1970, knocking Quarry out in the third round. Ali's battle over serving in Vietnam ended with a Supreme Court decision in 1971 that overturned his conviction on a technicality.

Ali lost a unanimous decision to Joe Frazier in a tremendous fifteen-round fight just before the Supreme Court decision. By then, Ali had become convinced that he was a fighter for the people, a champion of the poor and the disposed. "I'm fighting for me," he said. "I'm fighting for the black people on welfare, the black people who have no future, black people who are the wineheads and dope addicts. I am a politician for Allah."[10] After he returned to ring, Ali regained the title that had been taken from him by first beating Jimmy Ellis and Ken Norton and then Frazier in a rematch. In a thrilling fight evocatively called the "Rumble in the Jungle," Ali faced George Foreman in Kinshasa, Zaire, in 1974, the first heavyweight championship event ever held in Africa. The underdog again, Ali knocked out Foreman in the eighth round to regain the undisputed heavyweight title, six years after having been stripped of his championship.

No other athlete ever made the same kind of professional sacrifice in order to hold firm to his convictions. Ali gave up three and a half years in the prime of his boxing career in order to remain true to his beliefs. But Ali's stance against the war, so outside the mainstream in 1967, gradually took hold among other athletes and sports officials. His fight against the United States government reverberated throughout the sporting world, especially among younger athletes. UCLA basketball star and three-time Player of the Year Bill Walton was arrested at an antiwar protest in the early 1970s. After the National Guard shot to death four Kent State students at an antiwar rally, sparking massive campus shutdowns across the country, two Northwestern football players asked their coach for permission to wear black armbands. By 1971, fifty members of the University of Michigan's undefeated football team signed a petition asking that the halftime show at their game be devoted to antiwar themes and several promised to flash peace signs from the sidelines. Michigan athletic director Don Canham expressed no surprise at the players' decision, declaring that "who the hell is in favor of the war anymore?"[11]

Ali changed the perception of how athletes could act. His behavior was not the first challenge to the idea that sports created responsible citizens who always followed the rules. Sports had always had a place for good natured cut-ups and heavy drinkers, especially if they were white. Stars such as Detroit Lions quarterback Bobby Layne, Green Bay halfback Paul Hornung, and New York slugger Mickey Mantle had been known as serious partiers for their entire careers. These athletes represented something virile and exciting, a welcome break from middle-class values. African American boxer Sugar Ray Robinson, who favored pink Cadillacs and entourages filled with beautiful women, also fell within this tradition. But Ali turned African American styles into a political statement. He refused to kowtow to white standards and demanded to be taken seriously as an athlete and as a person while celebrating his black identity. He, more than any other athlete, made rebellion hip.

RACIAL STRUGGLES, COUNTER CULTURE, AND THE SILENT MAJORITY

The social and cultural unrest of the late 1960s exploded in 1968. After the Tet Offensive in January, student sit-ins at Howard University and Columbia University in March and April demonstrated the depth of student discontent with the status quo. President Johnson, facing defeat from challenger Eugene McCarthy in the Wisconsin primary, announced that he would not run for reelection. Then civil rights leader Martin Luther King Jr. was assassinated in Memphis, Tennessee, in April, leading to massive unrest in over a hundred cities. Presidential candidate Robert Kennedy was murdered in June after winning the California Democratic primary. In late August, the Democratic National Convention, with its theme, provided by demonstrators outside, of "The Whole World is Watching," opened in Chicago. Millions of viewers watched for five days as police beat antiwar protestors in the streets. In the presidential election, Richard Nixon narrowly defeated Hubert Humphrey, while former Alabama governor and white supremacist George Wallace took almost 10 million votes. The unrest was global. Students and workers in France and Mexico took to the streets, and Soviets tanks invaded Czechoslovakia, brutally ending that country's experiment in "socialism with a human face." It seemed that the world was coming loose from its moorings, spinning apart as one painful development followed another.

While the world of sports was never immune from many of the issues roiling the country, there were moments of pure sporting joy throughout the troubled years of the late 1960s and early 1970s. Off-the-field events did not impede fan interest, especially for "big games." When the University of Houston and UCLA basketball teams met in the Astrodome in January 1968, 52,693 spectators attended, then the largest crowd ever to see a basketball game in the United States. The contest also had the broadest television coverage ever for college basketball, airing on 150 stations in forty states. The spectacle featured Lew Alcindor and Elvin Hayes, the two best college players in the country, but fans could also watch three bands, two sets of pompom girls, UCLA students dressed as male and female Bruins, and a live cougar named Shasta. Thankfully, the game lived up to its hype. "Big E" Hayes had fifteen rebounds and thirty-nine points, including two crucial last-second free throws, and Houston won 71–69 to break UCLA's forty-seven game winning streak.

Culturally aware viewers would notice, of course, that Alcindor sported a large afro hairstyle, while those who read the sports pages might be aware of Alcindor and teammates Mike Warren and Lucius Allen's increasingly militant attitudes about the need to oppose racial injustice. They would also learn at the end of the year that Alcindor had converted to Islam and would soon change his name to Kareem Abdul-Jabbar. But the game also offered an escape, a chance to enjoy great athletes and well-coached teams at the top of their game. That same mix of social unrest and athletic prowess marked most of the year's best sporting events and characterized its top athletes. Fans appreciated games and athletic success for their excitement, competitive fervor, and skill, but they also read sports through the lens of broader social changes, making athletes cultural symbols for both radicalism and tradition and stability. In the heated atmosphere of the late 1960s and early 1970s, every event, every athlete, seemed to stand for something greater.

The issue of race was everywhere. During the 1968 baseball season, St. Louis Cardinals pitcher Bob Gibson dominated the competition. He went 22–9, with a fifteen-game winning streak, and an astonishing 1.12 ERA. His Cy Young–winning season helped to propel the Cards into the World Series against the Detroit Tigers, where, in the first game, Gibson struck out seventeen and won 4–0. Though he lost the deciding game seven, Gibson set a new strikeout record with thirty-five in three games. Nevertheless, when Gibson was asked about the pressure he felt as a pitcher in tight situations, he replied that "I face more pressure every day just being a Negro."[12] This was not the answer the interviewer expected, but by 1968, some African American athletes had begun to feel that it was their duty to speak publicly about racial issues or to at least acknowledge that being an athlete did not erase racial struggles. When Robert Kennedy was shot and killed in June 1968, *Sports Illustrated* used the occasion to meditate on the relationship between black athletes and sports. The magazine argued that sports had been one of the first arenas to give blacks social recognition and the opportunity for economic advancement, but wondered if sports had done enough. "Have the achievements of Negro athletes been beneficial to Negroes as a whole?" the editors asked. "Have sports drawn the races together, or have they made Negroes feel exploited?"[13]

UCLA illustrated the potential for racial harmony within sports. Basketball coach John Wooden had simultaneously created the most powerful college team in the country and an environment in which it was possible for racial militancy to exist without disrupting the program. After he graduated, Alcindor exposed the difficult racial environment he faced at the university, but even he admitted that the team usually got along. Wooden's teams won ten NCAA titles in twelve years, including seven consecutive championships from 1967 through 1973. It was a dynasty never equaled in college basketball. Unlike many college basketball coaches, Wooden rarely yelled on the sidelines, saying that he thought that would be a bad example for his players. As a university, UCLA had long had a relatively positive reputation among black athletes: Jackie Robinson was a three-sport star there in the 1940s, and Olympic track star Rafer Johnson had served as student-body president.

Just as with Alcindor and his teammates at UCLA, Ali's fight against the United States government reverberated throughout the sporting world, especially among younger athletes. Yet ironically, the widespread emergence of social activism on college campuses created new dilemmas for black athletes. By the late 1960s, the civil rights movement produced a new kind of activist—African American and other minority students on largely white campuses—for whom what happened on campus and what they learned in classes was a crucial part of the struggle for racial justice. "Afro-American" societies and black student unions emerged in force, demanding ethnic-studies and black-studies courses and departments, more black faculty, and changes in administration attitudes.

While the rebellion of black athletes must be understood as part of this new movement, militant activism placed difficult demands on black players. Black radicals eager to force change rightly saw athletes as the most visible African Americans on campus and sought to use their fame as an avenue toward social change. At the same time, athletes in colleges were often caught between their loyalty to a team and their desire to be a part of the black community on campus. Many athletes realized that sports was the only reason they had been accepted to college and that any activism could anger their coach and imperil their scholarship. But with so few African American students on most campuses, black athletes also depended on the support of other minority students for social interaction and support.

Two major issues played out simultaneously in college athletics, one based on older civil rights ideas about integration, the other drawing heavily on the tactics of civil rights and the language of black power. Many of the top colleges in the country continued to field all-white teams throughout the 1960s. In the South, especially the deep South, the emphasis remained on integration, as athletes tried to gain the right to win a scholarship and compete as a part of a team. Jackie Robinson may have integrated Major League Baseball in 1947, but no football team in the Southwest Conference fielded a black player until Southern Methodist University's Jerry LeVias and Baylor University's John Westbrook made their respective teams in 1966. For these schools, the era of the "racial pioneer" continued into the 1970s. For schools outside the South, the issues were different. Small numbers of black athletes had competed for colleges in the South and West since the nineteenth century. But by the late 1960s, these athletes had begun to chafe against what they saw as structural and individual racism within the intercollegiate athletic system. Widespread "black revolts" started to occur, inspired by the example of Ali and the tactics of SNCC and the Southern Christian Leadership Conference.

The unwillingness of Southern state schools to recruit black players and the limits on black athletes at other universities meant that many African American high school stars attended all-black colleges. Grambling State University in Louisiana became a football powerhouse under Coach Eddie Robinson, who signed on in 1941 and finally retired in 1997 after winning a record 408 games. Robinson's program sent its first player—Paul "Tank" Younger—to the NFL in 1949, then won the National Black College Championship in 1955, going 10–0 and outscoring opponents 356 to 61. Robinson played a national schedule—the team drew over 60,000 to a game at Yankee Stadium in 1968—and also helped develop the Grambling–Southern University game, which became an annual spectacle in New Orleans, known for both the game and the incredible halftime shows put on by the schools' bands. Urging his players to "put on strength and let weakness go to hell," Robinson and his teams won big throughout the 1960s and developed a national following among African Americans.[14]

Black athletes continued to be underrepresented on most college campuses and among scholarship athletes. In 1968, schools in the Atlantic Coast Conference (ACC), Big Eight Conference, Big Ten Conference, Southeastern Conference (SEC), and the Southwest Conference (SWC) awarded 10,698 athletic scholarships. Approximately 634 of those, or about 6 percent, went to African Americans. The large number of major universities in the South impeded the numbers; of the 2,236 athletic scholarships given in the SEC in 1968, a conference dominated by Deep South schools, only eleven went to African Americans.

Vanderbilt University had broken the color line in the conference in 1966 when they signed Perry Wallace Jr. to a basketball scholarship. At the time, freshmen were ineligible for varsity play, so Wallace's first season against SEC competition came in 1967. Opposing fans chanted "we're going to lynch you" when the team was on the road, and Wallace faced regular physical abuse from opposing players as well. Of the Southern-based conferences, the ACC was the first to feature an African American athlete on a major sports team. Football player Darryl Hill, who had integrated the United States Naval Academy's football team in the previous season, joined the University of Maryland squad in 1963. Still, in 1968, only thirty-four African Americans received athletic scholarships in the conference, with twenty of those at Maryland and nine at Wake Forest University. The University of South Carolina and the University of Virginia would not integrate their teams until the 1971 season.

In most of the South, the football field and basketball court seemed almost untouched by the decade's racial changes, and major teams remained segregated for several years after black undergraduates were allowed into classrooms and donned graduation robes. Many boards of regents and university presidents actively resisted the integration of intercollegiate athletics, despite threats that their schools might lose federal funding. As with the example of Ole Miss and Alabama, teams represented a school's, and sometimes a state's, public identity. Though

Alabama's governor George Wallace's "stand in the schoolhouse door" had failed to prevent desegregation at the university as a whole in 1963, Bear Bryant's dominating, all-white football team remained a potent image of white power and racial exclusion throughout the decade. But after enormous success throughout the 1960s, including playing in a major bowl every year between 1962 and 1968 and winning the national title in 1964 and 1965, Bryant's team went just 6–5–1 in 1970. The following season Wilbur Jackson became the first African American to earn a scholarship to play for the Crimson Tide.

The association between masculinity, racial identity, and sports was most powerful in the South, but the entire system of college athletics was designed and controlled by white men. Black athletes recruited to play for mostly white schools were expected to be grateful for the opportunity to play; they had no input into the economic, social, or political structure of intercollegiate sports. In the context of Ali's struggles, civil rights activism, and emergent calls for black power, the chance to play—to be a "hired hand"—no longer seemed enough for newly radicalized black athletes. The locker room became a site for civil rights activism and the assertions of black power, and athletes at schools as diverse as Princeton University and the University of Wyoming began to fight back against what they saw as systemic racism on their campuses. No longer content with the opportunity for integration, many black players grew angry at the regular slights and slurs they faced, including the widespread proscription against interracial dating, the almost total lack of black coaches and support staff, racist language from coaches and other players, struggles over housing, and the lack of opportunity to compete for starting positions. It was time, they said, to be treated like other students.

At Michigan State University, a majority of the twenty-two starters on the football team were black in 1967, and the university gave almost twice as many scholarships to African Americans—fifty—as any other Big Ten school. Nevertheless, African Americans complained vehemently that they were pressured to take nonacademic classes to stay eligible, that the school had not hired black coaches, athletic trainers, or athletic counselors, and had never had a black cheerleader.[15] Similarly, eighteen black football players at the University of Wisconsin boycotted the team's end-of-season banquet and presented a list of demands to the school's athletic board, including that the coaching staff undergo a reorganization. In other words, both schools had added black athletes to their squads but had made no structural changes to a system created and controlled by white men.

Two schools with very different academic histories and approaches to black athletes both experienced serious racial turmoil in 1968. The University of Texas at El Paso (UTEP) and the University of California at Berkeley were both state schools, but that largely ended the resemblance between the two. Berkeley was the flagship school of the California state system, a place the state's brightest students were eager to attend. The campus had been at the center of national student protest against racial injustice and the Vietnam War since 1964, when the Berkeley Free Speech Movement occupied the administration building, singing "We Shall Overcome." By 1967, students and antiwar protestors were attempting to shut down the Oakland Army Induction Center, a move that sparked several days of skirmishes between activists and the police. The UTEP campus, in comparison, was neither a high-powered academic center nor a hotbed for student protest. In sports, however, Berkeley had almost no tradition of recruiting black athletes, while UTEP had been working to attract African American players since just two years after the *Brown v. Board of Education* decision in 1954. Despite their divergent paths, both schools found themselves embroiled in controversy over their treatment of black athletes.

UTEP burst onto the national scene in March 1966, when, as Texas Western College, the school stunned the University of Kentucky in the NCAA basketball finals, beating the Wildcats 72–65. Texas Western, which joined the University of Texas system the following year, started five African Americans; the team's first two reserves were also black. Adolph Rupp's Kentucky squad was proudly all white and would remain so until 1970, although the school had integrated its student body in 1949. Like Alabama and Mississippi's football team, Wildcat basketball was a source of pride and identity for many in Kentucky, not just the school's students. And like the two Deep South state universities, the idea of a winning, all-white team remained powerful long after the schools had been at least nominally desegregated. Rupp himself believed that black athletes had natural talent but lacked the self-control and intelligence to succeed at a championship level, an attitude that Texas Western's ball-control offense and dogged defense belied.

The nationally televised upset looked like a clear victory for the forces of racial integration, but the real story was a bit more complicated. UTEP had made a conscious decision to recruit black athletes in an effort to win games and increase their national profile. The school used its sporting accomplishments to attract new students, doubling its enrollment from 1960 to 1968. Head football coach Bobby Dobbs admitted that black athletes helped tremendously: "we wouldn't have built this institution as quickly without the Negro." While UTEP offered black athletes an opportunity to play, the school seemed uninterested in modifying its racial attitudes, creating a situation in which the small number of African Americans on campus felt betrayed and abandoned. George McCarthy, UTEP's athletic director, regularly used the word "nigger" to refer to the scholarship athletes he recruited, explaining to *Sports Illustrated* that "it's a habit you don't change overnight."[16] With fewer than 250 African Americans in a student body of almost 10,000, black athletes at UTEP, as at many mostly white schools, had almost no social life. Much of the conflict between athletes and the athletic department emerged over the issue of interracial dating. McCarthy admitted that "one of our biggest detriments or handicaps with the nigger athlete right now is the shortage of, you know, girls."[17] By girls, McCarthy meant African American women, since of course there were a large number of white women on campus. But coaches often threatened to withdraw the scholarships of players who dated white women and sometimes ran off players who refused to stop seeing their white girlfriends.

By 1967, athletes had begun to protest UTEP's policies. Black players on the football team staged a sit-in to voice their complaints, without effect, largely because their coach convinced them not to share their story with the media. Then, in 1968, nine track athletes decided to boycott an Easter-weekend meet against Brigham Young University. They were concerned about the murder of Martin Luther King Jr., about their treatment on the UTEP campus, and about BYU's attitudes toward African Americans. Expected to challenge for their second national track title in three years, the UTEP team was loaded with talent, including Bob Beamon, the world's top long jumper. In response to the athletes' decision, UTEP dismissed them from the team and withdrew their scholarships.

In an atmosphere of increasing distrust, even the smallest incident could trigger revolt. At the University of California at Berkeley, a campuswide rebellion among athletes was sparked by rules over hair styles. Hair was the trigger, but it symbolized deeper concerns. The school's thirty-five black scholarship athletes had been admitted to Cal in a process of "accelerated recruiting."[18] Just eight years before, only five African American athletes played for Berkeley teams. Many of the black athletes recruited for college sports had attended segregated high schools and generally received inferior educational instruction—studying with fewer new books, in shabbier facilities, and under poorly paid teachers. Bob Presley, the basketball player whose complaints helped to start the black-athlete revolt at Berkeley, was from the ghettos of Detroit. At nineteen, he had not graduated from high school and thus attended several junior colleges before coming to Berkeley. Presley did not have the academic background to be a student at Berkeley, but he had the basketball talents that might make the team a winner. University programs depended on talent like this, with junior colleges emerging as what *Sports Illustrated* called "a new kind of Underground Railroad" for coaches looking for rapid infusions of talent.[19]

Signing academic risks was not new. CCNY's Red Holtzman and Long Island University's Clair Bee, two of the top coaches in the 1940s and early 1950s, sometimes had assistant coaches forge high school transcripts for desired players and routinely signed athletes with questionable academic abilities. Still, at many colleges in the 1950s and 1960s, most athletes graduated. More significantly, most white athletes graduated. All five of the starters for the all-white 1966 Kentucky NCAA basketball team graduated, for example. None of the top seven black players from Texas Western College did.

Whether colleges did offer less help and place larger demands on black athletes than on white is largely moot. A majority of African American players believed that they were "hired guns," admitted to play sports and easily discarded after their eligibility was completed. A UTEP basketball player avowed that while coaches gave lip service to the importance of education, "they want you to *win* first. All the sports requirements—practice, schedules, road trips—come first."[20] This win-at-all-costs attitude particularly harmed poor black players, who, without extra help, struggled within the system. Tex Winter, head basketball coach at Kansas State University in the 1960s, argued that schools exploited the black athlete, bringing "him into a white college environment with one purpose in mind—to get what we can out of him as a basketball player."[21]

Muhammad Ali toured college campuses and spoke out about what he saw as racial injustices, but sociology professor Harry Edwards proved to be the linchpin between the broader civil rights movement and the growing turmoil felt by college athletes. While teaching at San Jose State College in California, Edwards founded the United Black Students for Action (UBSA) to protest a wide range of discriminatory practices in the fraternity system, campus housing policies, social organizations, and athletics. This was a civil rights organization, one of the hundreds emerging on college campuses across the country in the mid- to late 1960s. A former track athlete, Edwards's innovation came in using sports to make his point. When the UBSA could not get the

school's administration to listen to their concerns, the group threatened to disrupt an early-season football game between San Jose State
and UTEP in 1967 "by any means necessary." When school officials
decided to cancel the game in order to avoid what they termed "mass
violence," the possibility of using sports as a vehicle for effective
protest became clear to Edwards. "We had seen, all too often, the spectacle of black people demonstrating and picketing groups, organizations, and institutions of limited concern to people in positions of
power," he said. "We therefore decided to use something more central
to the concerns of the entire local community structure—athletics."[22]

Edwards was a firebrand in the late 1960s, moving from campus to
campus to talk with athletes. He encouraged them to see their athletic
struggles as an important part of the push for racial justice, to understand their demands as linked to other forms of student protest and a
broader coalition of activists working for global social change. Edwards
explained to athletes that sports was a massive industry in which
African Americans thrilled consumers but reaped few long-term rewards
and lacked any power within the management structure. Nevertheless,
sports was a space in which African Americans had achieved widespread
visibility for their skills and talents. Edwards declared that athletes
could exploit this visibility to force change both in athletics and in an
American society that placed so much value on sports.

He was also the instigator of a national movement among black athletes that called for a boycott of the 1968 Olympics. He formed the
Olympic Project for Human Rights in 1967, a controversial development that joined the inchoate protests of black college athletes, the
legal struggles of Ali, and the racial discrimination of major athletic
clubs to the larger civil rights and black power movement. The movement also linked American struggles for civil rights with African struggles against colonialism and oppression, part of a movement toward a
pan-national black movement. A poster advocating the boycott featured two black fists raised in solidarity, one representing the United
States, the other Africa. The rhetoric noted that thirty-two African
nations had voted to boycott the Olympics, challenging black American athletes, "Can we do less?"[23] Edwards and his co-activists argued
that the Olympics provided a world forum for exposing racism in the
United States and around the world.

The organization's most successful boycott came in February 1968,
when they protested the one-hundredth Anniversary Games of the
New York Amateur Athletic Club, an organization that refused to admit
African Americans and restricted access for Jews. Amateur athletic clubs

had long limited access for African Americans. In a 1968 *Sports Illustrated* survey, only one ranking athletic club in twenty large cities admitted blacks. The St. Louis amateur athletic club's constitution included the adjective "white" in at least ten places. The Detroit Yacht Club had stopped handing out free passes to media and city officials because those sections of society were increasingly integrated. And the Olympic Club in San Francisco limited membership to "white male citizens" until February 1968.[24] For track athletes, this meant that they could win prizes in national tournaments at the clubs, but they could not eat in their dining rooms.

The protesters surrounded the prominent site of the Anniversary Games, Madison Square Garden, carrying signs and chanting slogans, including "Muhummad Ali is our champ!"[25] Edwards invited black power advocate and hothead H. Rap Brown to speak at the pre-meet press conference, where Brown suggested that the Garden be blown up. Despite Brown's exhortation, the boycott was peaceful and largely successful. Soviet athletes and many top-level American track stars, black and white, refused to compete, and the protest earned widespread media coverage.

World-class sprinter Tommie Smith believed that though the idea of top black athletes boycotting the Olympics was unpopular, African Americans were "using the best means we have" to publicize their struggles against racism.[26] The threat that the best American athletes might not represent their country—and help the United States beat the Soviets—made many take notice, even as the boycott remained unlikely. Smith was an early supporter of the movement, but the murder of Martin Luther King Jr. in April 1968 pushed some black athletes to more radical positions. The UTEP track team's decision to boycott the meet against BYU came just days after King's death, for example. Ralph Boston, one of the nation's top long jumpers and nearly a lock to make the Olympic team, expressed the uncertainty of many, admitting that King's death made him reassess the idea of competing as an American in the Olympics: "If I go to Mexico City and represent the United States I would be representing people like the one that killed Dr. King," he said. "And there are more people like that going around. I feel I shouldn't represent people like that. . . . It makes you think that Stokely Carmichael and Rap Brown are right."[27] Black power advocates Carmichael and Brown promoted forceful opposition to racism, arguing that African Americans should shun white Americans until the structures of racial injustice had fallen. In the agony of King's death, their answers appealed to some athletes.

Passions had cooled by the time the Olympics took place in November. The threat of an Olympic boycott proved useful, but the boycott itself never gained enough support to be viable. No American athletes boycotted the Olympics, although UCLA basketball stars Lew Alcindor, Mike Warren, and Lucius Harris decided not to try out for the Olympic squad, saying that they were too tired and busy to play. Edwards's plan contradicted what athletes had spent years working for—the chance to prove themselves the best against international competition. For athletes competing in track-and-field events, the Olympics were the pinnacle of their careers and could provide them with a brighter future and financial reward. Many also rightly believed that winning a medal gave them a better platform from which to fight against inequalities in sport and society.

Though the 1968 Olympics are best remembered for racial protests and the acrimony over whether to admit South Africa to the competition, a much more serious protest—with deadly results—happened just ten days before the Olympics began. Many Mexicans, especially college students, took to the streets to protest their country's spending millions on the Olympics when so many of the nation's citizens lived in abject poverty. With athletes already in the Olympic Village, readying themselves for the Games and adjusting to Mexico's high altitude, protestors prepared for one final march. Because of the massive numbers of police patrolling the city, however, the march was cancelled and activists gathered in a central plaza to talk and regroup. *Sports Illustrated* described the scene as having the flavor of "a student pep rally on the campus of the University of Kansas, seeking free love."[28] Then suddenly, a flare exploded overhead, lighting the scene. At that moment, machine gun fire exploded from the police and soldiers who had surrounded the plaza. Students and their supporters ran in panic, but an estimated 300 activists and bystanders were killed in the three hours of gunfire. Most athletes were too absorbed with preparations to notice. But changes to the Olympic posters advertising the Games tried to make the carnage clear. The poster featured a white dove, and all over town, Mexican activists who were horrified by the massacre added a small dot of red paint to the dove's breast, "creating the effect of a bird shot through the heart, blood dripping down."[29]

It was an inauspicious beginning for Games already so marked with political controversy. Yet the racial tensions and international disputes, together with great athletic performances and the packaging of the Games for television, made the 1968 Olympics an irresistible event for Americans. Though the Olympics had been televised since 1960, the

Mexico City Games were the first to attract a significant audience. ABC sports director Roone Arledge applied the lessons he and his network had learned in presenting *Wide World of Sports*, packaging the Games as a dramatic miniseries that featured in-depth personal profiles of athletes for the first time. In addition, new camera and satellite technology made the events easier to follow from the comfort of the living room, and Arledge decided to schedule thirty-four hours of coverage, more than three times the airtime given to the 1964 Games. Even without the merger of sports and politics before the Games, such expansive, personalized exposure guaranteed that the actions of athletes would be widely scrutinized and discussed.

There were many spectacular performances at the Olympics, particularly in track and field events. Every men's and women's race under 1,500 meters saw new world-record times, aided in part by running at over 7,000 feet. Long jumper Bob Beamon won the gold medal in his event and shattered the world record by more than two and one-half feet. Dick Fosbury added the "Fosbury flop" to sporting language by winning the high jump with his innovative technique. The incomparable Al Oerter won his fourth consecutive gold in the discus while setting his fourth consecutive Olympic record in the event. In 1956, he won with a throw of 184'11"; by 1968, his winning toss traveled 212'6". Led by freestyler Debbie Meyer, American female swimmers nearly blew the competition out of the water, taking twenty-four of the thirty-six individual medals available and winning gold in both relay events. The women were competing in six new races, as the IOC gradually expanded the number of events for female athletes.

But the Games' athletic performances would be overshadowed by perhaps the most famous black power demonstration ever. Tommie Smith and John Carlos, the gold and bronze medal winners in the 200-meter race, took the podium for the national anthem in black socks and one black glove each. As "The Star-Spangled Banner" played, the two athletes raised their gloved fists and bowed their heads, a powerful symbolic protest aimed at raising awareness of racial problems in the United States. Both men had been supporters of the boycott movement, and Smith had been booed by crowds at several pre-Olympic meets, including one in Los Angeles in January 1968. But in the fervid nationalistic atmosphere of the Olympics, their silent protest evoked a quick response, not from the crowd, but from United States officials. The USOC quickly suspended both sprinters from the team, revoked their visas, and gave them only forty-eight hours to leave Mexico City.

CONSERVATIVE HEROES: O.J. SIMPSON, ROGER STAUBACH, AND VINCE LOMBARDI

O.J. Simpson, the brilliant tailback who won the 1968 Heisman Trophy after gaining 1,654 yards in his senior season, publicly denounced the Olympic protesters and made sure to distance himself from campus protests. Simpson also made fun of hippies and long-haired youth, presenting himself in the classic image of the football All-American, clean-cut, sober, and traditional. When Simpson spoke of his idea of black power, he meant his ability to make money, announcing that "it's the material things that count" and emphasizing that his acquisitions would "give pride and hope to a lot of young blacks."[30] In contrast, Purdue running back Leroy Keyes, who finished second in the Heisman voting, was publicly militant, including hanging a banner from his dorm room that read "The Fire Next Time," a reference to African American author James Baldwin's scalding assessment of race relations in the United States.

In the voting, Keyes never had a chance. Simpson was black and conservative, a welcome respite for many Americans nervous about militant black athletes. Like Ali at the beginning of his career, Simpson benefited tremendously from television; he was the first great college running back to play in front of instant replay and slow-motion cameras that could follow his moves and then break them down so that viewers could see his style and skill. Unlike Ali, Simpson was able to combine television and his abilities to break into mainstream advertising campaigns. Historians Leola Johnson and David Roediger argue that black militancy "ensured that the first athlete to cash in on new possibilities would be anything but a militant."[31] In the late 1960s and early 1970s, American might have been intrigued by Ali and other militant black athletes, but most of the rewards went to those who matched more traditional ideas about how athletes should act.

Despite widespread social change, even within sports, the sporting world remained a site of conservatism. Sports were where "the silent majority" went to find respite from shifting cultural norms. As the president of the University of Connecticut took pains to explain, college football players were "the guys in the white hats—they keep their hair cut short, they're clean, they're orderly, aware of the importance of law and order and discipline."[32] Football, with its long-time emphasis on regimentation, discipline, and authority and its metaphorical links to warfare, provided many of the most popular figures of the decade. Green Bay quarterback Bart Starr and coach Vince Lombardi,

Baltimore Colts quarterback Johnny Unitas, Dallas Cowboys quarterback Roger Staubach, and Ohio State coach Woody Hayes were all celebrated for their "old-school" style nearly as much as for their winning ways. Other white, working-class sports, including hockey and stock car racing, also offered heroes who resonated with Americans hungry for traditional styles in a changing era.

Woody Hayes coached the Ohio State University team that defeated Simpson's USC squad in the Rose Bowl and finished atop the 1968 national polls. Despite starting eleven sophomore players (in a time when freshmen were ineligible for the varsity competition), the Buckeyes finished 10–0, crushing archrival Michigan 50–14 along the way. A veteran of World War II and a military buff, Hayes came to Ohio State in 1951. By 1954, he had driven the long-dormant program to a perfect season and a national title. The square-jawed Hayes favored a potent ground attack, what he called "three yards and a cloud of dust," that flattened opponents with its power. Like his fellow coach Bear Bryant, Hayes brooked no objection to his way of doing things, from either players or administrators. He demanded physical and mental toughness from his players and a total commitment to the program. Despite a ferocious temper, he earned the respect of most of them. Hayes spoke to groups across the country in the late 1960s, giving pep talks that emphasized the value of football in teaching lessons of discipline and self-control.

A 1971 story about legendary Texas high school football coach Gordon Wood and his Brownwood Lions echoed these sentiments, reminding readers of the traditional benefits of sports. Wood had led small-town football programs in Brownwood and Stamford to five state titles between 1960 and 1970. Wood stressed the virtues of dedication, determination, and positive thinking in shaping undersized players into champions. Most importantly, he made clear that discipline was a way of life for his football teams. As a result, he allowed no long hair, "loud dress," or talking back. Even as it covered racial unrest and changing social mores on the field, *Sports Illustrated* celebrated this more traditional version of sporting life, a place where authority still carried weight and where "the youngsters of the community spent their elementary days dreaming of the time they would wear the blue and white and do their part for the glory of the [Stamford] Bulldogs."[33]

Few football figures were more revered than Vince Lombardi. The Green Bay Packers won Super Bowl II, with Bart Starr repeating as the game's MVP. Lombardi and Starr both fit the mold of traditional sports heroes. Lombardi was a disciple of famed West Point coach Earl "Red" Blaik and, like Woody Hayes, demanded unblinking obedience to his rules. After he was named the head coach of Green Bay in 1959, Lombardi's disciplined teams won five NFL titles between 1961 and 1967. With his crew cut, gap-toothed grin, and squat, square body, Lombardi projected an image of powerful, authoritative masculinity. His demanding practices became the stuff of legend.

In a decade where "question authority" became the signal phrase of a generation, Lombardi's take-charge style and blunt approach had political ramifications. He believed the permissive attitudes of the decade were anathema to the "American Way" and that the discipline learned in football could provide the solution to most of society's problems. He found it "increasingly difficult to be tolerant of a society which seems to have sympathy only for the misfits, only for the maladjusted, only for the criminal, only for the loser."[34] Winning was the cure, not complaining. Though *Monday Night Football* announcer Don Meredith worried that "young folks won't buy the old Vince Lombardi stuff anymore," the Green Bay coach's emphasis on winning continued to find a ready audience.[35] In 1968, Robert Lipsyte called Lombardi "one of the few non-variables in American sports: tough, strict, sometimes petty, but capable of bringing a football player to the highest level of his ability, a talent for which he is loved."[36]

Lombardi's starting quarterback was also a classic football hero. Bart Starr was a Southern boy who played college ball for the University of Alabama, had strong religious convictions, a polite, controlled demeanor, and razor-sharp passing abilities that gave him a 57.4 percent career completion rate. Twice the MVP in the Super Bowl, Starr's greatest game may have come in the 1968 NFL Championship Game against Dallas, known as the "Ice Bowl" because it was 13 degrees below zero at game time. Down 17 to 14, Starr marched his team down the field. "This is it," he told his freezing teammates. "We're going in."[37] Then, with sixteen seconds on the clock and no timeouts, the Packers faced a third-and-goal situation from the one-yard line. Starr could have thrown the ball; if the pass failed, there would be time to go for a game-tying field goal. Instead, he called his own number and scored on a quarterback sneak. For fans who wanted to believe that sports taught players morality, citizenship, and self-discipline, the coach and quarterback of the Packers provided exceptional examples. In a decade fraught with changes, both men—and their team—seemed a throwback to a simpler, more straightforward world.

Few sports provided more throwback appeal than hockey, a sport dominated by white athletes and a powerful sense of tradition. The same "Original Six" teams made up the National Hockey League (NHL) from its founding until 1967. The sport, with nearly 97 percent of its players from Canada, had long struggled to find a wide American audience or to create national American heroes. Canadians, including Maurice "Rocket" Richard, might have been great players, but they were rarely major stars. Still, in the 1960s, NHL teams played in arenas filled to near capacity, and the league decided it was time to move beyond its regional roots and take hockey coast-to-coast. The NHL doubled in size in 1967, with new teams in Los Angeles, San Francisco, Philadelphia, Pittsburgh, Minneapolis, and St. Louis, and the league earned its first national television contract. Immediately competitive on the ice, most of the league's new teams attracted large audiences in their early years. Individual stars also found a wider audience. Chicago Blackhawk left winger Bobby Hull, whose shot was clocked at 120 mph, won three scoring titles during the 1960s and played with a joy that put fans in the seats. Called the "Golden Jet," his dashing breakaway attempts sent electricity through the crowd and terrified his opponents. His smile, complete with missing front teeth, expressed a masculine toughness that countered the perceived "softness" of the decade, but it also denoted a charisma that made him a natural ambassador of the game.

Long popular in the South, stock car racing also began to appeal to a national audience in the 1960s. Technological advances in car and engine design had moved the sport far from its rough stock car days on dirt tracks by the time the Daytona International Speedway opened in 1959. Just as with hockey, auto racing was dominated by white men, part of its allure for fans who wanted to avoid the racial tensions that were increasingly a part of college and professional team sports. Stock car racer Richard Petty brought the sport to national attention through a combination of his driving skills and out-sized personality. Petty won the Daytona 500 for the first time in 1964. In 1967, he drove car No. 43 to victory in twenty-seven of the forty-eight races he entered, including ten straight. Known as the "King," Petty's fierce determination to win and his cool sunglasses and cowboy hat look made him a hero to many working-class American men. "When I put the hammer down, some of those drivers just scatter," he said, describing his style. "They think, 'uh, oh, here comes No. 43.'"[38] He was not quite in the same heroic mold as Lombardi or Starr; his sport lacked the traditional association with moral virtue that was a part of football's tradition. Nevertheless, Petty's hard-charging rebelliousness and Southern charm rivaled that of Alabama governor George Wallace, attracting Northern fans to racing in much the way Wallace's message appealed to voters in the "silent majority."

Even the nation's president used sports to signify his conservatism. President Richard Nixon, elected in November 1968 on a promise to end American involvement in Vietnam, announced that he would be watching a football game while anti-Vietnam protesters occupied the Washington Mall in October 1969. His choice was a clear signal to Americans appalled by the protests that the president was "one of them," a man who appreciated the values that sports could teach. In his second acceptance speech in 1972, Nixon thanked his college football coach, along with mother and father, for instilling him with the right values. Though Nixon was merely a scrub on the Whitman College team, he repeatedly reminded voters of that experience and its impact on him. His enthusiasm for sports—Nixon was also a rabid baseball fan and was dismayed when the Washington Senators moved to Texas in 1972—offered the president multiple opportunities to associate himself with traditional American heroes. He made sure to call big winners or to invite them to the White House, trading on sports' conservative appeal to win voters.

Despite the emerging stories of racially based rebellions in college sports, federal and local government officials also continued to see sports as way to contain widespread urban unrest. In 1967, federal support of summer youth programs totaled $660 million. Though most of this went toward jobs and educational programs, the youth component of President Johnson's War on Poverty programs included a range of sports activities, sometimes enlisting professional teams to provide free tickets to games, at other times developing participant programs designed to get young people off the street. Most cities also believed that sports could make a difference in containing violence. In Washington, D.C., local high school, college, and professional basketball stars ran games and conducted clinics in poor neighborhoods, while the San Francisco Giants gave 400 free tickets to disadvantaged Oakland youngsters for every daylight game the team played. Mayor Richard Daley used a combination of local and federal funds to run an indoor recreation program that included opportunities to play basketball or volleyball and that taught inner-city youth judo, wrestling, and gymnastics.

The 1969 Rose Bowl confrontation between Ohio State and USC pitted Woody Hayes's hypercontrolled conservative offense against the hip but conservative stylings of O. J. Simpson. Commentators could read the game as a reassertion of traditional values, even if one of the stars was African American. The 1969 Super Bowl, on the other hand, was hyped as a classic battle between old values and new. The upstart AFL New York Jets, with former Alabama star Joe Namath at quarterback, faced the NFL powerhouse Baltimore Colts. Though Colts' quarterback Johnny Unitas had spent the most of the year injured and replaced on the field by Earl Morrall, the press used the contrasting personal styles of Unitas and Namath to tout the game. Unitas, said *Sports Illustrated*, "is crew cut and quiet," the classic laconic masculine hero. In contrast, Namath "has long hair and a big mouth," and a brash style—he personally guaranteed a Jet victory in the Super Bowl—that meshed well with the counter-cultural changes of the decade. Namath's flowing locks and fu-man-chu mustache made him a "folk hero of the new generation" with a persona that "spells insouciant youth in the jet age."[39]

The contrasting styles of masculinity made for great press, but Namath's rebellion was more about style than substance. Despite the penthouse, the mink coats, the number of women on his arm, or even his much-discussed hair, Namath had little interest in bucking the system, much less changing it. Namath had long hair, but he was no hippie. Instead, "Broadway Joe" was a sexy ladies' man, part of a long tradition of sports stars who both played and partied hard. As the Super Chicks sang at Super Bowl III:

> He's a hero
> He's a pro
> He's a mister something else
> He's Broadway Joe
>
> He's a groovy, super guy
> He can pass a football through a needle's eye
>
> What a feeling
> What a sight
> When we see that number 12 in green and white
>
> One two three, hip, go-go-go
> No one else can throw like Broadway Joe. [40]

A tremendous competitor and winner on the field, Namath did not use his fame to speak out on social issues but rather allowed his image to be linked to the counterculture. Unlike Ali or collegiate athletes in revolt against their coaches, Namath did not rebel so much as celebrate a lifestyle of conspicuous consumption that put him squarely in the mainstream of American society. He also kept fans riveted to football, a game that Lombardi insisted was a emblematic of "what this country's best attributes are; namely courage, stamina, and coordinated effi-ciency . . . the Spartan qualities of sacrifice and self-denial."[41]

THE TRIUMPH OF STYLE: THE NBA AND THE ABA

Professional basketball coaches rarely made that kind of claim, but Bill Russell's resolve and work ethic clearly would have made Lombardi proud. In late April 1969, with Russell as both player and coach, the Celtics beat the Los Angeles Lakers in seven games to take their eleventh NBA championship in thirteen years. It was an incredible dynastic run, anchored by Russell's defensive prowess and his absolute determination to win. In January 1969, Russell became the second black athlete to be named *Sports Illustrated*'s Sportsman of the Year. Like the Green Bay Packers and the UCLA Bruins, the Celtics seemed a model of racial harmony, yet Russell was a man proud of his racial identity and unafraid to speak his mind on racial issues. He blamed "the destruction of race pride" for many problems facing African Amer-icans, arguing that being black in a country where "all the emphasis is on being white" created psychological distress. For Russell, being black meant being proud and celebrating black cultural styles while still see-ing "people as they are no matter what their color."[42]

While Russell was an outspoken civil rights activist, the impact of a growing number of African American athletes generally had a greater impact on American styles than on American politics. Russell, Oscar Robertson, and Wilt Chamberlain had helped to transform the league over the course of the 1960s. The trio proved that black men could be league scoring champions and superstars, and their abilities shattered informal guidelines that had restricted teams to a maximum of four black players. By 1970, 50 percent of the league's players were African American. Chamberlain fundamentally changed the perception of league games as plodding and foul-filled when he scored 100 points in a game against New York Knicks in 1962. This was a far cry from the 19–18 slow-down between the Fort Wayne Pistons and Minneapolis Lakers in 1951. For the 1961–1962 season, Chamberlain averaged a record 50.4 points per game for the Philadelphia Warriors. In that same season, Robertson averaged a triple double—30.8 points, 12.5 rebounds, and 11.4 assists—for the Cincinnati Royals. Along with John Havelick of the Celtics, Elgin Baylor and Jerry West of the Lakers, and Willis Reed of the New York Knicks, Robertson, Russell, and Chamberlain moved the NBA into the modern era.

Still, in 1966, more than half of all NBA teams lost money, and the league did not receive the same level of television coverage as either the NFL or MLB. Nevertheless, the mere possibility of television revenues, a perceived local demand for teams, and the fact that one great player could create a winning franchise encouraged investors to start a new, rival league, the American Basketball Association (ABA) and also prompted rapid expansion within the NBA. As a result, professional basketball was fastest growing sport of the 1960s, going from ten teams in 1965 to twenty-six in 1968. Like the NFL and MLB, professional basketball's expansion followed the demographic shifts in the American population. Most of the new teams were in the fast-growing West. The Chicago Bulls joined the NBA in 1966, the San Diego Rockets and Seattle Supersonics in 1967, the Milwaukee Bucks and Phoenix Suns in 1968, and the Buffalo Braves, Cleveland Cavaliers, and Portland Trail Blazers in 1970. The ABA started its first season in 1967 with a decidedly Midwestern and Western flavor, with teams in Anaheim, Oakland, Denver, Dallas, Houston, New Orleans, Louisville, Indianapolis, and Minneapolis. Only the Pittsburgh Pipers and New Jersey Americans challenged in the East. In the league's nine-year history, several teams would be moved to the South—North Carolina, Miami, Virginia, and Washington, D.C.—but unlike the AFL's approach to confronting the NFL, the ABA almost never challenged the NBA in the major markets of the Northeast.

The NBA's first great big man, former Lakers star George Mikan, became commissioner of the ABA, as owners hoped that his reputation would provide respectability to the new league. By its second season, seven of the ABA's eleven franchises had signed some sort of television contract. The Indiana Pacers and Denver Nuggets drew the best gates in the first season, attracting an average of 4,000 spectators per home game. But like all rival leagues, the ABA lacked stability, as owners struggled financially and some teams changed locations almost every season. The Anaheim Amigos moved to Los Angeles in 1968, for example, and became known as the Stars. Few Los Angeles residents agreed, however, and the crowd at one game reached 1,800 only "because somebody from the Stars had gone out there to crank up the turnstiles."[43] Not surprisingly, the team moved to Utah in 1970 and then folded in 1975.

Despite its tenuous financial state, the ABA proved very important in the development of professional basketball. The ABA contributed to a transformation in both the style of play and the personal style of players. Its snazzy red, white, and blue ball signaled, for example, that the league would not take a staid approach to the game. The ABA made the three-point shot popular—introducing it with an exhibit at their first press conference—and created the slam dunk competition as half-time entertainment at the all-star game. They kept statistics on steals, blocked shots, and turnovers, something the NBA had not done. Their uniforms were also flashy and colorful, playing on the shifting standards of the decade. The afro hairstyles of some ABA players were legendary. Artis Gilmore, star center for the Kentucky Colonels, stood 7'2" before adding another six inches for his afro. It wasn't just the hair. Dressing styles changed so dramatically that sportswriter Frank Deford ridiculed the players' choices, arguing that they verged "on the effete and very nearly erase[d] all memories of locker rooms with tobacco chaws and pleated pants."[44] Marvin Barnes of the St. Louis Spirits favored what sportscaster Bob Costas called the "Super Fly image—the wide-brimmed hats, the long, floor-length mink coats, the platform shoes."[45]

The most famous afro belonged to high-leaping Julius Erving, who left the University of Massachusetts after his junior year and emerged as the transcendent superstar of the ABA. One broadcaster exclaimed that the young Erving was "like Thomas Edison. He was inventing something new every night."[46] When he came up with new dunk after new dunk, his teammates compared him a doctor digging into his medical bag, leading to the nickname Doctor J. Erving started his professional career with the Virginia Squires, where he averaged over thirty-one points per game in his third season. The Squires, like many ABA teams, found themselves short of money and traded Erving to the New Jersey Nets, where his electrifying moves gained major media coverage in the New York City market. He combined the flash of playground basketball with a profound on-court intelligence, making him an influential hero to many. Though Erving rarely spoke out against injustice in the ways that Russell had, he became the defining example of how African American styles and ability had fundamentally changed the nature of professional basketball. More than Ali and Russell, more than the Olympic boycotts or campus rebellions, players such as Namath and Erving define the changes in sports in the decade. Style largely triumphed over substance in the fight for a level playing field.

5. Walking the Picket Line and Fighting for Rights

*T*he Miami Dolphins swept through the 1972 NFL regular season and playoffs with a perfect 16–0 record behind running backs Larry Csonka and Mercury Morris, quarterback Bob Griese, and a dominating defense. The team was making a return trip to the Super Bowl, having lost to the Dallas Cowboys the previous season despite coaching assistance from the nation's highest office. President Richard Nixon had called the Dolphins' head coach, Don Shula, at home two weeks before the game with encouragement and a recommendation that Shula send wide receiver Paul Warfield on a down-and-in pattern during the game. Nixon was sure the play would lead to a score.[1] It didn't. Nixon also proved to be a fickle fan. For Super Bowl VII, on January 13, 1973, with home-team Washington in the Super Bowl for the first time, Nixon abandoned Shula and the Dolphins and came out as a staunch Redskin fan. Nixon's support again proved no help, as Miami overpowered Washington in a low-scoring affair, 14–7. The Dolphins, an AFL expansion team created in 1966, became the only NFL team to ever go undefeated. Despite the final score, the game—like so many Super

Bowls—was never close. Csonka rushed for 112 years in the contest, and the Dolphin defense forced three interceptions and a fumble. From a financial standpoint, however, the game was a hit, with the NFL earning an estimated $2.75 million in radio and television revenues.

There were other great moments—and other great undefeated teams—in 1973. Fullback Sam Cunningham scored four times as the University of Southern California Trojans trampled Woody Hayes's Ohio State team in the Rose Bowl on January 1, taking the college-football national title with a perfect 11–0 record. The UCLA Bruins continued their absolute domination of college basketball, going 30–0 for the season and stretching their winning streak to a record seventy-five straight. In the process, the Bruins won their seventh consecutive NCAA title, and center Bill Walton won his second Player of the Year award. Led by stars Reggie Jackson and Jim "Catfish" Hunter, the Oakland A's defeated the New York Mets to take their second straight World Series. O. J. Simpson, now with the Buffalo Bills, broke Jim Brown's single-season rushing record by finishing with 2,003 yards in fourteen games. But in a season of great performances, the year's top athlete was a horse. Over 134,000 fans watched at the Kentucky Derby as Secretariat won the first leg of racing's Triple Crown in May. After taking the Preakness, the horse made the cover of *Time*, *Newsweek*, and *Sports Illustrated*, but Secretariat saved his best performance for last. He thrilled the racing world by winning the Belmont Stakes by thirty-one lengths, smashing the course's record time by nearly three seconds to become the first Triple Crown winner since 1948.

Undefeated teams, appealing stars in a wide array of fields, major media coverage, even a deep interest in football from the president of the country: everything seemed wonderful in American sports. But the picture wasn't so rosy off the field. By 1973, with the Watergate scandal dominating the news, even presidential support was suspect. Multiple political concerns intruded on the sporting world in other ways. At the 1972 Olympic Games in Munich, eight Palestinian terrorists slipped into the Olympic Village, killing two members of the Israeli national team and taking nine others hostage. As a tense global audience waited and listened, broadcaster Jim McKay finally announced "they're all gone," killed in a shootout between the terrorists and German police.[2] Though IOC head Avery Brundage declared that "the Games must go on," the spirit of international harmony had been destroyed. Mark Spitz, who won four individual and three relay gold medals in swimming at Munich, didn't help matters by announcing that he planned to cash in on his success. After the Games, a beefcake poster of Spitz in his swimsuit sold over 300,000 copies, making him the most popular pin-up figure since Betty Grable. He admitted that "it's like a game to see how much money I can make. It's amazing to me . . . I know I'm lucky, but I also feel entitled to make a buck."[3] Bitter labor disputes between owners and players also contributed to the sense that everything was big business now, even the nation's most popular games. And tensions in the Middle East intruded again in 1974 when competitors in the Daytona 500 completed only 450 laps; the OPEC oil crisis forced organizers to shorten the race.

Fans heard much more about these issues than before. The Watergate scandal and the concurrent rise of investigative journalism contributed to a dramatic shift in media attitudes, meaning that many sportswriters now reported on behavior they once would have covered up. "When I came up, people who covered baseball were fans," said Tommy John, a pitcher for the Los Angeles Dodgers. "They probably knew so and so was hung over when he pitched, but they didn't expose it to the whole world. . . . Now reporters aren't holding back to protect the image of ballplayers."[4] "Tell all" books from players themselves, including Jim Bouton's *Ball Four* and Dave Meggyesy's *Out of Their League*, also altered the spit-and-shine image of athletes and revealed the sometimes sordid nature of professional leagues. A scene in the 1979 film *Breaking Away* reflected how many fans felt. Dave, an avid amateur cyclist and great admirer of Italy, comes home from a race with skinned knees instead of an expected trophy, having fallen when the Italian national team stuck a bike pump in his spokes. "Where's the trophy?" asks his dad. "No trophy," he says, broken-hearted. "Everybody cheats."[5] By the early 1980s, *Sports Illustrated* began to run multiple articles on the "problems" of sports, best represented by William Oscar Johnson's 1983 article "What's Happened to our Heroes?"

The mostly male heroes of sports faced other challenges as well. African American athletes had made it clear that sports could be a powerful platform for expressions of dissent as well as an indicator of social change. The same proved true for the female athletes whose every rebound, shot, and serve reminded people of the rapidly shifting ideas about gender roles in American society. As the country debated whether women belonged in the house or in the Senate, female athletes embodied the social dislocations caused by the feminist movement. The passage of Title IX in 1972, which mandated equal opportunity for female participation in high school and college activities, revolutionized the landscape of sports and created fierce—if often one-sided—battles over athletic funding between men and women.

As more and more women began to enjoy the benefits of sports, spectator tastes began to change, if only slightly. Nineteen-year-old ice skater Dorothy Hamill became a fashion celebrity as well as a gold medalist in 1976—her short, bobbed haircut, called a "wedge," encouraged women to cut their hair and turned into one of the hottest styles of the decade. Tennis, long a sport followed by a mostly upper-class crowd, found the mainstream, aided by the enormous audience who watched the "Battle of the Sexes," a match featuring female star Billie Jean King against self-proclaimed male chauvinist Bobby Riggs. Both the men's and the women's circuit developed new stars—Jimmy Connors, John McEnroe, Chris Evert, and Martina Navratilova—whose personalities and rivalries kept audiences enthralled. Women's golf also unearthed a new star, Nancy Lopez, and a wider audience. Soccer, the most popular sport worldwide, tried to break into the American market with limited success. Auto racing, long a sport mostly favored by Southerners, found a growing national audience. And, increasingly, Americans turned off the TV, got up off the couch, and went outside to play. Getting fit, whether through running marathons, practicing karate, or playing Ultimate frisbee and tennis on the weekend, became a priority for many.

This chapter looks first at the challenges facing professional sports in the early 1970s. Despite the emergence of several dynastic teams, labor strife grabbed a piece of the spotlight. Players continued to make crunching tackles on the field, but now they also sued in court and carried picket signs in an effort to change what they saw as unfair labor practices. Those crunching hits sometimes extended beyond the field of play, as violent behavior became more prevalent, earning players opprobrium in the press for being both greedy and thuggish. These image problems were compounded by mounting claims from women that they deserved a slice of the sporting pie. The chapter's second section examines the long-standing gender bias against women in sports—the assumption that active competition was unfeminine—and charts the ways that those notions began to change in the late 1960s. The third section explores the impact of Title IX legislation on college sports for both women and men. Ironically, college football, which athletic directors and coaches claimed would be irreparably damaged by Title IX, grew tremendously in the decade. The discussion around Title IX proved a referendum on both female equality and the state of collegiate football, as boosters declared that its ability to create revenue meant that football deserved special status. By the mid-1970s, football proponents rarely mentioned the sport's educational mission. The chapter's fourth section looks at how tennis and golf benefited from a changing social climate, and the chapter closes with a discussion of shifting attitudes about participant sports.

CHANGING THE SPORTS LANDSCAPE

The Watergate scandal dominated the front pages from late in 1973 until President Nixon resigned in August 1974. On October 20, 1973, Nixon fired special prosecutor Archibald Cox, who had been in charge of investigating the possible scandal. In response, Attorney General Richardson and Deputy Attorney General William D. Ruckelshaus resigned their positions in protest and pressure for impeachment of the president mounted in Congress. What was called the "Saturday Night Massacre" competed for coverage with game six of the World Series between the powerhouse Oakland Athletics and the New York Mets, a 3–1 victory for A's pitcher Catfish Hunter over Met ace Tom Seaver. Eventually, the scandal surrounding the presidency touched baseball directly. In 1974, MLB Commissioner Bowie Kuhn fined New York Yankees owner George Steinbrenner $15,000 for illegal campaign contributions to the Nixon reelection campaign and forced the Yankee owner to withdraw from any contact with the team for a month. Kuhn and Steinbrenner had another run-in in 1977, when Steinbrenner admitted to making illegal campaign contributions and was suspended from baseball for two years. Steinbrenner proposed diluting the power of the commissioner's office, arguing that baseball's system needed to be revamped. "No one man should have the power the baseball constitution gives the commissioner's office," the Yankee owner explained. "There's a lot in baseball that's against the whole democratic system of the United States."[6] In response, Kuhn explained that "an essential element of a professional team sport is the public's confidence in its integrity. If the public doesn't believe that a sport is honest, it would be impossible for the sport to succeed."[7]

In his criticism of Steinbrenner, Kuhn invoked a standard trope about the meaning of sports. Despite gambling scandals in college sports in the 1950s and again in 1961, sports had long been touted as a space where honesty, fair play, and tradition reigned supreme. Some fans had been stunned when their teams left for more profitable pastures. Others watched, in either horror or delight, as black athletes used sports as a platform to discuss social change. Despite these changes, and despite the exploding television revenues that further linked sports to the bottom line, an air of innocence remained. Players were heroes, tied to their team by both contract and, it was presumed, loyalty. Then the players began to fight for their piece of the financial pie, forcing sportswriters and fans to realize that sports was a workplace as well as a place where heroes were made.

Sometimes players sued, as Baltimore Colt tight end John Mackey did in 1973. NFL owners exerted almost total control over their players, employing what came to be called the "Rozelle Rule" in order to stifle player movement. This rule required that any club that acquired a free agent compensate the player's former club with a commissioner-determined amount of money, draft picks, or players. Technically, the NFL enjoyed the benefits of free agency, but in reality player movement was almost nil because the uncertainty of the cost of a free agent impeded players from changing teams unless they were traded. Mackey maintained that the Rozelle Rule stifled competition and restricted salaries by limiting players' bargaining power. He had plenty of on-the-field credentials to help him make his case. A five-time Pro Bowler, Mackey had revolutionized his position, turning the tight end into a major offensive weapon for the first time. He also played in two Super Bowls, going seventy-five yards for a touchdown in Super Bowl V. Off the field, he served as head of the players' union and was willing to challenge the entrenched power of the owners.

Despite the labor disputes, professional football flourished, particularly in Dallas and Pittsburgh. Though the team had gone winless during coach Tom Landry's first season as coach in 1960, the Cowboys gradually become a powerhouse in the NFL, winning the Super Bowl in 1972 and 1978 and losing to the Steelers in 1975 and 1980. The franchise, owned by Texas millionaire Clint Murchison, proved a fascinating mix of innovation and conservatism, both on the field and off. Landry coached from the sidelines dressed in a sports coat and slacks and wearing a fedora—not a cap. He had made his name as a professional coach in the late 1950s with the New York Giants, inventing the 4–3 defense that would ultimately be adopted as the standard defense for NFL teams. Dallas hosted a televised Thanksgiving Day game each year, creating a national audience that thrilled at the passing of quarterback Roger Staubach and a dominating defense featuring Ed "Too Tall" Jones, Randy White, and Harvey Martin. The Cowboys, despite their location in the heart of the Bible Belt and Landry's personal conservatism, also provided a sexy new innovation to the game, the Dallas Cowboys Cheerleaders. Other teams copied the lurid combination of skimpy uniforms and choreographed dance numbers as quickly as they mimicked Landry's innovative defensive sets. Pittsburgh lacked the cheerleaders, but sold-out crowds waved black and gold "terrible towels" for their stars, who surpassed even Dallas in their on-the-field success. Behind coach Chuck Noll, the Steelers went to eight consecutive playoffs between 1972 and 1979 and won the Super Bowl four times.

Success on the field could not mask the labor troubles off of it. Mackey and the NFL players' union, which won its decision in 1976, were part of a much larger labor revolution in professional sports. With television revenues increasing at an astonishing rate, players became ever more resentful of the restrictions placed on their bargaining positions. Acrimonious labor disputes, lawsuits, walkouts, and strikes became regular topics for the sports page. To an extent these were part of a sixties legacy that encouraged players to challenge authority. Many of the players who emerged as leaders in the fight against traditional labor practices were black—Curt Flood, John Mackey, Oscar Robertson, and Spencer Haywood—and drew on the heritage of civil rights activism and the black power movement.

Baseball players who wanted some measure of control over their own work faced daunting legal obstacles as well as owners committed to maintaining the reserve clause. Alone of the major professional sports in the United States, baseball enjoys a legal exemption from antitrust action. Baseball players gained one significant advantage when Marvin Miller became the head of the Major League Baseball players' association (MLBPA) in 1966. Unlike the powerful United Steel Workers union, where Miller had served as chief negotiator, the MLBPA was weak and unorganized. His decision to work with the players' union was based in part on his love of the game, since the new job was an obvious demotion. Miller worked slowly and carefully to transform the association into a robust advocate for players' rights. Though he wanted to abolish the reserve clause from the beginning, arguing that players signed the worst contracts in labor history, he started with smaller actions designed to gain the players' trust. Miller met with almost every player during the 1966 season, trying to convince each one that a strong union could help them. Many players were fearful of reprisals from baseball owners, who had blackballed previous players who had actively questioned the reserve system. Others thought of themselves as professionals, not as workers who needed the help of a union.

But times were changing. Black athletes had started to speak out about injustices they faced, providing a model for all athletes to follow. Player salaries had not kept pace with inflation, much less the tremendous jump in revenues that owners received. In the twenty years from 1946 to 1966, the major-league minimum salary rose from $5,000 to

$7,000. In approximately the same period, from 1952 to 1971, television revenues alone soared from $5.4 million to over $40 million. Players did not even receive a raise in their minimum salary when the number of games they played per season jumped from 154 to 162.

Once hired as executive director of the nascent union, Miller started by working to improve two key issues, player salaries and retirement pensions. In 1963, the average salary for a player stood at $19,160, with only two players—most likely Willie Mays and Stan Musial—making more than $75,000 per year. In the first collective-bargaining agreement between the owners and the players' union, in 1968, Miller got the starting salary raised to $10,000, and in 1969 the average annual salary reached $24,909. Retirement pensions were so important to players, who realized their careers would likely be over when they reached their midthirties, that the union organized its first strike over the issue in 1969. Owners had just signed a new $40-million television contract but had no incentive to share the revenues with players. Miller convinced a majority of the players to refuse to sign their yearly contracts—because the reserve clause bound a player to a team for life there was no need for multiyear contracts—and the union threatened not to play the season. Taken by surprise, the owners agreed to contribute more to the pension fund and to lower the requirement to participate to four years of major-league service.

Then, in 1969, St. Louis Cardinals owner August Busch traded all-star outfielder Curt Flood to the Philadelphia Phillies. Flood had been with the Cardinals since 1958 and had been a star since 1961, winning seven Gold Gloves for his defensive prowess and batting over .300 five times. But the Cardinals starting lineup made $565,000, including Flood's $72,500, and Busch was looking to trim the payroll. At thirty-one, Flood hit only .285 during the 1969 season and had been a vocal leader of the push for more player autonomy; he was an obvious choice to go. The trade devastated Flood. The racism he faced during the two years he had spent playing minor-league baseball in the South had deeply affected him, leaving him fearful of joining a Philadelphia club that had a reputation for struggling with star black players. He also believed that, as a ten-year veteran, he should have some say over where he played. Knowing that he might never play baseball again, Flood refused to report to the Phillies and decided to fight the reserve-clause system in the federal courts.

In a letter to baseball commissioner Bowie Kuhn, Flood explain that "I do not feel that I am a piece of property to be bought and sold irrespective of my wishes." The civil rights movement had helped Flood see the link between racial oppression and labor injustice, so, by 1969, he could believe that the reserve clause amounted to little more than well-paid slavery and that he had a moral responsibility to challenge the system. Flood explained that "in the Southern part of the United States we were marching for civil rights and Dr. King had been assassinated, and we lost the Kennedys. And to think that merely because I was a professional baseball player, I could ignore what was going on outside the walls of Busch Stadium [was] truly hypocrisy, . . . all of those rights that these great Americans were dying for, I didn't have in my own profession."[8] Flood's case reached the Supreme Court, where the Court again upheld the reserve system in a five to three vote. Supreme Court Justice Harry Blackmun included a list of eighty-eight notable ballplayers as a part of his legal decision, choosing to wax nostalgic about the meaning of "America's national game" rather than view MLB as an interstate industry. Justice William O. Douglas, one of the three dissenting judges, noted in contrast that baseball was a "big business that is packaged with beer, with broadcasting, and with other industries."[9]

Despite this seeming victory for the owners, Flood's fight had important ramifications. The court admitted that it had "grave reservations" about MLB's exemption from the Sherman Antitrust Act, and it encouraged other means of overturning the reserve system, whether through a congressional law or a federal labor arbitrator. Miller, who had encouraged Flood in his struggle, had stayed busy in other ways as well. The players' union staged a thirteen-day strike at the beginning of the 1972 season, earning higher salaries and a better pension plan, as well as what came to be called the "Flood rule," the right for ten-year veterans who had at least five years with the same team to refuse trades.

The decision also made it clear to the players' union that lawsuits were not the answer to their struggle, so Miller turned instead to the concept of arbitration as a possible solution. A cantankerous owner gave the players an easy first victory. In 1974, an arbitration panel ruled that Oakland A's owner Charles O. Finley had knowingly violated the terms of Catfish Hunter's contract, making the ace pitcher baseball's first free agent. Because Hunter had won twenty-five games for the A's in 1973, he commanded top dollar on the open market, at least from New York Yankees owner George Steinbrenner, who agreed to pay Hunter $750,000.

Miller then convinced two pitchers, Montreal Expo Dave McNally and Los Angeles Dodger Andy Messersmith to play out a year without signing a contract. The labor leader believed that the answer to overturning the hated reserve clause lay in the language of players' contracts.

The contract stated that owners enjoyed the automatic right to renew for one year, not, as most owners and players assumed, for perpetuity. In 1975, McNally and Messersmith declined to sign contracts with their clubs, playing the season without one. At the end of the year, both players then claimed they had played out the option year required by the standard contract and were now free agents, able to negotiate with any team they chose. MLB commissioner Bowie Kuhn presented the question to arbitrator Peter Seitz, who ruled in December 1975 that the two players had fulfilled their contracts and were free to bargain with other clubs. After more than eighty years, free agency had arrived in baseball.

The owners immediately fired Seitz and appealed his decision to the federal district court. Though Seitz lost his job, his ruling stood. Miller and the players had forever changed the landscape of MLB. When Atlanta Braves owner Ted Turner was banned from managing his own team in 1977 in "the best interests of baseball," he exclaimed that he should have signed himself to a player's contract. Then he would have been "under Marvin Miller's protection. The man people in baseball fear most is not Bowie Kuhn but Marv."[10]

Despite the feuding between players and owners, the level of play on the field helped to spark a renaissance of interest in the game. Finley's A's fought their way—sometimes literally—to three straight World Series titles, only to be supplanted in 1974 by the "Big Red Machine" in Cincinnati. The Athletics had brought the mustache back to baseball, part of the rebellious image their owner cultivated. Cincinnati featured, on the other hand, a team of clean-cut stars who combined speed and power in a devastating offensive attack that averaged more than five runs per game. In 1975, Johnny Bench and Tony Perez each drove in more than one hundred runs, while Bench, second baseman and season MVP Joe Morgan, shortstop Dave Concepcion, and centerfielder Cesar Geronimo all won Gold Gloves for their defense. The team won 108 regular season games and then faced the Boston Red Sox in one of the most memorable World Series ever played. Games three and six both went to extra innings, with the sixth game won when Boston catcher Carleton Fisk willed his twelfth-inning home run to stay fair over the Green Monster in Fenway Park. It made for great television. In the final game, Morgan singled home Ken Griffey in the ninth inning and the Reds took the Series.

Atlanta Braves slugger Hank Aaron hit the first homerun in Cincinnati's Riverfront Stadium, which opened in April 1974. It was Aaron's 714th career homer, tying him with Babe Ruth for the record. Two evenings later, at home in Atlanta, Aaron sent a solo shot into the left-field bullpen, breaking a record that many had assumed would stand forever. Far from celebrating the accomplishment, many Americans—and some sportswriters—belittled Aaron as a consistent but never great player, someone who passed "the Babe" only because of the length of his career. Others were less subtle in their objections to Aaron's accomplishments, especially those who could not imagine a black man as the all-time homerun leader. He received an enormous amount of hate mail as he grew closer to the record, most of it filled with racial invectives and threats of violence. The experience made Aaron much more outspoken about what he felt were the continuing racial problems facing MLB, especially the reluctance to hire African Americans in front office or managing jobs.

Even as Aaron and the Cincinnati Reds shined on the ball field and the Steelers and Cowboys vied for NFL team of the decade, labor strife continued to plague both leagues. After several years of acrimonious negotiations, MLB players went on strike on June 10, 1981, ending fruitless negotiations with owners who vowed to eliminate salary arbitration and demanded free-agent compensation. Players, who remembered the salary scale of just ten years before, were united behind Marvin Miller and the union. "The owners think our salaries will make us selfish," said Yankee union representative Rudy May. "Don't they understand that this is the first labor generation in baseball? The majority on every team remember how it used to be."[11] On the other side, team owners had taken out a $2 million strike-insurance policy, which allowed them to maintain a hard line without fear of losing money. But after taking a firm stance for months, they yielded just as their insurance ran out and the final agreement included most of the demands set out by Miller and the players' union. The following year, NFL players walked their own picket line, striking for fifty-seven days at the beginning of the 1982 season.

Fans hardly knew what to make of the strikes, the rapid escalation in player salaries, and the rancorous disagreements between owners and players. Black athletes had caused some consternation when they rebelled against structural racism in the 1960s, but labor disputes seemed even more disruptive to the classic myths about sports that so many fans cherished. In general, most sportswriters and fans favored the status quo and supported the owners in labor disputes. Many believed that athletes who fought so publicly for higher salaries and better benefits were ungrateful for the opportunities they had been given. After all, they played a game for a living, a dream most Americans could never reach.

The rapidly rising salaries that accompanied free agency exacerbated the disconnect between spectators and players, especially because union activism in non-sports-related industries ebbed during the 1970s. Trade unions declined in numbers as members lost their jobs to factory automation and increasing competition from foreign markets. Even those Americans who did not lose their jobs found themselves losing ground against rampant inflation; the cost of living increased nearly 250 percent between 1967 and 1979 while real income declined by 15 percent from 1973 to 1980. The fastest-growing section of the United States economy was the low-paying fast-food industry. In comparison, MLB's top salary jumped from $200,000 in 1975 to $560,000 in 1977, earned by Philadelphia's third baseman Mike Schmidt. These were circumstances bound to cause anger in the stands. Fans who resented the money players made heckled players, and even the players sometimes admitted, as light-hitting Kansas City shortstop Freddie Patek did, that "deep down I know I'm not worth it." He added, however, that "I have to admit I asked for it."[12]

In addition, violence—on and off the field—became more pronounced, or at least more discussed in the 1970s. On-court brawling had long been commonplace in the NBA—superstar Kareem Abdul-Jabbar broke his hand hitting another player—but even fans who enjoyed the occasional fight were appalled by what happened in a game between the Houston Rockets and the Los Angeles Lakers in 1977. When Laker forward Kermit Washington and Rocket center Kevin Kunnert began fighting, Kunnert's teammate and Rocket all-star Rudy Tomjanovich moved in to break up the altercation. Instead, Washington leveled him with a punch that left a fist-shaped cavity on Tomjaovich's face, fractured his nose, jaw, and skull, and caused spinal fluid to leak from his brain. On the baseball field, Texas Ranger infielder Lenny Randle slugged his manager Frank Lucchesi, breaking his cheekbone and sending him to the hospital before the start of the 1977 season.

Ohio State coach Woody Hayes, an icon for those who saw sports as a place of tradition, discipline, and hard work, lost his temper on the sidelines in 1978, punching a player from the opposing team who had made an interception. The sixty-five-year-old Hayes was fired the following morning. It was a sad ending to a long coaching career. But the most frightening example of on-the-field violence was legal, not a brawl or an outburst of temper, but part of the game. During a 1978 preseason football game between the Oakland Raiders and the New England Patriots, Patriot wide receiver Darryl Stingley ran a slant pattern across the middle of the field and leapt for an overthrown ball.

Jack Tatum, who had played college football under Hayes at Ohio State and who was celebrated in the press as a ferocious hitter, met Stingley with full force. Tatum's hit fractured two vertebrae in Stingley's neck, leaving him a quadriplegic. Tatum expressed no remorse for the hit, explaining in his autobiography, *They Call Me Assassin*, that it was "what the owners expect of me when they give me my paycheck."[13]

The fans themselves sometimes ran amuck, reflecting the increasing social violence of the decade. The rate of violent crime in the United States more than doubled from 1965 to 1975, and violent actions by fans—including a 1978 incident at New York's Shea Stadium where spectators attacked a security guard and dropped him fifteen feet onto a concrete walkway below—mirrored this rapid rise. At a 1976 all-star benefit football game in Chicago, fans rushed the field during a rain delay, harassing officials and players and tearing down the goalposts. During a 49er football game at Candlestick Park, one section of drunken fans threw so many cherry bombs on the field that umpires had to call the opposing team off the field.

In the 1976 playoff series between the New York Yankees and Kansas City Royals, Royal manger Whitey Hertzog was struck by a flashlight battery and Yankee third baseman Chris Chambliss needed a police escort to round the bases after his pennant-winning home run. The following year, the Yankees again earned a trip to the World Series, a high point in an otherwise grim year. Like many Northeastern and Midwestern cities, New York faced tremendous financial stress from an economic recession, forcing city officials to make deep cutbacks to city services. A citywide electrical blackout in July only intensified city dwellers' fears of crime, especially the murderous rampage of David Berkowitz, known as the "Son of Sam" killer. And the cost of the city's planned renovations of Yankee Stadium soared to $240 million, even as the neighborhood around the ballpark lay in ruins. When the Yankees met the Dodgers for the world championships in October, some fans lost control. Fans threw batteries, fruit, rubber balls, ice, bricks, and bottles onto the field, aiming at Dodger relief pitchers and outfielders. Game six featured three home run blasts by "Mr. October," Reggie Jackson, but it also ended in a riot, as fans rushed the field and police tried in vain to hold them back.

SPORTS AND GENDER IDENTITY

Despite the increasing incidents of violent behavior on and off the field and despite labor strife, men's team sports, especially football and baseball, continued to be the place where heroes were made. Fans might complain about Steinbrenner's free-spending ways and Jackson's salary, now inflated by free agency, but they feted him as a masculine hero nevertheless. At a time when traditional notions about gender roles were under fire, sports remained a bastion of masculine identity and a source of comfort for many Americans. In 1967, for example, a psychiatrist argued that it was "small wonder that the American male has a strong affinity for sports. He has learned that this is one area where there is no doubt about sexual differences and where his biology is not obsolete. Athletics help assure his difference from women in a world where her functions have come to resemble his."[14] When fans watched Mr. October hit home runs on television or when they braved subzero weather to cheer a ferocious hit by Chicago Bears linebacker Dick Buttcus, they were also celebrating traditional gender norms. Sports heroes, with only few exceptions, were men.

Because sports had long been associated with the development of masculine characteristics, there remained a widespread assumption that sports were slightly unnatural for women. Girls who wanted to play athletic games were "tomboys" expected to outgrow their interest, especially since some doctors continued to believe that sports harmed women's physical and social development. One 1967 article asserted that "the female breasts and other organs can be injured seriously by a sudden blow. The danger of scars, broken teeth, or other results of injury probably are more of a psychological hazard for girls than for boys."[15] Others worried that participating in such a public sphere would make women sexually promiscuous. Women's teams often included chaperones who were supposed to ensure that women behaved in properly feminine ways. Just as with the All-American Girls Baseball League, most women's teams, whether professional or amateur, insisted on certain standards of femininity for their players. The first women's basketball team to compete in the Pan American Games in 1955 posed for their team photograph in skirts, hats, and white gloves. One player held her purse. Except for the team patch on their matching blazers, they looked more like tourists to Mexico City than a basketball team.

Sports were also believed to make women unattractive to men or, worse, create lesbian desires. Pervasive homophobia forced lesbians who did play sports to hide their sexuality and could keep women from competing at all, impeded by the fear that the "inappropriate behavior" of playing sports would call their sexual identities into question. The president of the Association of Intercollegiate Athletics for Women, first organized in 1966, admitted that the group tread lightly in the beginning because members believed that being outspoken on issues signaled an aggressiveness that might be mistaken for sexual deviance. The fear of being labeled a lesbian also pushed female athletes to a hyperawareness about their femininity, an attitude encouraged by the physical educators, both male and female, who ran women's sports.

In September 1968, *Sports Illustrated* ran a final pre-Olympic story about the potential of the women's track team. "Dolls on the Move to Mexico" noted, almost in passing, that the team would probably be the best American squad ever assembled for the Olympics. But athletic excellence was not really the point. Instead, author Bob Ottum breathlessly declared that "there was a youthful touch of femininity in the air, perhaps a faint breath of hairspray . . . a great many more girls who look great in those warm up suits, almost as if they were modeling them for heaven's sakes, instead of just keeping their muscles warm." One coach explained that he thought young women enjoyed running because it did "great things for the legs" and brought them lots of positive attention from young men.[16] American women wanted to win, of course, but they wanted to look good while doing it. As a result, coaches assured spectators that this Olympic team would be young, shapely, and lovely, athletes who could keep viewers entertained with their looks alone. For coaches and sportswriters alike, equating athletic excellence for women with sexual desirability seemed the best way to sell the Olympic track-and-field program to a wide audience. The story fairly screamed "no lesbians here."

"Dolls on the Move to Mexico" did not mention that the 1968 Olympics would be the first to test the genetic makeup of all female competitors to assure that they were women, a sure sign of the fear that at least some female athletes were moving away from a hairspray-and-shapely-legs approach to sports. When women did play, stereotypes about the manner in which they should compete and which sports they should play continued. On the college level, most women's sports were noncompetitive, and intercollegiate opportunities for women remained rare, except at smaller schools such as Immaculata College and West Chester College. Instead, women competed in intramurals or in what were called "play days," usually with the rules modified to ensure that the competition did not grow too heated.

There were exceptions to this, of course. In Iowa, high school girls' basketball teams routinely outdrew boys' teams in the 1950s and 1960s. On a professional level, women such as Althea Gibson and Maureen Connolly competed in the traditionally upper-class sports of golf and tennis. On the Olympic level, swimming, diving, gymnastics, and running events attracted disciplined athletes who wanted to win, and the United States Olympic Committee continued to gradually increase funds for women's sports. A clear sign of female interest in sports before the passage of Title IX was the continued expansion of Olympic events for women. One new event was added in each of the 1956, 1960, and 1964 games, and then six new events joined the women's program in 1968. Women's volleyball became an Olympic sport in 1972; women's basketball, handball, and rowing events were added in 1976. There were 384 female participants in 1956, a number that more than tripled to 1,247 in 1976.

Attitudes on campus were also beginning to change by the mid-1960s. Physical educators and coaches created the Commission of Intercollegiate Athletics for Women in 1966, a group that would become the Association of Intercollegiate Athletics for Women in 1971. By 1969, the organization had scheduled the first national championships for women. Long-distance runners emerged, almost covertly, since the Amateur Athletic Union (AAU) prohibited women from entering any race that covered more than 2.5 miles. Kathrine Switzer, who registered for the 1967 Boston Marathon using only her first initial and thus avoiding the question of her gender, was the first women to run the race. Switzer's participation so enraged race organizer Jock Semple that he tried to physically force her out of the race. In response, Switzer's boyfriend and other male friends pushed Semple away and then formed a protective wall around Switzer so that she could complete the marathon. Switzer declared that it was time for both the Boston marathon rules committee and the AAU to change their rules about women. "Women can run, and they can still be women and look like women," she said. "I think the AAU will begin to realize this and put in longer races for women. . . . I'm glad I ran—you know, equal rights and all."[17]

FEMINISM AND FOOTBALL

There was a complicated relationship between the women's movement—what Switzer called "equal rights and all"—and female advancement in sports. Like black athletes, female athletes increasingly used a language of equality and rights that had been created by the civil rights movement and fostered by other movements of 1960s and 1970s. Nevertheless, many female athletes and coaches were extremely wary of being called feminists. Already participating in a field that made their femininity suspect, female athletes feared that too close of an association with the feminist movement would only lead to being called a "man-hating lesbian" and thus could undermine their already limited opportunities to play.

Still, by the early 1970s, feminist activism encouraged many Americans to question long-held assumptions about the roles of men and women in society. Should women take part in the workplace as more than secretaries, nurses, and teachers? Did they need to be sheltered and protected by their husbands? Did they deserve equal opportunities in areas previously reserved for men? Could women compete with men at all? Because the prevailing rhetoric about sports maintained that they developed both physical and moral strength in men, there was a deep resistance to providing athletic opportunities to women. Women made easier headway into law and medical schools in the 1970s than they did into college sports. Nevertheless, women proved eager to play, despite limitations and insinuations, even before changes in the law. Sports had become too important to American society to exclude half the population. Although most physical educators and female athletes were not feminists, the women's liberation movement and the legal changes of 1960s and early 1970s aided both structural and symbolic changes in women's sports.

Legal changes came slowly and faced enormous resistance. During congressional debates over the 1964 Civil Rights Act, Republican Howard Smith moved to add "sex" to Title VII of the Act. Title VII prohibited discrimination in employment, and Smith reasoned that women as well as African Americans deserved federal protections in the workplace. When the newly established Equal Employment Opportunities Commission (EEOC) publicly refused to enforce the provisions banning sexual discrimination, female activists formed the National Organization for Women (NOW) in 1966 to apply outside political pressure. NOW and other women's organizations argued that gender discrimination was as pervasive as racial discrimination in American society and that similar remedies could be used to ensure equality for women.

The "Battle of the Sexes" between Billie Jean King and Bobby Riggs became a physical enactment of many of the fierce debates roiling the country. The fifty-five-year-old Riggs, a former star and long-time hustler, proclaimed that women were naturally inferior to men and that female tennis players were overpaid. He called himself the "undisputed number-one male chauvinist in the world" and decreed that his goal was "to keep our women at home taking care of the babies—where they belong."[18] King was less inflammatory, but she had already made a name for herself as both a great tennis player and a tireless worker for equality within the tennis world.

Certainly, some of Riggs's words were bluster, designed to appeal to national uncertainty about the role of women in society in a way that might make him money. But whether it was an act or what he truly felt, Riggs pursued the idea of a male-female match with gusto, repeatedly challenging King to play him. When she refused, Riggs took on Margaret Court, the top-ranked female player, and beat her decisively, 6–2, 6–1, on Mother's Day, 1973. Riggs, delighted by both the victory and the television coverage that it brought him, taunted King in the press. As his comments about the superiority of men grew more inflammatory, and King worried that his views and the victory would threaten the recent advances made by women in the sport. The recognized leader of women's tennis, particularly in its efforts to equalize tournament paychecks, King now felt compelled to play Riggs. The offer of more than $100,000 for a winner-take-all match, plus a share in $300,000 in endorsements, certainly influenced decision as well.

Riggs argued his case with gusto. He admitted that King was a stronger athlete than he was and could execute several tennis shots with more élan. But he was sure the pressure would destroy her game. Oddsmakers agreed, installing Riggs as the favorite. "I wonder if she'll even show up," he said. "When the pressure mounts and she thinks about 50 million people watching on TV, she'll fold. That's the way women are."[19] By 1973, Riggs was forced to acknowledge that women could be good athletes, that they were both strong and skillful. Instead of the physical, it was the mental aspects of the game in which he claimed men had the natural advantage. For many men struggling to maintain their long-established dominance in an office setting, Riggs's words resonated. But for the more than 50 percent of American women who worked outside the home by 1973, the claim that they could not withstand pressure situations must have been galling.

The match was made for television, literally. The "Battle of the Sexes" was a media-created event that was hyped into a spectacle designed to attract millions. Until the match started, the Astrodome seemed to be hosting a circus rather than a sporting event, with midgets dressed as teddy bears and cheerleaders dancing to music of "Jesus Christ Superstar" on the sidelines. Four bare-chested men carried King into the stadium on a litter and watched as King presented Riggs with a baby pig before the start of the match. A crowd of more than 30,000 bought tickets to the event, then the largest audience to ever watch a tennis match in person, while more than 50 million people watched the event on television. Playing by male tennis rules that required winning three of five matches for a victory, King beat Riggs in straight sets, 6–4, 6–3, 6–3. Her victory did not demonstrate that women could compete with men since there was no doubt that reigning champion Jimmy Connors would have dispatched King easily. But the match did show that King, and by extension, the women she represented, could concentrate and win under extreme conditions.

The "Battle of the Sexes" also seemed like a referendum on Title IX legislation. Title IX was modeled on Title VII of 1964 Civil Rights Act that outlawed discrimination in education based on race and national origin. It required that no individual "shall, on the basis of sex, be excluded from participation in, be denied the benefits of, or be subjected to discrimination under any educational programs or activities receiving federal funding."[20] Title IX never mentioned athletics, of course, but the pervasiveness of federal funding to colleges and universities ensured that intercollegiate sports would come under its purview.

Though Title IX was hailed as a major boon to equal opportunities for women in sports, it took more than seven years to create a system for interpreting the rules of enforcement. Signed by President Nixon in June 1972, Title IX regulations did not become effective until July 1975, after extensive deliberation in congressional committees and at the Health, Education, and Welfare (HEW) Department over interpretations of the law. The 1975 regulations drafted by HEW gave postsecondary institutions three additional years to comply before they risked termination of their federal funding. Fearful of this step, many university and college sports administrators complained that the regulations were vague, forcing the Office of Civil Rights to issue another policy statement in 1979 that set out the final criteria and tests that would be used to enforce Title IX.

Title IX regulations covered far more than sports. One telling way to understand how deep resistance ran to women playing intercollegiate sports is to compare sports programs to legal, medical, and business schools. In 1970, only 5 percent of law students, 8 percent of medical students, and 13 percent of business students were women. Nine years later, those percentages had risen to 29 percent, 23 percent, and 31 percent. Before the passage of Title IX, many graduate programs had quotas that limited how many women would be admitted, usually a tiny percentage of each incoming class. At Cornell University's medical school, for example, each entering class averaged about two women per year. By the early 1980s, the program regularly admitted classes in which 60 percent of the students were women.

Change happened more slowly in athletic departments, perhaps because women were even less likely to already have a toehold. At the University of Washington in the 1973 to 1974 school year, men's sports received $2.5 million in funds. Women's teams had a budget of $18,000. The numbers were similar at the University of Minnesota: $2.2 million for men, not quite $16,000 for women. The five most powerful athletic conferences in country combined—the Big Ten, the Southeastern Conference (SEC), the Big Eight Conference, the Southwest Conference (SWC) and the Pacific Athletic Conference (PAC)—gave fewer than fifty athletic scholarships to women in 1971. The same conferences awarded more than 5,000 scholarships in football alone. On the high school level, one school district in Texas allocated $250,000 for its boys' sports program, $970 for girls' physical education. School district officials banned female use of its stadiums, athletic fields, or gymnasiums for either interscholastic or intramural competitions.

These numbers and attitudes would gradually begin to change, but money—and the perceived threat to the supremacy of football programs—was a constant issue in the first seven years of Title IX implementation. Even HEW administrators, whom the NCAA and male athletic directors vilified for forcing athletic departments to consider providing equal opportunities for female athletes, were reluctant to jeopardize college football. A HEW staff member responsible for drafting the 1974 regulations remembers "working with a set of high-level administrators at HEW" who did not want "to let football be attacked, as they saw it, by the prospect of diverting funds or efforts into women's athletics."[21] John Tower, the senior senator from Texas, sponsored an 1974 amendment to Title IX that would have exempted football and men's basketball—the so-called "revenue-producing sports"—from being included when determining Title IX compliance. The amendment failed, as did two other congressional attempts to exempt football from federal regulations, but lobbyists and coaches continued to press congressional leaders to give special leeway to money-making intercollegiate sports.

For the majority of men involved in sports, women had not earned equal status because female athletes did not attract crowds and could not make money for their departments. Male athletic directors, NCAA leaders, and most sporting-news commentators assumed that female athletes should not achieve equality—as measured by scholarship dollars and other financial support—until their sports attracted a fan base that rivaled that of men's sports. Many feminist scholars have written that this argument masked a more deep-seated rejection of the very concept of the female athlete by vigorously protecting the most "masculine" of collegiate sports, especially football.[22] But that was only part of the story—football was both an embattled icon of traditional gender norms and a major business venture to be protected. Most men involved in college athletics elided questions of gender equality by dividing athletic departments into revenue-producing and non-revenue-producing categories. Seen from this "business" angle, women's sports were simply an inferior product in the marketplace of sports consumption and therefore deserved less assistance from college athletic departments.

The NCAA, led by Walter Byers, opposed Title IX and actively lobbied Congress to pass the Tower Amendment. The NCAA sent a delegation of representatives to Congress to ask that revenue-producing sports be exempted from Title IX, with John Fuzak, president of the NCAA, arguing that if revenue-producing sports had to share their funds with women, the quality of the "public entertainment product" would be diminished and universities would fall behind in the competition for "the public's financial support."[23] The NCAA would reap more than $24 million in television revenues from football and basketball in 1977, with about $18 million of that from football alone. Opposing Title IX made good business sense for the organization and its members.

A host of top football coaches, including Darrell Royal of the University of Texas, Bear Bryant of the University of Alabama, Bo Schembechler of the University of Michigan, and Tom Osborne of the University of Nebraska, testified at congressional hearings on the amendment. For the football coaches who traveled to the capitol in 1975, it was about the money and tradition. To a man they maintained that if universities funded women's intercollegiate athletics at an equitable level, male sports programs would be doomed. Royal testified that Title IX would "eliminate, kill, or seriously weaken the programs that we already have in existence."[24] Jim Kehoe, the athletic director of the University of Maryland in 1978, had "no philosophical objections to equality, but the only two revenue-producing sports here are football and basketball. If you divert money from visible operations to support women's teams and give scholarships to women in sports like tennis, swimming and lacrosse, you may be robbing Peter to pay Paul."[25] Equality was a fine philosophy, but men's sports paid the bills.

Over and over, proponents of weakening Title IX argued that federal regulations would "kill the goose that lays the golden eggs." Football was the goose that allowed universities to compete in the sports-entertainment world. Schembechler insisted that if Michigan cut back funds for its football programs, then "the football program in competition with professional teams in Detroit would not bring in an average of 93,000 people per game to watch our team or generate revenue of somewhere around $2.8 million." Michigan's head coach then added that because his program competed with professional sports "for the dollar . . . either you bring in the money or you don't have a program."[26] In their testimony, the coaches took great pains to explain that their programs were separate from their universities. Not one claimed that revenue-producing sports had educational benefits for the student-athletes who played.

Instead, football provided entertainment and a sense of tradition and identity for a huge range of sports fans, not just university students. Osborne argued that, unlike women's sports, "football has been in existence for a number of years [and] a lot of tradition has grown up around" it. Roman Hruska, a senator from Nebraska, reinforced Osborne's testimony. Hruska provided a detailed list of the Cornhusker football team's accomplishments and asked his congressional colleagues to "appreciate that Nebraska football has become a great source of pride to the citizens of the state." For Hruska, as for the coaches and for millions of fans around the country, the question of athletic revenues involved "traditions and values far beyond the basic concerns of the athletic budget."[27] State pride, traditions and values, rather than any academic objective, explained why football coaching salaries at Nebraska were $301,981 in 1974 while the combined coaching and support personnel salaries for all women's sports were $42,522.

As long as the focus was neither equality nor education, these arguments made sense. The coaches who testified against Title IX enforcement believed winning mattered most, and all of them did a lot of it. The Cornhusker football team won back-to-back national titles in 1970 and 1971. Nebraska also outlasted the University of Oklahoma 35–31 in a much-hyped "game of the century" in 1971, bringing extensive media attention to the state. At the University of Texas, where Royal roamed the sidelines, the football team claimed six consecutive SWC titles and six straight Cotton Bowl appearances between 1968 and 1973. Schembechler's Michigan team posted a 96–10–2 record in the 1970s, the best regular-season mark in the country. Finally, a thrilling end-of-game goal line stand gave Bryant and the Crimson Tide the 1979 national title over Penn State University, ending a great decade for Alabama football. Victorious football teams at large state schools created a sense of identity among fans across the state, not just at the university. For their coaches, this meant they deserved more money and more perks than other collegiate sports.

Even as football programs continued to grow larger and more important in the 1970s, Title IX legislation and regulations had a tremendous impact on female opportunities in high school and college athletics. Despite uncertainties over interpretations and implementation, as well as the concerted lobbying effort against Title IX, the inherent threat of a federal law gradually reshaped women's sporting opportunities. By 1980, women made up 30 percent of college athletes, participating in an average of five sports per school. Women's teams also enjoyed 16 percent of collegiate sports budgets. While this may seem small, in 1972, it was less than 2 percent.

College sports for women moved quickly toward the spectator-based vision of sports favored by male sports leaders. Some leaders within the AIAW, and many physical educators on campus, had hoped to avoid what they saw as the evils of men's intercollegiate athletics—the hype of recruiting, the big-money aspects of scholarships and financial benefits for athletes, and the emphasis on winning at all costs. But female athletes wanted the chance to compete within the same environment as men, and after a lawsuit by female athletes in 1973 charging that the prohibition on women's scholarships discriminated against women, the AIAW to began to award athletic grants-in-aid. Historian Mary Jo Festle argues that female athletic leaders involved in the AIAW moved gradually toward a "male model" throughout the 1970s as they sought increased opportunities for women in sports. Intercollegiate women's sports had long frowned on aggressive competition and overt consumerism, but AIAW delegates "did not want to deny athletes and coaches benefits that men already had; and they wanted to build the best, which increasingly meant the winningest, team possible."[28] Competing successfully on the court or field required a commitment to accumulating resources off of it. To compete, women had to be "serious" about sports and treat it as a business, and most proved eager to win their competitive stripes both on and off the court.

Women's basketball became the clearest marker of change on the high school and college levels. The Olympic sports of track and field and swimming also attracted larger numbers of athletes but, except in Olympic years, failed to attract much attention in the United States for either male or female participants. By 1978, *Sports Illustrated* was already worrying about the state of women's intercollegiate basketball, arguing that it was moving "too far, too fast" in its imitation of the men's game. Some, such as Rev. Oral Roberts, president of his own college in Oklahoma, realized the publicity that a good women's team might supply and promised that his university would "get the best women's basketball team that money can buy . . . within the rules, of course."[29] Because of these attitudes, the story added that the sport had the potential to become the third women's sport, after tennis and golf, to capture a substantial share of the public's entertainment dollar and to attract significant television revenues.

The make-up of the Pan American women's basketball teams from 1955 to 1979 is one good indicator of the massive changes in the nature of the women's game. Because almost no major universities offered intercollegiate basketball for women, stars from small colleges and independent teams who competed in regular AAU tournaments dominated the national team. Two all-white teams from the 1950s— 1955 and 1959—featured a majority of players from tiny Wayland Baptist College, whose Flying Queens team dominated women's competition in the United States. Other Pan Am players played for the powerful Hanes Hosiery team, with the rest from an assortment of business or small Midwestern colleges and company teams. Nashville Business College players dominated the team in 1963; the Raytown Piperettes in 1967. These teams won gold in their first three Pan Am appearances against Latin American competition, but they struggled against better European teams in international competition. American women were hampered internationally because the United States was the only country to use special rules for the women's game, forcing its players to adjust when they played abroad.

A dominant 1975 team ended a twelve-year gold-medal drought for the Americans at the Pan Am Games and also featured several players who would help to change the face of women's basketball. Delta State University's 6'2" Luisa Harris was the team's leading player, the first African American to star for a national team. (African American players had first played for the Pan Am team in 1971.) Seventeen-year-old high schooler Nancy Lieberman, who would be named the top collegiate female player while at Old Dominion University in 1979 and 1980, also played, as did UCLA star Ann Meyers and twenty-two-year-old Pat Head, already the head coach at the University of Tennessee as a graduate assistant. Harris would also star for the first American team when women's basketball finally became an Olympic sport in 1976. Behind Harris and Meyers, that team took the silver medal, their best showing ever in an international competition.

The most dominant women's teams of the 1970s continued to represent smaller schools, although the game was now firmly under collegiate control rather than being promoted by the AAU. When the AIAW began sponsoring college basketball championships in 1972, tiny Immaculata College from Pennsylvania reeled off three consecutive titles, playing their third championship game in front of approximately 12,000 fans in New York's Madison Square Garden. Delta State, behind the talents of Harris and the coaching abilities of Margaret Wade, took the crown from Immaculata in 1975 and then won again in 1976 and 1977.

While Lieberman, Meyers, and Montclair State College's Carol Blazejowski emerged as the best-known female players in the 1970s, it was Head, under her married name of Pat Summitt, who would have the greatest impact on the college game. She took advantage of AIAW rules that allowed players to transfer without penalty and recruited two of her 1976 Olympic teammates to join the University of Tennessee team for the 1976–1977 season. That season, the Volunteers offered female players scholarships for the first time. Summitt's team won twenty-eight games and made the AIAW championship semifinals, starting nearly three decades of triumph for women's basketball at the school. At first, Summitt did it on the cheap. All the women's sports at the university shared a budget of $126,000 for the 1976–77 season, and Summitt made less than $9,000 as the head coach. Though tiny, this represented enormous progress. When Joan Cronan served as the Volunteers' coach in the 1960s, she made $500 per year and had a $500 budget for the team. Donna Lopiano, the women's athletic director at the University of Texas, noted in 1975 that the annual telephone bill for the men's athletic department was larger than the entire operating budget for the women's programs.

Eight female athletes at Temple University in Philadelphia filed suit against the university in 1980, charging that the athletic department offered fewer scholarships for female athletes, gave women's teams no publicity for their sport, provided inferior facilities and equipment, relegated women to off-hours practice times, and provided male athletes with better accommodations for road trips. These female athletes could easily see the inequalities of material resources on their college campuses. When women ran bake sales to raise money for equipment and men received new uniforms every year, the relative importance of male and female athletes was clear. Perhaps most galling for female athletes at Temple, their uniforms never seemed to match. While men's teams "always had nice sweat suits with just the right colors," women got second-hand uniforms that did not match.[30] They might represent their university on the court, but the school colors were never quite right.

George Ingram, a vice president at Temple University, maintained that the school could not be guilty of discrimination because "in a period of austere finances, no other program has grown as much as women's sports."[31] And indeed, between 1975 to 1980, the women's sports budget at Temple rose an astonishing 216 percent, from $147,000 to $465,000, while the men's budget increase was only 23 percent. Nevertheless, total expenditures for men reached 1.25 million, dwarfing the fast-growing, but still small women's program. The growth in women's sports did not come at the expense of male athletic programs; the number of male teams remained constant and expenses for those teams increased. By 1981, feminist lawyer and activist Bernice Sandler, who had lobbied hard to have Title IX passed in 1972, argued that "things have gone from absolutely horrendous to only very bad" for female athletes.[32] Equality had not arrived, but a major revolution in attitudes and experiences had begun.

TENNIS AND GOLF IN THE 1970S

The same revolution occurred on the professional level, particularly in the individual sports of tennis and golf. The "Battle of the Sexes" had a tremendous impact on both men's and women's tennis in the 1970s. Millions watched as a strong, well-muscled, competent female athlete tracked down shots and hit winners. While the match demonstrated that female professionals could be viable entertainers, it also showed off tennis itself as an entertaining sport that could attract a mass audience. "The Battle of the Sexes" brought tennis out of the country club and into the mainstream. Combined with a new crop of dominant American players, the much-publicized match helped to make tennis one of the most watched sports of the 1970s and early 1980s. In addition to King, Chris Evert and Martina Navratilova emerged as major stars on the women's circuit, while Arthur Ashe, Jimmy Connors, and Bjorn Borg kindled increased interest in the men's tour.

King emerged as the most visible symbol of feminism in sports, even though she was reluctant to call herself a feminist. Much like Muhammad Ali, King was not just a great athlete. She was articulate, confident and assertive, and willing to take a stand on issues that she felt were important. As an athlete, she would be remembered as one of the top female tennis players of all time. But she was perhaps more important for the structural and symbolic changes she helped make in women's tennis and in American society. Harassed by reporters for frank pursuit of tennis as profession and her decision not to have children, she insisted on her right to be a full-time athlete: "Almost every day for the last four years, someone comes up to me and says 'Hey, when are you going to have children?' I say 'I'm not ready yet.' They say 'Why aren't you at home?' I say 'Why don't you go ask Rod Laver why he isn't at home?' "[33] For Americans with traditional notions of femininity, such remarks seemed revolutionary and King became a poster girl for broader social transformations happening in the workplace. She fought for equal pay for female players, helped to organize the Virginia Slims circuit for women, led in the foundation of the Women's Tennis Association, which represented the interests of female professional players, and, along with former Olympic swimmer Donna da Varona, founded the Women's Sports Foundation in 1974. "Sometimes," she sighed, "I felt like a 1930s labor organizer."[34]

King had also been part of a concerted effort to end what was called "shamateurism" in international tennis play. Before 1968, most tennis players competed as amateurs and part of the game's snobbish appeal was that its tennis players competed for the "love of the game," not because they wanted make money. In reality, tournament organizers paid many players, including most of the men, under the table for tournament appearances and victories. Some amateurs earned up to $20,000 in appearance fees, nearly equal to money made by the few professionals on the tour. King hated the secrecy and shame of receiving money in a paper bag at the end of a tournament and, together with other stars, pleaded for "open" tennis where professionals and amateurs could compete together. The players' moral opposition to shamateurism was aided by a growing number of businessmen who saw the financial potential of tennis and signed top players to professional contracts and then sponsored tournaments for them. The combination proved too much for the International Lawn Tennis Federation (ILTF). Worried about its reputation and the growing drain of top amateur players, the ILTF voted in 1968 to allow professionals to compete at the major tournaments, including Wimbledon, the U.S. Open, and the French Open.

King and Ashe emerged in the late 1960s as two new, appealing American stars and helped move the sport away from its exclusive country-club roots. Both attended UCLA, where Ashe led the men's team to the national title and attained a number-three world ranking. After graduation he joined the military, and while serving as a first lieutenant in the Army, he won the 1968 U.S. Open and became the top player in the world. In 1975, he beat Connors to become the first African American man to win Wimbledon. Ashe became the sport's first black millionaire and, more significantly, used his position as a top player to argue eloquently for civil rights. Like King, he believed that he had an obligation to try to make change, applying for a visa to play in South Africa, for example, in order to demonstrate the racist policies of the South African government.

King was the top international amateur player in 1966, was named "Female Athlete of the Year" in 1967, and won Wimbledon for the third straight time in 1968. Ultimately, she won a combined 168 singles and doubles titles. Her matches sometimes attracted audiences as large as those for men's tennis, yet she and other women made only 10 percent what male players earned for their victories. When King won the Italian tennis championship in 1970, she realized that she had won $600 while men's champion earned $3,500. Then she learned that the next tournament on the tour would award the male winner $12,500 and the female winner $1,500. For King, this was a question of "equal pay for equal work," a pressing issue for the growing numbers of working women across the United States. King and some of her fellow female players called for a boycott of the tournament, but the United States Lawn Tennis Association (USLTA) had little interest in changing the system.

In response, King and Gladys Heldman organized the Virginia Slims Circuit, a separate series of tournaments for female players that proved enormously successful. Crucially, the women's tour also enjoyed a substantial TV contract and the deep pockets of the Phillip Morris Company, which saw the feminist image of women's tennis as a way to promote smoking for women. The combination of an advertising base and television revenues meant that the women's tour could compete in the open sports marketplace. Within three years, the circuit offered tournaments in twenty-two cities and awarded more than $775,000 in prize money. And by threatening to withdraw from the U.S. Open and Wimbledon, newly empowered female players forced these tournaments to begin to equalize purses for men and women at the annual major tournaments. In 1975, after much wrangling, the women rejoined the USLTA circuit, though Virginia Slims retained sponsorship.

New American stars followed Ashe and King, though few of them felt any obligation to speak out on issues not related to tennis. Nevertheless, the rivalry between the divergent styles of Evert and Navratilova riveted the American public. At the same time, the "bad boy" antics and stellar play of Jimmy Connors and John McEnroe contrasted with the calm demeanor and deadly backcourt play of Swedish star Bjorn Borg, creating a constantly appealing competition between the players. Technology also changed the way players approached the game, as well as making it easier for casual players to improve their games. Connors, for example, used a steel racket developed by Rene Lacoste in the early 1960s and introduced in the United States in 1967. In 1975, graphite-reinforced rackets became available for the first time, and, in 1976, the Prince and Howard Head Companies introduced oversized aluminum rackets. These racquets made the two-handed backhand a potent weapon for men and women and generally increased the power and speed of the game.

Connors emerged as the top men's star of the 1970s, though Ashe, Borg, and a young McEnroe provided plenty of competition. Connors was ranked number one in the world for five consecutive years in the mid-1970s, breaking out in 1974 by winning fifteen tournaments, including three of the four Grand Slam events. Yet the media coverage of Connors often focused as much on his rude behavior on and off the court as on his tennis abilities. Connors fought with everyone—line judges, opponents, umpires, the players' union, even fans—and frequently engaged in on-the-court temper tantrums. His brash and sometimes vulgar approach earned him a reputation as the "bad boy" of tennis, though that title, as well as Connors's number-one ranking, would be contested by McEnroe before the end of the decade. Connors and McEnroe both aggressively attacked their opponents and were capable of moments of brilliance on the court, yet neither player seemed able to control their emotions or take adversity in stride. Their petulant outbursts outraged some, but, for other fans, both players brought a welcome edge to a sport that prided itself on tradition and restraint.

On the women's circuit, King was gradually eclipsed by two very different newcomers. Evert emerged as a challenger in 1970, when she was just sixteen. She was a pert young player in ribbons, nail polish, and makeup who used a patient baseline attack to wear down her opponents. Her conscious decision to appear and act feminine—early in her career she insisted that no point was worth winning if she fell down in pursuit of the ball—made her a media darling, especially as she backed up her looks with plenty of wins. Evert, who had a brief but very public romance with Connors in 1974, served as a sort of "anti-King" on the women's tour, reassuring spectators worried about the feminist overtones of women's accomplishments in tennis. Evert ultimately won eighteen Grand Slam titles, though she would be more than matched on the court by Navratilova. The Czech immigrant struggled early in her career, but by 1978 she dominated the women's tour. Yet though Navratilova won more often than Evert, she never captured the endorsements or the popularity that Evert maintained throughout her career. Questions about Navratilova's sexuality dogged her throughout the 1970s, in part because of her aggressiveness on the court. She attacked the net with a serve-and-volley game that depended on a level of power never seen before in the women's game. She ended speculations when came out as a lesbian in 1981, ensuring that despite 330 career victories in singles and doubles, she would never win big with advertisers.

The women's game proved so popular that even whispers about players' sexual preferences had little impact on the overall state of the tour. Playing what *Sports Illustrated* called "a unique amalgam of sport and spangles," the Virginia Slims tour found a ready audience.[35] Evert, with her pig-tails and two-handed backhand, inspired a new generation of teen-aged prodigies in the late 1970s, including Tracy Austin and Andrea Jaeger. Tennis offered top female athletes the opportunity to become millionaires, and, across the country, adolescent girls joined their male counterparts on tennis teams and in tennis academies, eager to cash in on their talent.

Women's professional golf had a longer history than women's tennis, but, until the late 1970s, golf lacked a player who captured the public imagination in the ways that King and Evert did. As a result, women's golf never achieved any sort of parity with the men's tour in the 1970s. Jack Nicklaus, the top male golfer in 1972, earned more than $300,000 while playing in nineteen tournaments; in the same year, Kathy Whitworth dominated the women's tour, but picked up just $65,000 from twenty-nine tournaments.

On the men's tour, Nicklaus emerged as a superstar in the early 1960s. Though Arnold Palmer remained the most popular player, by 1966 Nicklaus had already won three Masters titles. He would add two more in the 1970s, winning the event in 1972 and 1975, and changing his image from a pudgy upstart to a golden-boy sex symbol in the process. Nicklaus was challenged by a host of great players in the late 1960s and 1970s, including Lee Trevino, Gary Player, Johnny Miller, Tom Weiskopf, and an up-and-coming Tom Watson. Watson made his name in 1977, besting Nicklaus at both the Masters and the British Open tournaments. Throughout the decade, the men's tour sizzled with outstanding performances and audiences followed the sport avidly.

On the women's tour, Whitworth emerged in the 1960s as the best female golfer in history. After turning pro in 1959, the Texan was the leading money winner on the women's tour in eight of the nine years between 1965 and 1973. She won forty-two tournaments between 1964 and 1969 and was twice named Associated Press Female Athlete of the Year. Yet almost no one knew who she was. Looking back on her career, she acknowledged that few cared much about women's golf in the 1960s. "Back in the old days, it took ten years to know your name," she said. "You could win twenty-five tournaments and nobody cared."[36] Whitworth became president of the Ladies Professional Golf Assocation in 1971, taking charge of the organization just as the women's game began to expand, helped by corporate money from the Colgate-Palmolive Company and a gradual infusion of talent from colleges, where Title IX was beginning to take effect. Only thirty-seven golfers had played in the U.S. Women's Open in 1953. By 1976, the field had grown to 205 players and sectional qualifying was introduced for the first time.

But it was Nancy Lopez who finally brought the women's game a level of attention comparable to the men's game. She turned pro in July 1977 after completing her sophomore year in college. The fresh-faced rookie finished second in each of her first three professional tournaments. By the following year, she was the top money winner on the tour, winning a record-setting five tournaments in a row. Of course, Whitworth had been a dominant player for years, without attracting much media attention. Lopez combined "a pretty swing and a pretty smile," making her the Chris Evert of women's golf, a player who both played well and had the appropriate feminine looks. *Sports Illustrated* found that Lopez "seems so good as to be unreal," though Lopez herself admitted that she would prefer "to lose a little more weight."[37] These sort of self-deprecating comments reminded fans that Lopez shared many of their own concerns. She may have been a top-notch athlete, but she worried about her appearance just like other women. By the time she turned thirty, Lopez had won thirty-five tournaments, and the attention her career received had helped to boost the women's game into the media mainstream.

FITNESS AND NEW SPORTS AND COMMERCE

Fans who watched Chrissie and Jimmy or Nancy and Jack increasingly picked themselves up off the couch and grabbed their own racquets or golf clubs. These appealing golf and tennis stars helped the sports increase their market shares, but they also contributed to a national fitness boom in the 1970s. A growing number of Americans played tennis, practiced aerobics, learned karate and other martial arts, competed in the newly invented triathlon event, or played frisbee, anything to keep active and get fit. In 1973, the sports-leisure market racked up sales of over $100 billion, and the number of fitness clubs in the country grew from 350 in 1968 to over 7,000 by 1986. Americans bought 400,000 power boats and 200,000 canoes in 1972, impressive numbers that nevertheless paled in comparison to the 10.5 million bicycles sold. Ten-speed bikes became so popular that some states began to create networks of bike paths for amateur cyclists to use. Winter sports found new devotees as technological improvements made it easier for part-time athletes to compete. Snowmobiling grew in popularity, as did skiing, as new plastic boots and fiberglass skis transformed the slopes.[38]

New sports also emerged. Wind surfing made its debut in California, creating a new industry that sold enormous sky-surfing kites to enthusiasts. The invention of polyurethane wheels in 1973 gave skateboards a stable base and spurred the growth of a free-spirited industry aimed mostly at young men. Skateboard parks boomed, and, by the end of the decade, high-flying new tricks had been created. In New Jersey, high school students invented Ultimate frisbee in 1967. By the mid-1970s, the game had spread to colleges across the Northeast. A cross between football, soccer, and basketball, ultimate offered participants a nonstop aerobic game that nevertheless promoted a more mellow, slightly less competitive experience. A college player in 1977 explained that "the joy of the game lies in being imaginative and adaptable. The emphasis is not on competing as much as on cooperation and creativity."[39] Frisbee golf made its organized debut in 1969, and, by 1974, a disc golf course opened in Pasadena, California. For young Americans disillusioned by the problems facing traditional sports, the low-key nature of these new games was appealing.

Frank Shorter's gold medal in the 1972 Olympic marathon also contributed to this personal "fitness revolution." Long-distance running had never held much appeal for most Americans. American male runners did not dominate Olympic distance events in the same way that they excelled in the sprints. (Until the 1500-meter race was added in 1972, female competitors ran nothing longer than the 800-meter race.) Billy Mills had set an Olympic record in a thrilling come-from-behind victory in the 1964 10,000-meter race, and Jim Ryun took silver in the 1968 1500-meter race behind Kenya's Kip Keino. But until Shorter won the marathon event, most of the publicity went to American sprinters. Television coverage of the 1972 marathon indirectly benefited from the terrorist tragedy that had taken place at the Olympics. Because the marathon was one of the games' final events, television viewers, who had found the drama of the Munich games irresistible, watched in enormous numbers.

Shorter's victory, along with the efforts of new fitness experts such as Jim Fixx and Kenneth Cooper, changed the way people thought about long-distance running and its potential for personal fitness. Suddenly, running was popular. In 1968, *Sports Illustrated* had noted that Americans "tend to regard the Boston Marathon as a ludicrous exercise engaged in each April by some 700 runners who don't appreciate the proper joys of spring."[40] Just ten years later, 4,391 runners competed in the 26.2-mile race, and not nearly so many Americans found long-distance running a silly waste of time. In an even more impressive explosion, the New York City marathon went from 126 entries in 1970 to more than 16,000 in 1980. Nationwide, the number of cities hosting marathons jumped from less than forty in 1969 to almost 200 by 1977.

Shorter and fellow marathoner Bill Rodgers proved critical to the development of the New York City marathon. Paid under the table to compete in the 1970s, the two marathoners' images as fit and healthy men encouraged many middle-class New Yorkers to run the race themselves. Shorter and Rodgers's participation was part of a larger effort to reconfigure the New York City marathon to attract runners who had no chance of winning. Fred Lebow and other race organizers encouraged participants to see running the race—not winning it—as a worthy and exclusive goal. According to the *New York Times*, some runners claimed that the race gave them "a special sensation that attunes them close to the world yet also raises their consciousness and provides a sense of elation."[41] Lebow's efforts were echoed by Jim Fixx, a doctor whose best-selling book, *The Big Book of Running*, sold more than one million copies. Fixx argued that heart disease and other modern ailments resulted from overcivilization and recommended running as a way to recapture a more natural, physical self. For Fixx, running was not merely physical exertion but a way of life that encouraged spiritual awareness and individual growth.

Women were a significant part of the running boom. New York organizer Lebow also encouraged women to run by starting a six-mile run (what he termed a "mini" marathon) in 1972. The first race featured six Playboy Bunnies in an attempt to convince women that racing could be sexy. The Bunnies were a flop, but by late 1970s over 6,000 women annually ran in the race. These shorter races would ultimately prove even more popular than the marathon with both men and women. Women's running exploded in the late 1970s, as the first generation of women attending high school and college under Title IX became adults and ideas about female self-empowerment through sports became more commonplace. The President's Council on Physical Fitness estimated that there were fewer than 1 million female runners in 1973. Ten years later, national surveys indicated that there were more than 19 million women who ran regularly. *Sports Illustrated* named long-distance runner Mary Decker its Sportswoman of the Year in 1983. Decker held seven American records in distances ranging from 800 to 10,000 meters, had broken seven world records in the previous two years, and was undefeated in twenty finals in 1983. Decker, whom the magazine labeled "young, beautiful and sexy," promoted exactly the image that corporations such as the Avon Company hoped to associate themselves with when they sponsored races for female runners.[42]

The Avon Company was not alone in realizing the marketing potential of athletes such as Decker. Even the weekend runner was a potential adverting boon. Runners competing in organized races also received a T-shirt for participating, marking them as part of an elite group while allowing companies to advertise to a target audience. As one company explained, "what better way to sell an image than by identifying with a healthy amateur sport?"[43] Weekend joggers and marathoners alike also bought plenty of specialized equipment. In Oregon, track coach Bill Bowerman and his partner Phil Knight started a store called Blue Ribbon Sports, selling running shoes imported from Japan. Then, in 1971, Bowerman invented a new "waffle" shoe that Knight marketed under the brand name Nike. Using charismatic local track star Steve Prefontaine, whose startling talent landed him on the cover of *Sports Illustrated* at eighteen, as an early spokesman, the company flourished. Nike marketed running shoes as a key aspect of a vigorous lifestyle, a purchase that could improve both physical and mental health. Prefontaine was just the start. By the mid-1980s, Nike and other sporting goods companies would—by combining the appeal of elite athletes with the notion that *everyone* should "just do it"—make millions.

6. Competing on the Open Market

*E*ric Heiden should have been the biggest story of the 1980 Winter Olympic Games. The speed skater from Wisconsin won five individual gold medals—something no athlete had ever accomplished—and set a world record in his final race. A six-footer with shaggy brown hair and twenty-nine-inch thighs, he radiated a casual boyish charm that made his on-ice abilities even more appealing. But while his looks and exploits earned Heiden plenty of coverage, the biggest story of the Lake Placid Games was hockey, specifically the victory of the American hockey team over a dominant Soviet squad in the tournament semifinals. The game was supposed to be a rout; the Soviets had trounced the United States team 10–3 in an exhibition just a week before the Olympics. Instead, Mike Eruzione scored the go-ahead goal midway through the third period and the Americans hung on for a stunning 4–3 win, with announcer Al Michaels yelling "do you believe in miracles? Y-e-s-s-s-s!" A postgame photograph of goalie Jim Craig draped in an enormous American flag had special resonance for a country weary from an economic downturn and worried about fifty-three Americans held hostage in Iran. When the U.S. team then beat Finland for the gold medal, Dudley Clendinen, a sportswriter for the *New York Times*, explained that "it was, in a time of great international tension and fatigue, as if the nation had been given a great present."[1]

It would be the last chance to beat the Soviets for several years. In March 1980, President Jimmy Carter asked the United States Olympic Committee to boycott the 1980 Summer Games to be held in Moscow that summer. Carter's request came in response to the Soviet Union's invasion of Afghanistan. Rather than using the Olympics as an international platform for demonstrating American superiority—as the "Miracle on Ice" had done—Carter believed that allowing American athletes to compete in Moscow would send the wrong message to the Soviets and that a boycott had more symbolic value than gold medal victories. NBC, which had bid $87 million for the right to broadcast the games from Moscow, paid the steepest price for Carter's decision, but many American athletes were furious that they would be denied an opportunity for Olympic glory. "It was like somebody had just taken a prize from you that you hadn't collected yet," said sprinter Evelyn Ashford.[2] Rower Anita DeFrantz and other athletes unsuccessfully sued the United States Olympic Committee in federal court, trying to have the organization's decision overturned. In a meeting with a representative from the White House, DeFrantz asked whether the Olympic boycott would save even one Afghani life. Though the answer was no, American athletes stayed home for the first time since the beginning of the modern Olympics in 1896.

Despite this stance against Soviet aggression, Carter lost the 1980 presidential election to former Hollywood star and California governor Ronald Reagan. Reagan's campaign promised voters an aggressive return to American patriotic glory, along with an end to "big government" regulations and an increasing reliance on the free market. At least on the surface, Reagan's laissez-faire approach worked. Four years later, when Los Angeles hosted the 1984 Summer Games, the economic gloom of the late 1970s seemed a distant memory, replaced by a can-do enterprising spirit. Olympic organizer Peter Ueberroth raised half a billion dollars by selling advertising rights to more than thirty companies, including refuse companies that bid for the right to pick up Olympic garbage. By making commercial sponsorships a significant revenue stream, the first-ever privately financed games paid for themselves, turning a profit of $215 million. Like his fellow entrepreneurs Lee Iacocca, Donald Trump, and Ted Turner, Ueberroth was widely celebrated as the living embodiment of a new ethos of capitalist success, an example of what could happen when government got out of the way and let markets operate freely. *Time* magazine named Ueberroth its "Man of the Year" for devising a privatized model to finance the Olympics that transformed them into a money-making spectacle. The 1980 Olympics had served as an advertisement for state socialism; the 1984 Olympics touted the benefits of private enterprise.

What this meant for the future of the Olympics as an amateur international event was less clear. Even more than two decades of television coverage had, Ueberroth and the Los Angeles games fully reshaped the Olympics as a packaged spectacle, an ideal medium through which corporations could sell their products. ABC broadcaster Jim McKay called Los Angeles "the Olympics of *right now*, all glitz and glamour, state of the art, Hollywood on parade."[3] In retaliation for the 1980 boycott, the Soviets and thirteen of their Eastern Bloc allies stayed home, a decision that only heightened the patriotic glow of the games, since American athletes dominated amid the weakened competition and viewers at home heard the American national anthem again and again. Sprinter Carl Lewis duplicated Jesse Owens's feat at the 1936 Olympics by winning gold medals in the 100, 200, 4x100 relay, and the long jump, but West Virginia gymnast Mary Lou Retton was the surprise superstar of the games. Retton earned a perfect 10 on her final vault to capture the individual all-round gold medal, the first gold medal ever won by an American woman in gymnastics. The performance earned her *Sports Illustrated*'s "Sportswoman of the Year" honors.

Her wide smile and fresh-faced enthusiasm made Retton a natural promoter for a huge range of products; she was the first woman to grace the cover of a Wheaties cereal box. Her ability to sell her image was aided by a number of new developments in American sports, most of them aimed at increasing revenues and expanding the audience for sports and sport-related products. Marketing companies such as ProServ and the International Management Group (IMG) transformed the reach and scope of the sports agent, creating new opportunities for athletes in a wide range of sports. Broadcast rights for the Olympics almost tripled from 1980 to 1984, jumping from $87 million to $225 million, meaning that ABC needed to sell more commercials and devote even more air time to the games. And while network television continued to play a vital role, for the first time network stations competed with new cable stations for viewers. Cable network owners, including TBS's Ted Turner and ESPN's Bill Rasmussen realized that sports remained a relatively inexpensive way to attract viewers, and the number of televised sporting events exploded in the 1980s.

Retton's wholesome image also proved a big draw for advertisers who had grown somewhat wary of the negative publicity surrounding professional sports. A great athlete who had excelled under enormous pressure at only sixteen, Retton avoided the taint of the drug scandals that were affecting every level of sport. Reagan had declared a "war on drugs" in a 1982 speech to the Justice Department, and athletes as well as Hollywood stars found themselves in the glare of the media spotlight for their use of both performance-enhancing and recreational drugs. A popular "Just Say No" campaign hammered home the message that drugs were a national disgrace, but for athletes looking for any advantage that bring might them victory, using drugs, especially performance-enhancing drugs, made sense: American audiences liked winners best. Winners made the most money. And some drugs helped athletes win.

This chapter looks first at the impact of deregulation on sports, especially college sports. Reagan's push to disengage the federal government from the oversight of private institutions and the marketplace had critical ramifications for the way that Title IX was enforced. It also encouraged powerful football programs to sue for their independence from a long-standing NCAA-negotiated television contract, leading to a mid-decade free-for-all as hundreds of televised football games came flooding onto the marketplace. And as the potential for new revenues emerged, the rate of recruiting violations and other forms of misconduct rose. The federal government's decision to back away from civil rights enforcement also trickled down to affect opportunities for minorities in sports. African American athletes made up the majority of athletes in several professional team sports, but some on-the-field positions remained hard to break into and postretirement careers in management were rare. In a country where race remained a contentious issue, the influx of African American athletes also affected the coverage of drug use in sports, the topic of the chapter's second section. The press may have overlooked Mickey Mantle's drinking binges in the 1950s, but they proved less likely to ignore examples of marijuana and cocaine use among minority athletes in the 1970s and 1980s. Recreational drug use nearly proved the undoing of the NBA. Perhaps even more common, especially among Olympic athletes and football players, were performance-enhancing drugs such as steroids, though leagues proved more reluctant to crack down on their use.

Yet even as steroid and cocaine use among athletes became common knowledge, sports remained a space to find all-American heroes. Marketers, shoe companies, and television and cable executives made sure of that. The third section of this chapter explores the exponential rise of televised sports and the concomitant promotion of sporting goods and sports heroes in the 1980s. Nike sold its products by encouraging part-time athletes to "just do it" and by explaining new NBA superstar Michael Jordan's success with "it's gotta be the shoes." These popular commercials made Nike and Jordan millions and made sports marketing central to the American cultural vocabulary. Commercials that marketed sports stars such as Jordan offered viewers dual messages, however. On one hand, they solidified the connection between athletics and the American dream that hard work and sweat led to individual triumph. On the other, they promised fans they could "be like Mike" if they just bought the right products. No sweat required. In making sports more central to American identity, advertisers and TV executives also created a fiercely competitive market among cities for teams and sporting events. The idea of deregulation and a belief in the free market trickled down to professional teams. As high-powered stockbroker Gordon Gecko proclaimed in the 1987 movie *Wall Street*, franchise owners operated in a world that celebrated the fact "that greed, for lack of a better word, is good. Greed is right. Greed works."[4] Owners placed their teams on the open market and encouraged urban officials to bid for the right to serve as host cities. The chapter's final section explores the increased movement among professional teams in the 1980s and 1990s and why fans continued to welcome new teams with open arms—and massive subsidies—even amid the rapid turnover.

SPORTS AND THE REAGAN REVOLUTION

The nation's new president had attended Eureka College on a partial football scholarship and started his career as a radio announcer for college football games in the Midwest. As a Hollywood star, one of Reagan's most famous role was playing football star George Gipp in the 1940 classic *Knute Rockne—All American*. In the movie's most poignant scene, a deathly ill Gipp urges his coach to have the boys "win one for the Gipper." After Reagan won the presidency, this phrase became part of the American political lexicon. All of Reagan's experiences with sports, whether real or make-believe, promoted the by-now near-mythic connection between sports and masculine citizenship. Despite an awareness that sports were big business, for the president, the playing field remained a space where young men "joined together in a common cause and attained the unattainable." In his 1981 commencement speech at the University of Notre Dame, Reagan echoed the rhetoric of the 1940s and 1950s, extolling sports as a proving ground because "there will come times in the lives of all of us when we'll be faced with causes bigger than ourselves, and they won't be on a playing field."[5] Just as in previous decades, this view held sway even as revelations about cheating, drug use, and violent behavior in college sports flooded the news. Despite the multiple scandals, Reagan and much of the country continued to believe that sports, especially football, turned boys into men and prepared them for the larger challenges of governing a nation or managing a business.

In the same speech, Reagan maintained that the federal government had usurped powers that belonged to local and state governments and had enmeshed private institutions such as Notre Dame in a "network of regulations and [a] costly blizzard of paperwork." Reagan explained to the graduating seniors that "almost every aspect of campus life is now regulated—hiring, firing, promotions, physical plant, construction, recordkeeping, fundraising and, to some extent, curriculum and educational programs."[6] In his view, this was a major problem that needed immediate attention. Elected on a promise that he would dismantle "big government," Reagan pushed hard for less government interference in every aspect of American life, including intercollegiate athletics. This approach would seriously weakened Title IX regulations, while encouraging major college football programs to rebel against the "private government" regulations of the NCAA. Deregulation became the watchword of intercollegiate sports.

The changes started immediately. In early 1981, Vice President George Bush announced that the administration intended to review federal guidelines set up by Title IX to determine whether they were among the "burdensome, unnecessary or counterproductive Federal Regulations" that Reagan planned to eliminate as a means of stimulating the economy.[7] In the same year, United States district court judge Charles W. Joiner of Michigan ruled that Title IX laws against sex discrimination did not apply to interscholastic and intercollegiate sports. Though Joiner's decision was overturned on appeal, the Office of Civil Rights (OCR), the agency in charge of investigating Title IX complaints, began to relax the pace and rigor of enforcement of the regulations on college campuses. Some labeled this new approach "common sense." Sportswriter Thomas Boswell argued that since "the Justice Department didn't pick nits or try to force the creation of ritzy programs [for women] where no common-sense reason for them existed," schools could more carefully allocate financial and material resources, a move that he believed would improve both men and women's programs.[8]

The deregulation of college athletes was a positive step for the many athletic directors who believed the federal government had no right to oversee their programs. University of Michigan athletic director Donald Canham was joyous at Reagan's new direction. For Canham, it was enough that women got an "equal opportunity" to buy tickets to watch the Michigan football team. He found Title IX a dangerous intrusion into the private affairs of an athletic department, arguing that if his program raised "$800,000 in gifts, I go right through the roof when the government tells us how to spend it."[9] Similarly, Tom Hansen, assistant executive director of the NCAA, focused on Title IX as a government intrusion into private affairs, arguing that institutions should have "the power to mold their programs as they see fit." He was eager to work with the Reagan administration because of its promises "to get government out of our lives, to reduce regulations. The O.C.R. tries to bluff and scare you. They've been out there counting showerheads and locker stalls. Now the institution will be in a much more solid negotiating position. They don't have to acquiesce to everything the investigators say."[10] The "institution" of college athletics for both Hansen and Canham remained an all-male domain. With only nine years since the passage of Title IX and even less time of active enforcement, athletic departments continued as the private bailiwicks of male directors, who believed that they deserved total control over the spending decisions of the department.

As Hansen's concerns demonstrated, the NCAA remained largely opposed to Title IX enforcement. Nevertheless, the organization voted in 1981 to hold championship tournaments for women in basketball, cross-country running, field hockey, gymnastics, swimming, tennis, track and field, and volleyball. This meant the NCAA would compete directly with the Association of Intercollegiate Athletics for Women (AIAW) for control over women's sports, a decision that quickly spelled the end for the smaller, female-run organization. The AIAW was out of business by 1982, and the future of women's sports now rested in hands of a male-dominated NCAA.

In 1984, Title IX's application to women's sports suffered further setbacks when, in *Grove City v. Bell*, the Supreme Court affirmed that Title IX regulations only applied to programs and departments that directly received federal resources.[11] Because very few athletic departments received direct federal funds, the *Grove City v. Bell* decision meant that Title IX lost almost all of its regulatory bite in intercollegiate athletics. In response to the *Grove City* case, the federal government dropped or suspended over 800 active investigations and compliance reviews. Until

1988, when Congress passed the Civil Rights Restoration Act (overriding a presidential veto), athletic departments that wanted to maintain the status quo had little to fear from Title IX regulations. Though public opinion increasingly held that girls and women deserved a chance to compete and that playing sports benefited both sexes, male leadership within college athletics saw female athletes almost exclusively as a financial threat to the success of their male programs.

Antipathy to Title IX was also part of a larger backlash against the aims of feminism. A new brand of conservatism that focused its efforts on the promotion of family values reshaped the Republican Party's approach under Reagan. In 1980, for example, the party eliminated its longstanding endorsement of the Equal Rights Amendment (ERA). Partly as a result, a decade-long drive to approve the ERA as a constitutional amendment dramatically lost momentum and even with the deadline extended to 1982, it proved impossible to gain the required number of states for ratification. The debate over the ERA often centered on perceived gender differences between men and women and the ways in which these differences should affect the roles they played in society. Opponents of the ERA argued that women should not be drafted for military service or allowed to play contact sports, for example, because these were masculine pursuits unsuited to women. The spurious belief that the ERA would require unisex bathrooms also illuminated a pervasive fear that feminist gains meant the complete elimination of gender difference. Obviously, this made advancements for women in sports a highly contested terrain.

Conservative arguments for upholding the *Grove City v. Bell* decision compared giving equal money to women's sports programs to the idea of accepting transvestites in government work. Both seemed patently "ridiculous."[12] This argument combined the "economic unfairness" of women benefiting from financial proceeds they had not earned on the field with the fear that women were moving too far beyond their traditional gender roles. Rev. Edmund Joyce, vice president of the University of Notre Dame, also lashed out at feminists, whom he believed were waging a "strident, irresponsible, and irrational campaign" against football. Joyce was "dismayed at the publicity and apparent support the militant women have received on their irrational attack of football as their bugaboo."[13] For Joyce, feminists hated football because it demonstrated a natural masculine superiority, not because its costs impeded feminist efforts for equality in college sports.

Some male athletic directors spoke openly about disbanding women's programs. At the NCAA's Special Convention in New Orleans in 1985, an athletic director from a university in New England admitted that his school planned "to drop some women's programs as soon as possible. They don't bring gate receipts, and the [women] don't want to compete anyway."[14] Even more than in the 1970s, when athletic directors testified that Title IX would destroy the "golden goose" of football, athletic departments countered claims for equality with a "rational" approach that emphasized "meeting the demands of the marketplace."[15] A 1992 editorial in the *Houston Chronicle* put it bluntly, declaring that college sports programs had to succeed not just on the field but in the marketplace. The editors urged federal judges to balance "our wish for fairness on the one hand and our devotion to capitalism on the other" because American society had "never rewarded anyone, no matter how hard he or she worked, for producing a product void of market appeal."[16] Revenue had privilege over the less easily quantified—and often dismissed—notion of equal opportunity.

Given the uncertain political climate, many female sports advocates worried that the gains they had made since the passage of Title IX would be lost. Yet some women's programs flourished despite adverse conditions. The University of Texas women's basketball program boomed amid fierce arguments over what level of support female athletes deserved from their universities and from the federal government. Advocates for women's sports, such as the Longhorns' women's athletic director Donna Lopiano, managed to hold the line during the 1980s, building programs despite the abandonment of Title IX enforcement by the federal government. The Lady Longhorns won the NCAA women's basketball national championship in 1986, beating Cheryl Miller and the University of Southern California Lady Trojans in the title game to go a perfect 36–0 for the season. The Lady Longhorns used more than on-court talent to build an unusual women's basketball program; regular promotions, fan clubs, and popular team T-shirts helped Texas lead all women's programs in attendance between 1986 and 1988. Lopiano testified regularly in favor of preserving Title IX, but she also worked to create women's programs that could attract fans and make money. In a decade when terms such as economic viability, revenue production, and fiscal responsibility dominated public discussions over the future of female sporting opportunities, equal opportunity became feasible only if it was also economically profitable.

After the passage of the Civil Rights Restoration Act, Title IX regulations were more strictly enforced and other schools began to duplicate the early accomplishments of programs at the University of Texas and the University of Tennessee. The University of Connecticut became the

second women's program to finish a NCAA Division I season undefeated, winning the national title behind the dominant play of forward
Rebecca Lobo in 1995 while averaging nearly 8,000 fans per game. Over
90,000 women participated in intercollegiate athletics by 1996, nearly
triple the number from 1972. At the 1996 Olympics, 39 percent of the
American athletes were women. Whether at the Olympics or playing
soccer in a community league, by the 1990s female athletes were competing seriously at every level. Though female team sports continued to
be largely ignored by television networks, Jennifer Azzi, a basketball star
at Stanford University, linked the growing strength of women's sports to
their entertainment appeal. "Crowds are getting bigger," she said. "The
Final Four will be in Knoxville this year [1990], and there's already a big
billboard on the Interstate advertising it."[17] Azzi was right. Attendance
at Division I women's basketball games more than doubled from 1982 to
1992, from just over 1 million fans to more than 2.5 million. By 1998,
Lopiano, now the director of the Women's Sports Foundation, declared
that "every college and university exists in a capitalist environment . . .
you want all these schools to maximize the revenue. If there's a public
demand, that's good."[18] Over 4.5 million spectators agreed.

Women's programs were not alone in their efforts to take advantage
of a "capitalist environment" in sports. Nothing mattered more than
television dollars. In 1982, with just five days notice, the University of
Houston shifted the starting time of its homecoming game from 7:00
P.M. to 11:30 A.M. in order to appear on national TV. Though a wide
range of traditional activities for students and alumni had to be resched-
uled, the school gained valuable exposure and collected $140,000 for its
trouble. With the relationship between winning and revenue production clear, the NCAA found itself in constant struggle with its most powerful members, trying to regulate illegal behavior among its members
while also trying to maximize revenues. An unincorporated association
comprising a wide range of public and private colleges and universities,
the NCAA acted as a private government within college sports. The
organization took responsibility for promulgating rules governing all
aspects of intercollegiate athletics, including recruiting, the eligibility of
student-athletes, and academic standards. At least in theory, member
institutions agreed to abide by and enforce these rules, though the
behavior of booster clubs and alumni associations and the sheer desire
to field a winning team meant that many NCAA regulations were regularly disregarded.

In 1980, the NCAA found basketball coaches at the University of
New Mexico guilty of tampering with athletes' transcripts and creating

phony summer classes in order to keep players eligible. The same year, the University of Florida, winner of the Southeastern Conference football title, was charged with over one hundred infractions, ranging from paying athletes to spying on its opponents. Neither school was alone in its willingness to cheat. So many schools were caught violating NCAA rules that most punishments lost the sting of public embarrassment. With just one notable exception, being placed on probation came to be part of the price of fielding a winning team.

The exception was Southern Methodist University, which received what came to be called "the death penalty" in 1987. The school had been punished for infractions by the NCAA five times between 1958 and 1981, a record among universities. Like other programs, SMU largely accepted this punishment as part of the business of football. Between 1980 and 1984, the team had the best winning percentage in the country. The Mustangs went undefeated in 1982 behind the running of the "Pony Express" backfield of Eric Dickerson and Craig James. But victory only increased the level of cheating. The scandal at SMU started at the top, where Bill Clements, the chairman of the Board of Trustees and former governor of the state of Texas, endorsed alumni and boosters who paid off players, first for their performances on the field and, later, to keep them from talking to investigators. By the mid-1980s, recruiting violations, regular payments to players, and transcript tampering were so rampant within the SMU football program that the NCAA officially suspended the school from competition for 1988 and, in effect, for 1989 as well. The program never recovered. Perhaps because of this, the NCAA never used the "death penalty" again, despite multiple examples of rampant, and repeated, cheating in other programs.

The NCAA adjusted other rules to put a good face on the sometime sordid nature of college sports. In 1982, professor Jan Kemp filed suit against the University of Georgia because she had been fired after protesting the preferential treatment given to academically unqualified athletes. A jury awarded Kemp $2.5 million, and her case turned academic integrity in college sports into a national debate. As a result, the NCAA eventually passed a rule requiring members to run formal academic support programs for athletes. The organization also passed what was called Prop 48 for the 1986 academic year, raising first-year eligibility standards for incoming athletes. Controversial, and especially opposed by black coaches who argued it disproportionately affected African Americans, Prop 48 required that recruits earn a 2.0 grade point average in eleven core high school courses and that they achieve a minimum combined score of 700 on the SATs. (In 1982, of the 1.5 million high school students who took the SATs, approximately 83 percent met this standard.)

The NCAA struggled to control revenue-producing sports in other ways as well. Schools with dominant football programs grew increasingly unhappy about the share of the profits they earned from the NCAA's television contract. Led by Big Eight conference commissioner Charles Neinas and Notre Dame's Edmund Joyce, sixty-one major football schools formed the College Football Association (CFA) in 1976 to better represent their interests. Neinas declared that "the major football playing universities are opposed to financing a welfare system for intercollegiate athletics," while Joyce reminded member schools that "we must never forget that we are in competition with the pros for the entertainment dollar."[19] In other words, teams such as the perennially successful Nebraska Cornhuskers and Notre Dame Fighting Irish believed they operated in a different sporting universe than schools such as the Ivy League's Columbia University Lions, who lost forty-four straight football games between 1983 and 1988. Powerhouse programs saw no reason to share revenues with losers. The NCAA took several steps in an effort to placate these schools, voting in 1978 to realign Division I football, splitting competition into Division I-A and I-AA, and effectively giving big-time football powers more independence. In the same year, the NCAA and ABC reached an out-of-court settlement with an Ohio-based cable company. The settlement allowed the cable company to show five Ohio State University football games to audiences in Columbus. This kind of niche broadcasting allowed schools a new way to produce revenues and continued to expand the split between football powerhouses and other NCAA schools.

The organization also tried to satisfy these powerful members by signing larger television packages. Walter Byers negotiated the NCAA's first four-year package in 1977, signing an agreement with ABC that brought in $120 million. That deal expired in 1981, and, still worried about a possible CFA breakaway, the NCAA responded by signing a two-year package deal with three networks—ABC, CBS, and TBS—for an annual total of $74.3 million. At the same time, the governing organization offered top programs and networks more concessions; teams could now appear on television six times per season, while the networks got five additional commercial minutes per game. In a further division between the "haves" and "have-nots" of college football, the NCAA agreed that teams whose conference did not appear in a televised game would be cut out of any revenue sharing.

None of this bargaining was enough. The CFA sued the NCAA, accusing the organization of violating antitrust laws. In 1984, the Supreme Court ruled in a 7–2 decision that the NCAA was behaving as a cartel in illegal constraint of trade. The Court also found the NCAA guilty of price-fixing, arguing that the organization set the amount to be received by televised football teams in advance, independent of the quality of the teams or the popularity of the contest. A game between top-ranked teams from the University of Southern California and the University of Oklahoma carried on over 200 stations and a game between Appalachian State and The Citadel run on only four stations earned each school the same amount of money. For the Supreme Court, the NCAA's approach obstructed the market, and encouraged the "overproduction" of football at second-rate football schools and the "underproduction" of football at top-quality schools.

The 1984 decision heightened the potential for revenue in college football and encouraged universities to devote even more resources to achieve winning programs, although its immediate results actually cost many schools money. Deregulation meant that the "product" of college football games flooded the market and depressed the price of television contracts. The CFA signed a last-minute deal with ABC and ESPN that was worth $35 million a year, while the Big Ten and Pac-10 Conferences signed their own contract with CBS for about $10 million. Though roughly twice as many games appeared on television, the combined value of both contracts did not approach the value of the 1983 contract that the NCAA had negotiated for its members.

Still, money flowed into college sports in many other ways. In 1988, the U.S. Congress revised the 1986 tax code to permit an 80 percent tax deduction for contributions to college athletic programs, even when the contributions entitled the donor to preference in purchasing choice seats at sporting events. As *Sports Illustrated*'s Rick Telander quipped, "Pay big bucks, get nice seats, write it off."[20] Jerry Tarkanian, basketball coach at the University of Nevada–Las Vegas, signed the first sneaker sponsorship in 1977, agreeing to a two-for-one deal with Converse in exchange for having UNLV players wear its shoes. Nike upped the ante in 1978, offering Tarkanian free shoes and warmups for the team plus $2,500 for himself. (Tarkanian was probably happy to see the money, since he regularly pleaded that his program was cash poor. He once joked he preferred to recruit junior college players because someone else had already paid for their cars.) By the early 1990s, many coaches had deals with sneaker companies that paid them over $100,000 per year.

Universities and athletic departments also began to realize the possibilities of selling university-related products to the general public. In 1983, nationwide sales of university logo products was $250,000. Sales rose gradually to $1 million in 1989 and then more than doubled in four years, reaching $2.1 million in 1993. In the mid-1990s, the University of Wisconsin had nearly 300 licensed vendors selling sweatshirts, hats, key chains, blankets, car horns, and a huge variety of other products emblazoned with the Wisconsin logo. Some schools even licensed their logo for use on caskets. All this branding could be a profitable decision; after going to the regional finals of the NCAA basketball tournament in 1994, the University of Michigan took home $6 million in licensing revenue.

As the money the Wolverine basketball team earned reveals, college basketball had also developed into a cash cow for the NCAA and its member schools. In part, this was because college basketball "deregulated" its approach to television much sooner than football. Realizing that nationally televised regular-season games would not draw enough fans, individual universities and conferences put together their own broadcast packages for regional or local audiences. In North Carolina, for example, Rick and Dee Ray convinced the Atlantic Coast Conference that increasing the number of locally televised games would create new revenue sources for the conference. The Rays create Raycom Sports in 1979 to televise all of North Carolina State University's games. By 1983, the company, together with another local company called Jefferson Pilot, had signed a three-year deal worth $18 million to broadcast ACC basketball games regionally. Selling ACC basketball games to ACC fans proved easy money, and these regionally telecast games contributed to a dramatic rise in the game's popularity and level of play.

The growing revenue streams available in college basketball led schools to make decisions based more on finances than on what might be best for their student-athletes. Dave Gavitt, the athletic director at Providence College and Jack Kaiser, the athletic director at St. John's University, put together the Big East Conference in large part because they believed it could generate substantial revenues from eastern television markets. Their plan called for a conference of eastern colleges that would dominate college basketball in four of the nation's top markets: New York City, Philadelphia, Boston, and Washington, D.C. The conference's name was chosen in consultation with a public relations firm, which thought the Big East would sell well. Walter Byers, then executive director of the NCAA understood that "the conference's mission was singular—the pursuit of wealth. Of its eight stated goals, almost all of them were about money: originate a TV network, run a post-season tournament, be successful financially, sell and create identity, and promote the conference name for merchandising and corporate sponsor income."[21] The plan worked. The money and exposure the Big East generated from television helped to create some of the top basketball programs in the country. Three of the four teams in the 1985 NCAA tournament's "Final Four" were from the Big East: Georgetown University, which had won the national title the previous year, St. John's University, and Villanova University. In a near-perfect performance, eighth-seeded Villanova stunned heavily favored Georgetown in the finals.

Regional coverage of college basketball helped the NCAA turn the season-ending NCAA tournament into a megaspectacle that attracted huge audiences and provided an enormous revenue stream for participating schools. The tournament expanded from forty-eight teams in 1980 to sixty-four in 1985. More impressive was the transformation in ticket sales and total revenues. In 1980, when Denny Crum's University of Louisville Wildcats won the national title behind a thirty-four point effort by Darrell Griffith, ticket sales totaled just over $3.1 million. The NCAA took home $4.9 million and participating teams shared $6.3 million. These weren't shabby figures. But ten years later, when Glen Rice and the University of Michigan defeated the Big East's Seton Hall University in an electrifying 80–79 overtime victory, ticket sales had reached $10.9 million. Revenue for the NCAA had jumped to just over $25 million, while Michigan and the sixty-three other schools shared $37.7 million for participating. Even the basketball itself was sponsored; the Rawlings Sporting Goods gave the NCAA more than $1 million for the right to impose its logo on the ball. In 1991, recognizing the tournament's potential to draw vast audiences, CBS offered the NCAA a seven-year contract worth $1 billion, marking college basketball's complete arrival as a revenue-producing sport.

THE "JUST SAY NO" CAMPAIGN

The widespread national attention that followed the death of University of Maryland star Len Bias is a clear indicator of the growing popularity of college basketball. Bias died just one day after being drafted by the Boston Celtics. Celebrating his status as the draft's number two pick, he spent an evening doing cocaine and drinking alcohol, a lethal combination that caused convulsions and heart failure. In the late

1970s, cocaine had became increasingly popular, as a powder among middle-class users and in the cheaper form of crack cocaine in poorer, inner-city neighborhoods. Bias's sad ending resonated with many because he had had major financial and social achievement in his grasp. A superstar player at Maryland, Bias had personified self-discipline and hard work and was held up as a classic example of the American dream, a role model who pushed his body to the limits in order to achieve victory. As someone who had thrown away his chance to "make it big" for one night of fun, Bias seemed the perfect example of why Americans should "just say no," the slogan coined by Nancy Reagan to urge American teenagers and schoolchildren to avoid drugs. The most covered drug story of the 1980s, Bias's death focused renewed national attention on the issue of cocaine abuse and helped to spur the passage of a federal Anti-Drug Abuse Act in 1986.

As the coverage of Bias's death revealed, there were widespread fears about the effects of recreational drugs on American society. One of the underlying assumptions about drug use in the 1980s was that it was primarily an inner-city, African American problem, even though a majority of cocaine users were white. Bias was black, and Peter Ueberroth, who had parleyed his financial triumph with the 1984 Olympics into a job as commissioner of MLB, argued on national television that drug use by people like Bias was "un-American." In a language of us-versus-them, Ueberroth declared that "We've got to educate them so that they know what they are doing can terminate life, mostly rearrange and disarrange their families, their children. It causes most of the crime [and] we've got to stop it."[22] Recreational drug use had the greatest impact on the NBA's image, where a majority of players were black and where observers estimated that anywhere between 45 and 75 percent of players used drugs in 1980.

But despite Ueberroth's comments, "America's national game" was not immune, nor was the problem limited to minority athletes. The Los Angeles Dodgers' Steve Howe had an amazing fastball that made him a star relief pitcher, but he also had an addiction to cocaine. Howe's on-the-field victories brought him one kind of fame; his record seven suspensions from baseball for drug violations during the 1980s brought him another. In the 1985 trial of accused cocaine trafficker Curtis Strong, who supplied a number of major leaguers with drugs, all-star Keith Hernandez estimated that he and close to 40 percent of players used cocaine in 1980. In other testimony, evidence emerged that several Pittsburgh Pirates players regularly distributed amphetamines in the locker room, while the Kansas City Royals' Lonnie Smith and the

Cincinnati Reds' Dave Parker also admitted to using cocaine. Ultimately, twenty-one players would be implicated.

Like Bias's death, Howe's travails and the Pittsburgh trial received widespread coverage. In part, such attention reflected an incredulity that "pure" athletes could be so tainted. Americans expected stories of drug use in Hollywood and among rock-and-roll stars. But as Reagan had conveyed in his commencement speech at Notre Dame, athletes were supposed to have stronger morals and values. They were role models, not drug addicts. Teams and leagues worried about how fans would react to these stories. NFL commissioner Pete Rozelle started drug testing players with "reasonable cause" in late 1982, justifying his decision by explaining that because millions of children admired and looked up to NFL players, the league had a responsibility to make sure its athletes behaved. Rozelle's anxieties were perhaps misplaced. While many fans expressed disgust with news that top athletes sometimes snorted coke, more remained deeply committed to their favorite team's success, especially if the team was winning. Before the 1983 season, a female Dallas Cowboys fan who had read a year's worth of stories detailing drug use by several Cowboys players declared that "I don't have any respect for anybody involved in drugs or anything like that. But I'm still a Cowboy fan, as crazy about them as ever."[23] More significantly, given the importance of advertising dollars, the director of sales for ESPN could not cite a single instance "where an advertiser has expressed any hesitancy at all to get involved in sports programming because of some idea that it represents something morally distasteful."[24]

Bias had died using cocaine to celebrate a moment of professional victory. Taking steps to eliminate widespread recreational drug use became a key focus of both intercollegiate and professional sports in the 1980s, with "get-tough" policies adopted by the NCAA and most professional leagues. NCAA members voted in 1986, for example, to begin random drug testing for student-athletes, who could be declared ineligible if they tested positive for marijuana or cocaine. Their fellow students faced no such tests. Sports proved to be one of the most successful fields for Reagan's war on recreational drug use precisely because athletes were supposed to be more moral and better behaved than the rest of society. The NCAA and professional leagues alike had a vested interest in making sure that image continued to hold.

Harder to eradicate, and perhaps even more prevalent, was the use of performance-enhancing drugs in sports. Olympic weightlifters had been the first to adopt performance-enhancing drugs as a part of their training rituals, but it was the stunning triumph of the East German women's team at the 1972 Games that confirmed the potential of drugs. In Munich, the East German women, who had hardly been competitive in 1968, medaled in every track-and-field event and won all but two swimming gold medals. A state-run, systematic drug program, administered unknowingly to many of the athletes, was responsible for much of their success. Though the drug program was a secret, many competitors commented on the physical appearance of East German athletes and rumors about the impact of doping raced through the athletic community. The price seemed severe, but the East Germans had taken home the glory.

A need to keep up with opponents was only part of the story. The use of performance-enhancing drugs was also closely related to changing ideas about drugs in mainstream society. Beginning in the 1960s, testing personal limits and challenging authority met with increasing approval in both sports and American society in general. "Steroids are needed by people who wish to set themselves apart from the rest of our weakling society," said one advocate. "Steroid users aren't suicidal; they're adventurers who think for themselves and who want to accomplish something noble before they are buried and become plant food."[25] In addition, scientific breakthroughs promised cures for ailments ranging from headaches to cancer, making a turn to the science of sport a natural development. By the mid-1980s, athletes could purchase at least nine books and pamphlets that explained how to use steroids and human growth hormone (hGH) to improve their performances.

Tom Waddell, a decathlete on the 1968 U.S. Olympic team, estimated that at least a third of the athletes at the pre-Olympic training camp had used steroids. At the 1972 Olympics, an unofficial poll of track-and-field contestants found that 68 percent of the competitors admitted to steroid use. Sixteen years later, the *New York Times* estimated that more than 50 percent of all the athletes participating in the 1988 Olympics used performance-enhancing drugs. One former track star from Great Britain, convicted for his role in a steroid-trafficking ring, claimed the figure was much closer to 99 percent. This was despite more than a decade of warnings about the negative physical ramifications of using steroids and increased drug testing of athletes.

Ben Johnson, Canadian winner of the 100-meter sprint in the 1988 Olympics in Seoul, South Korea, was the most famous athlete found guilty of steroid use. Johnson had blazed to a world record in his event, but two days later officials came into his room in the Olympic Village and stripped him of his gold medal. Despite having passed twenty-nine doping tests between 1985 and 1988, he admitted that he had been using steroids for six years, with the team doctor giving him the drug. American Carl Lewis, who had finished second in the race, was awarded the gold. As it turns out, Lewis, a nine-time Olympic champion, had tested positive three times at the 1988 Olympic trials for small amounts of banned stimulants. Lewis pleaded with the USOC that his use was inadvertent and was let off with a warning.

Though Johnson was caught, there were multiple problems with trying to stop performance-enhancing drug use. For one, athletes who chose to use drugs consistently remained several steps ahead of the testers, depending on a wide network of underground research to find new drugs. "The athletes are ahead of us and have stuff we don't even know about; I know that for a fact," said Dr. Robert Voy, the chief medical officer of the United States Olympic Committee in 1988. "We are not deterring use at all, as far as anabolic steroids are concerned."[26] The Pittsburgh Steelers' Steve Courson recalled that he and his fellow linemen sometimes sounded like pharmacists "talking shop" in the locker room. In addition, each individual sports federation tested its own athletes. This meant that the same governing body that negotiated for television rights and promoted the sport adjudicated the drug testing of athletes. This was often a severe conflict of interest, since, as one athlete explained, "Whether it's a country or a federation, it is not in their vested interest to lose their competitors."[27] The USOC wanted a top athlete such as Lewis to compete, for example. In addition, drug tests that caught too many offenders might permanently damage the image of the sport.

For some athletes, especially in sports that demanded brute strength, this translated into a tacit acceptance—and sometimes even encouragement—to continue steroid use. "I don't think the coaches are looking for it, anyway," said one former NFL linebacker. "And you can bet the trainers knew."[28] Bill Curry, head football coach at the University of Alabama in the mid-1980s and briefly a steroid user while an NFL player, added that "the system is saying, do whatever it takes to win. It is saying, 'We'll make you rich, famous and put you on TV.' "[29]

Tommy Chaikin, a college football lineman at the University of South Carolina in the mid-1980s, admitted in a *Sports Illustrated* exposé that he "was taking all kinds of steroids, including Equipoise, a horse steroid designed to make thoroughbreds leaner and more muscular." The steroids made his behavior much more aggressive and erratic, which should have made his drug use obvious to coaches and staff, except he estimated that at least forty teammates were also injecting themselves. After an argument with a team trainer, Chaikin went to his locker, jammed his hands through the metal mesh, and ripped the door off its hinges. "After I ruined my locker, I went back to the dorm and took a baseball bat and demolished my refrigerator, smashed it to pieces, and then ripped the phone off the wall," he added. During practice, he attacked a teammate who cut in line for a drill, knocking him down, pulling up his helmet, and then punching him in the eye. Chaikin said that as his teammate "got up, bleeding and humiliated, I felt sympathy for him. But then the steroids kicked in and I said to myself, alright! You're a tough guy!"[30] Being a "tough guy" and being "massive," with enormous bulging muscles, was the name of the game for Chaikin and his South Carolina teammates.

With Arnold Schwarzenegger and Sylvester Stallone appearing as action heroes in films such as *The Terminator* and *Rambo*, this sort of behavior could seem almost normal. Schwarzenegger broke into Hollywood from the world of competitive bodybuilding, where he admitted to using steroids in order to build bigger and more well-defined muscles. Steroid use enhanced performance, but it also augmented the markers of masculinity. The 1977 documentary *Pumping Iron*, which recorded Schwarzenegger's victory at the 1975 Mr. Olympia contest, made him a star. Appearing in a number of blockbuster movies in 1980s and 1990s, his pumped-up body became the measure not just for body builders, but for other actors and for a generation of American men. Stallone, who had become a star in the Oscar-winning boxing movie *Rocky*, continued to develop his body over the course of the decade. When he appeared as the psychologically unstable Vietnam veteran John Rambo in 1983, the young Rocky Balboa looked flabby and out-of-shape by comparison. In a cultural moment in which bodily displays of hypermasculinity sold millions of movie tickets, steroid abuse was not only about enhancing performance but also about meeting gender norms. Looking "strong" signaled internal strength and masculine power as much as it signaled athletic prowess.

Steroid use was also related to the growing reliance on weightlifting in sports. For decades, conventional wisdom held that weightlifting made athletes "muscle bound" and impeded their natural abilities. These attitudes changed dramatically in the 1970s and 1980s, when even casual athletes discovered the benefits of pumping iron. After the University of Georgia opened its $12 million Heritage Hall in 1987, mammoth training complexes featuring ultramodern weight rooms and indoor practice fields developed into required recruiting showpieces for all major football programs. For some football programs, weight training became a near obsession. The University of Nebraska made an early commitment to using weights as part of their regular program. By the time their football team played in the 1989 Orange Bowl, the school sent along a tractor trailer filled with weight-training equipment, which team trainers then set up under the stadium at the team's practice field. All these hours in the weight room encouraged a fixation on body image, not to mention that body builders and weight-lifters were among the most devoted fans of steroids and other performance-enhancing drugs.

Finally, managing pain was part of the story. Though not officially performance-enhancing drugs, painkillers that helped athletes perform were the most widespread, and most sanctioned, drug in every professional league. Playing through pain was crucial to being an accomplished athlete. Sandy Koufax, for example, made a near-unique decision to retire at the peak of his career in order to preserve the health of his left arm. At the press conference to announce his retirement, a reporter asked Koufax why he was walking away. "I don't know if cortisone is good for you or not," Koufax replied. "But to take a shot every other ballgame is more than I wanted to do and to walk around with a constant upset stomach . . . and to be high half the time during a ballgame because you're taking painkillers, I don't want to have to do that."[31] For other players, it seemed a short jump between the regular injections of painkillers that team doctors dispensed and postgame recreational drugs that dulled the pain in a different way. "The drug problem in sports is not about the 10 percent who are abusing cocaine, marijuana or alcohol," said Jack Scott, a sports therapist. "It's about the 100 percent confronted with Butazolidin and Xylocaine," two popular drugs injected to relieve pain.[32]

ATHLETIC SUCCESS, PACKAGED FOR SALE

Cocaine and steroids were two of the bugaboos of sport, much bemoaned for their deleterious effects. Drinking a cold brew at the ballpark, on the other hand, was promoted as nothing but fun, even though an estimated 18 million Americans abused alcohol in 1989, far more than used illegal drugs. Commercials for Miller Lite featured a roster of famous former athletes, including Mickey Mantle, John Madden, and Bubba Smith, taking opposing sides in a "tastes great, less filling" debate. The often-funny commercials played against gender stereotypes, featuring big, macho men promoting a beer that promised fewer calories, and Miller's sales surged. The tequila company Jose Cuervo went a step farther, deciding in 1978 to sponsor an entire sport. Cuervo's money helped to transform beach volleyball into a sport with television coverage, endorsement contracts, and more than $6 million in prize money. "We created a legitimate sport with a party lifestyle," said the company's public relations director. "We couldn't ask for a better combination."[33] By 1989, Anheuser-Busch spent approximately $450 million to advertise during sports programs, while its major competitors—Miller, Coors, and Stroh's—added another combined $300 million to network coffers. All told, the four breweries accounted for about a third of the advertising revenues that networks earned. The $1 billion that CBS paid in 1990 for the rights to the NCAA basketball tournament depended heavily on advertising revenues from Anheuser-Busch, which then used college basketball games to promote its product.

Beer companies were a small but significant part of a potent trio of market forces that reshaped the way that Americans understood sports. Cable television, powerful sporting-goods companies, and companies eager to market their products reshaped American sports heroes by combining traditional ideas about the character-building aspect of sports with an over-the-top approach that made athletes part of an ubiquitous televised spectacle. Tim Brosnan, who ran MLB's efforts to expand internationally in the 1990s, explained the approach that became the norm in the 1980s: "It's all about hero worship," he said.[34] Companies used a long-standing fascination with sports stars to reach new markets and to sell new products. Cable television and new marketing techniques transformed athletes into larger-than-life superstars, famous not just nationally but worldwide.

This marketing revolution was clearest in the NBA. The emergence of an electric rivalry between Larry Bird and Earvin "Magic" Johnson helped the league begin to overcome its negative image. The two had played for the NCAA basketball title in 1979, with Johnson's Michigan State team taking the crown over Bird's Indiana State squad. The game earned a 24.1 share on television, the highest rating ever for a college basketball game, and set the stage for the fierce NBA battles to come. Bird joined the storied Boston Celtics; Johnson became a 6'9" point guard for the Los Angeles Lakers. Bird won Rookie of the Year honors in their first season in the league, but the twenty-year-old Johnson scored forty-two points in game six of the NBA finals to carry the Lakers to victory over Julius Erving and the Philadelphia 76ers. Of course, Bird led the Celtics to the title the following year. Between them, Bird and Johnson won six MVP Awards (three each) and eight league titles in the 1980s. The Celtics and Lakers met each other three times in the finals, with Johnson's "Showtime" attack taking two of three.

Still, the two stars weren't enough to completely change the perception that the league was "too black" and filled with drug-addicted, lazy, overpaid players. The NBA remained in trouble. Its television contract was so weak that NBA fans had to watch Johnson's magical 1980 playoff performance on tape delay. Always the shakiest of the three major professional sports, the league nearly went under in the early 1980s, with an estimated seventeen of the twenty-three teams teetering on the brink of bankruptcy. By the end of the 1983 season, three franchises—Cleveland, Indianapolis, and Utah—seemed doomed, undermined by poor ownership, lack of cash, and lack of interest. A 1983 labor agreement that introduced a per-team "salary cap" and revenue sharing between owners and players helped. The advent of revenue sharing meant that players had a particular interest in policing their own behavior, and they agreed to the strongest drug policy of any professional league in late 1983. Bob Lanier, head of the Players' Association, declared that players resented "being tarnished with the brush of 'all being hopheads' " and instead wanted to demonstrate their suitability as role models.[35] With the support of the players' union and NBA commissioner Larry O'Brien, David Stern, the league's vice president for business and legal affairs, hammered out both of these agreements.

Stern became commissioner in 1984. The league had faced such struggles that when Stern read a newspaper article previewing the 1984–1985 season, he beamed because there was a "whole section on our teams, players and coaches. Nothing about drugs or runaway salaries or ownership problems!"[36] To transform the league, Stern took much the same approach that had worked for Roone Arledge at ABC; he focused attention on the players and their oversized personalities and skills. It helped tremendously that Stern took control of the NBA just four months before the Chicago Bulls drafted twenty-year-old Michael Jordan with the third pick in the draft.

Jordan had been an excellent college player, hitting the game-winning shot for the University of North Carolina in the 1983 NCAA title game and earning College Player of the Year honors in 1983 and 1984. But his collegiate career did not prepare people for the kind of professional Jordan became. In his rookie season, he thrilled fans with his electrifying dunks and his prodigious scoring ability. Jordan averaged just over twenty-eight points per game, earning Rookie of the Year honors and making the NBA All-Star team.

Off the court, Jordan was an even bigger sensation. He had signed a promotional contract with ProServ and agent David Falk before he joined the Bulls, though it wasn't obvious that he would be a marketing star. In general, advertisers favored stars in individual sports, especially golf, over those who were part of a team. And despite the breakthroughs achieved by O. J. Simpson and Magic Johnson, most companies still preferred white athletes to hawk their products. But Falk and ProServ were convinced that Jordan would be different. He combined astonishing athletic ability with charisma and an all-American image burnished by his participation on the 1984 Olympic basketball team. ProServ turned Jordan into a corporation for tax purposes, calling the company Jordan Universal Marketing and Promotions (JUMP). Jordan needed the tax break. In his first two seasons, he earned more than three times his $600,000 salary in endorsements, royalties, and appearance fees. The disparity between Jordan's salary and his off-the-court endorsement revenues would grow larger in the seasons to come. In 1992, he took home about $25 million; only $3.8 million of that came from the Bulls.

The agency to which Jordan entrusted his financial future was itself part of the revolution in sports marketing. Founded in 1969 to represent tennis players, ProServ, and its even more powerful competitor, Mark McCormack's International Management Group (IMG), reshaped how the business of sports was done. Both companies had made their fortunes representing tennis and golf stars, but turned to team sports athletes in the 1980s. With agencies in major cities around the world, ProServ represented over 200 athletes in addition to Jordan and also ran a lucrative practice that matched corporate clients with appropriate sporting events. In addition to representing clients, IMG owned and operated a large number of golf and tennis tournaments and also created sport academies, with the hope that they could develop top athletes the company would manage and sell to sponsors or sport teams. In 1986, ProServ earned an estimated $100 million, while IMG, which developed the sports agent business by turning Arnold Palmer into a national star in the late 1950s, took in $300 million every year. To represent Jordan, ProServ charged him an estimated 15 percent of his endorsements, an hourly charge for negotiations, and an annual retainer.

It was quickly worth it. ProServ convinced the shoe company Nike to develop a "signature shoe" for Jordan called the "Air Jordan." The company promoted the red-and-black high top sneakers with television advertisements that featured a slow-motion leap from Jordan as jet engines roared in the background. The tagline read, "who says man was not meant to fly?"[37] Sales for the shoes, which included a silhouette of Jordan preparing to dunk that became called the "Jump Man," totaled $130 million in 1985, and the shoes developed into an international sensation. Nike continued to market the shoe aggressively, teaming Jordan with film director Spike Lee to create a series of spots that insisted that "it's gotta be the shoes" that made Jordan so great. Slick, funny, and flavored with an urban edge, the commercials turned the shoe into a must-have item, especially for young people.

Jordan and Nike's success fed off of each other. For Jordan, his on-the-court abilities and his off-court polish combined to make him the most famous athlete in history. With his Chicago Bulls teammates, he won six NBA titles, including consecutive championships in 1991, 1992, and 1993, and then, after a brief detour to play minor-league baseball, again in 1996, 1997, and 1998. He pitched products for McDonald's, Coca-Cola, and Wheaties, as well as hot dogs, cars, Hanes underwear, and Gatorade, to name only a few. But Nike was the fulcrum around which the rest pivoted. "Air Jordan paved the way for all the other deals," said Falk.[38] For Nike, the benefits of the association were perhaps even greater. Because of Jordan and the other major athletes they signed to promote their products, Nike mastered the myriad intricacies of hip style and uncompromising cool. The company's sales doubled between 1987 and 1989 to $1.7 billion. By the early 1990s, Nike controlled 40 percent of the sporting-goods market.

The new atmosphere of sporting spectacle even turned several female athletes into advertising icons, though never at the level of Jordan or other male superstars. Florence Griffith-Joyner, who blistered the track at the 1988 Seoul Olympics to set world records in both the 100-meter and 200-meter dash, combined great speed with a sense of style rarely seen in sports. Many reporters spent as much time talking about Griffith-Joyner's outrageous outfits as they did her races. "Flo-Jo" might wear a bright orange and purple unitard with one leg cut out, or perhaps one in electric blue with her extra-long nails painted in rainbow colors. This made her an advertising natural since, as *Sports Illustrated* reported, "the idea that a beautiful woman in lingerie can run as fast as all but a handful of men in the NFL" stirred widespread interest.[39] Griffith-Joyner hawked enough products—including Agfa film, Mizuno sporting goods, Mitsubishi and Toshiba products—that some people took to calling her "Cash-Flo." Winter Olympic star Bonnie Blair never captured the imagination in quite the same way, but she was marketed as the classic "girl next door" after winning speed-skating gold medals in three consecutive Olympics. And the Kellogg Corporation started printing Special K cereal boxes emblazoned with Kristi Yamaguchi's face just hours after she won the 1992 gold medal in figure skating.

Even with the marketing efforts of ProServ, IMG, and Nike, this spectacle would not have been possible without critical transformations in television, particularly the rapid development of cable TV in the early 1980s. Television had already had a profound impact on how Americans understood and consumed sports: Roone Arledge's *Wide World of Sports* and *Monday Night Football*, the much-hyped "Battle of the Sexes" between Billie Jean King and Bobby Riggs, the hugely popular *Superstars* program that featured top athletes from different sports competing for the title of "best athlete." With all of the emphasis on spectacle and the need to sell excitement, athletes such as Joe Namath and Muhammad Ali had already "caught onto the theory that they're show business people."[40] But Namath and Ali performed when watching television was limited to a choice between three major networks. The advent of cable television exploded the amount of sports on television, and created new niche markets. In the medium's first years, the most successful American cable operator was Ted Turner, a businessman who owned MLB's Atlanta Braves and the NBA's Atlanta Hawks. Turner also owned WTBS, a local independent station. In 1976, he decided to have his local signal transmitted by satellite to cable systems all over the country. Turner's idea for a "superstation" was quickly followed by WGN, broadcasting Bulls and Cubs games from Chicago, and WWOR in New York, which carried Nets basketball and Mets baseball.

Three years later, Bill Rasmussen launched ESPN. Originally, Rasmussen envisioned a company much like Raycom in North Carolina. He wanted to broadcast the basketball games of local Connecticut teams, but in investigating new satellite distribution technology, he discovered it was cheaper to rent space around the clock than five hours at a time. Much like Arledge's approach with *The Wide World of Sports*, Rasmussen ranged far and wide to find programming to fill the space. Early sports included hurling, slow-pitch softball, Australian rules football, and college wrestling, not the standard network fare. Despite the slow beginning, ESPN, like MTV, which launched its twenty-four-hour-a-day video format with the Bugles' "Video Killed the Radio Star" in 1981, would change the way Americans watched and thought about television.

ESPN earned the rights to broadcast the America's Cup yachting competition in 1983. While this might not sound like a blockbuster sporting event, and certainly not one that lends itself easily to television, advertisers liked the demographics of the potential audience, and the network was able to charge more for commercials. This marked a serious breakthrough for the young cable station, and, by 1987, it had signed on as part of the NFL television contract. ESPN reached 37 million subscribers by 1986 and was the most popular cable network on prime-time TV. Its success helped to spawn a host of imitators and secondary sports channels. By the year 2000, ESPN channels carried approximately 23 percent of all televised sports in the United States, and the cable company broadcast in more than 160 countries and nineteen languages. No program was more important than *SportsCenter,* the network's oft-broadcast sporting-news show. With its innovative coverage, often irreverent sportscasters, and in-depth focus, *SportsCenter* transformed both the language and visuals associated with sports reporting.

Even as Jordan and other black athletes made millions as advertising icons and had their images beamed around the globe, some spaces in sports remained largely off-limits to African Americans. Blacks had come to dominate American professional sport teams: in 1986, they made up 63 percent of NFL players, 33 percent of MLB players, and 75 percent of NBA players. Opportunities to compete had come a long way since 1946. Nevertheless, black athletes continued to struggle to gain access to certain positions, on the field and off. In 1988, for example, more than three-fourths of all African American baseball players played first base or an outfield position. Black quarterbacks remained rare in the NFL. As a result, when former Grambling University star Doug Williams led the Washington Redskins to a Super Bowl victory over the Denver Broncos in 1988, it was so unusual that one reporter asked Williams how long he had been a black quarterback. Williams's abilities—and his Super Bowl victory—helped to dispel the myth that African Americans were too dumb to excel at the so-called thinking positions on the field, but it did little to open coaching and management positions to minority candidates.

Two televised conversations, one with Los Angeles Dodgers' general manager Al Campanis in 1987 and the other with CBS personality Jimmy "the Greek" Snyder in 1988, exposed some of the underlying assumptions that impeded minority advancement. Campanis, speaking on *Nightline* on the fortieth anniversary of Jackie Robinson's major-league debut with the Dodgers, explained that there were almost no African Americans in baseball management positions not because of prejudice but because "they may not have some of the necessities to be, let's say, a field manager, or perhaps a general manager."[41] The Dodgers fired Campanis, who had been with the organization since the 1940s, the following day. The following year, Jimmy "The Greek" Snyder, a Las Vegas oddsmaker who appeared regularly on the CBS pregame show *The NFL Today* to predict winners and losers, maintained that the African American athlete dominated American sports "because he has been bred to be that way." Snyder, who was speaking on Martin Luther King's birthday, then added that if minorities "take over coaching like everybody wants them to, there's not going to be anything left for the white people. . . . The only thing the whites control are the coaching jobs."[42] Like Campanis, Snyder lost his job after his remarks.

Snyder was right about one thing. White men did control management positions; minority coaches, managers, and owners remained rare. The Cleveland Indians had named Frank Robinson the first black MLB manager in 1975. In 1976, Robinson led the also-ran Indians to only their third .500-plus season since 1959, but he was fired when the club started slowly the following season. As late as 1999, MLB had hired only a total of nine black managers and two general managers. In the NFL, only five African Americans held executive positions within franchises in 1984; none of them were general managers. In the same year, 31 of the league's 258 assistant coaches were black, with only 2 holding offensive or defensive coordinator positions. African Americans had little legal recourse to push leagues to make change, since during Reagan's first four years in office, the number of lawyers in the Justice Department's Civil Rights Division shrank from 210 to 57. Jesse Jackson, a long-time civil rights activist who ran for president in 1988, tried to organize a boycott of MLB in 1987, but it had little impact. Jackson was no more successful in his efforts to shame Nike into hiring more African Americans in positions of authority. His nonprofit organization took to answering their phone with "Operation PUSH—say no to Nike," cleverly amending Nancy Reagan's "just say no to drugs" mantra for a new purpose. In response, the company added Georgetown University basketball coach John Thompson to their board of directors.

Jackson was not the only one taking Nike and Jordan to task. The urban cool that Jordan and Nike sold was hard for poor kids to afford; before Nike, sneakers did not come with a $125 price tag. The combination of high price and the fashion hype surrounding the shoe could lead to violence, and stories of young people being mugged or even killed for their Air Jordans began to surface in the late 1980s. Spike Lee, who made the "it's gotta be the shoes" commercials for Nike, insisted that, in this case, the problem was *not* the shoes, but dismal inner-city conditions that left teenagers with few viable economic opportunities. Others were not so sure. "Advertising fans this whole process by presenting the images that appeal to the kids, and the shoe companies capitalize on the situation, because it exists," said Elijah Andersen in a 1990 *Sports Illustrated* story. "Are the companies abdicating responsibility by doing this? That's a hard one to speak to. This is, after all, a free market."[43]

FRANCHISE FREE AGENCY

By 1990, sports fans understood the idea of a "free market" all too well. Starting with the move of the Oakland Raiders to Los Angeles in the early 1980s, the NFL embarked on a roller-coaster ride of team movement. Several developments encouraged owners to consider moving their teams to new locales. First, the coming of free agency dramatically raised player salaries. Player salaries escalated rapidly in the 1980s, from an average of $90,000 in 1982 to $650,000 by 1993. When New York Giant linebacker Lawrence Taylor signed a $1.45 million contract as a rookie in 1981, veteran teammates talked about walking out of training camp in protest. Just two years later, Taylor himself held out for the first three weeks of camp to protest being "underpaid" in comparison to 1983 rookies. In addition, Congress revised the tax code in 1976, no longer allowing owners to write off player contracts as a business expense, a practice that had previdously made team ownership a tax shelter. Both of these developments meant that owners spent more money and thus became much more interested in finding new sources of revenue. Owners also worried about the possibility of declining television revenues. Because the market was over-saturated with games, ratings for all sporting events fell, even for the ever-popular NFL.

The NFL grew much more aggressive in licensing and marketing its products, and all clubs agreed in 1982 to give NFL Properties exclusive use of all team logos and league marks. NFL Properties then sold logo rights to companies such as Coca-Cola and Reebok for use in advertisements, raking in approximately $3.5 billion in revenue by the late 1990s. Nevertheless, the best way for individual owners to raise extra money was to secure a new stadium deal. Unlike marketing deals, television revenues, or gate receipts, money made from a new stadium did not have to be shared with other owners. This financial reality coincided with a renewed emphasis on an individual owner's right to play the market and a continuing desire by residents and leaders of American cities to prove their "big-league" status by hosting a professional team.

An editorial in the *Los Angeles Times* starkly laid out the cutthroat environment in which urban leaders and team owners competed, explaining that the "sports business is rough-and-tumble competitive business. Self-interest rules. We hope the Oakland Raiders will come to Los Angeles even though we know the move would hurt Oakland. Both cities need the team for the same reasons—to provide a sense of identity and some economic benefit . . . sorry, Oakland, but we'd like to have your Raiders."[44] Just as in the 1950s, when the Dodgers left a trail of broken hearts in Brooklyn, this idea distressed fans who viewed the local team as part of their city's identity. Lionel Wilson, the mayor of Oakland, testified in Congress that the Raiders were "a creative and vital part of our community" and that the city needed "the pride and identity it gets from the Raiders." Fans had "taken the team into our hearts."[45]

Looking closely at his revenue stream, owner Al Davis found arguments about local pride and identity unconvincing. Unable to force to the city to pay for improvements to the stadium, he delighted the editorial staff at the *Los Angeles Times*—and Los Angeles officials—by agreeing to move his squad to Southern California. The free-thinking Davis bucked tradition and decided to move his team without gaining permission from the NFL and his fellow-owners. When the league tried to block the team's move, Davis and the Los Angeles Coliseum, where the Raiders had signed to play, both sued. The circuit court ruled that any attempts to block the Raiders' move violated the Sherman Antitrust Act, and it awarded monetary damages to both Davis and the Los Angeles Coliseum. The decision signaled a shift in the balance of power between the league and franchise owners. Deregulation was now the rule in the NFL.

The Raiders were an immediate sensation in Los Angeles, going 8–1 in the strike-shortened 1982 season and 12–4 in 1983. In 1984, behind a 191-yard rushing effort by Marcus Allen, Los Angeles crushed the Washington Redskins 38–9 in Super Bowl XVIII. Though their post-move success proved hard for other teams to emulate, Davis nevertheless started a powerful trend in the NFL. The league's revenue-sharing agreement, which allowed large- and small-market teams to compete on equal footing, made it particularly easy for owners to entertain offers from a wide range of suitors before moving their teams to new locales. NFL commissioner Pete Rozelle called the new developments "franchise free agency." Urban officials across the country constantly upped the ante in their efforts to lure franchises to their city, creating intense competition between cities for teams. Just as networks were willing to overpay in order to broadcast the Olympics, cities were will-ing to overpay in order to claim major-league teams. And though some economists promised a wide range of economic benefits and urban revi-talization with new stadium construction, the prestige of big-league sta-tus remained the preeminent reason for wooing team owners.

The United States Football League (USFL) began as a rival league in 1983, with owners attracted by "the glamour, hype and ego" of profes-sional football, "plus the chance to make some money."[46] In their one innovative move, USFL owners conducted polls and found a majority of fans more interested in watching football than baseball in the spring and so decided to play its games during the spring and summer. In other regards, they continued many of the same tactics practiced by previous rival leagues. The league located teams in a mix of cities, chal-lenging the NFL in the most important markets, but also placing teams in several smaller cities, including Memphis, Jacksonville, and San Antonio. Most significantly, they hired Chet Simmons, a veteran tele-vision producer with NBC and ESPN, to act as league commissioner.

Despite the evidence from polling data, many fans were dubious. One Los Angeles man knew that his wife would probably draw the line at spring football, so that even though he was "as big a pro-football honk as anyone—Sundays in front of the TV, going to the Rams games, the Monday night parties," he could not imagine year-round football. Another did not need his wife to tell him to stop watching. "By the end of the Super Bowl, I feel relatively saturated with pro football," said Bill Dwyre, sports editor of the *Los Angeles Times*. "I don't believe the USFL will catch on. The public places a premium on status and tradition and these guys don't have any of either."[47] For fans animated by the repu-tation of the NFL, this new spring league lacked cachet.

During its first season, the USFL inked television contracts with ABC and ESPN that brought in $16.5 million, important to league stability, but a tiny sum compared to the $316 million income that the NFL received from its TV contracts. Still, three consecutive Heisman Trophy winners—Georgia's Herschel Walker, Nebraska's Mike Rozier, and Boston College's Doug Flutie—signed with the league, lending it some much needed credibility. In 1984, the Los Angeles Express signed Brigham Young University quarterback Steve Young to a record $40 million contract. Just as with Joe Namath's contract with the AFL's New York Jets, Young's salary became a sign of the league's seriousness and a new benchmark for players in every league to reach. The league earned even more publicity when New York financier and multimil-lionaire Donald Trump bought the New Jersey Generals in 1984. Trump then convinced other league owners to switch to a fall schedule in order to compete directly with the NFL. In this, Trump's business acumen deserted him and the league folded before the 1986 season.

The threat from the USFL, though never serious, added new impetus for owners to relocate in search of greener pastures. In March 1984, three years after the Raiders left Oakland, the Baltimore Colts abandoned their home city under the cover of darkness. Owner Bob Irsay had found a superior arrangement in Indianapolis. Irsay had no sympathy for enraged Baltimore fans. "I know one thing," he exclaimed. "I have a stock certificate and at the bottom it says that I own the team." The mayor of Indianapolis was only a bit more conciliatory. He acknowledged that Baltimore fans might be upset that the Colts had left Baltimore, but he added that he did not "think any city has an inherent right to a sports franchise. We didn't steal the Colts. Baltimore lost them."[48] In his view, Indianapolis and Baltimore were competing freely on the open market, and he dismissed any notions that the Colts somehow "belonged" to residents of Baltimore.

Both public and private local businesses contributed to luring Irsay and the Colts to Indianapolis. The Mayflower Corporation of Indianapolis donated the use of fifteen moving vans, at a cost of $50,000, to help the Colts in their furtive overnight move. The Lilly Endowment provided a $30 million grant to help build the Hoosier Dome. Built before the city even signed a deal with the Colts, the stadium was the first of many to be constructed on the hope that "if you build it, they will come." Blue Cross/Blue Shield offered to sponsor the Colts' cheerleaders. And, bending to pressure from city officials, local church leaders agreed to Irsay's demands that Colts games be allowed to start earlier than two o'clock in order to keep television networks interested in broadcasting them. Though game traffic disturbed Sunday services, convincing an NFL franchise to relocate to Indianapolis overcame all spiritual objections.

While Indianapolis residents cheered their rise to "big-league" status, Baltimore residents were devastated; one explained that "the only feeling I can compare it to . . . was the Kennedy assassination."[49] *Sports Illustrated* sportswriter Frank Deford, himself a Baltimore native, described "how much they meant to that working-class city, forever in the lee of Washington and New York. . . . The Colts were like a high school team for a city of a million people."[50] Colts fans remained bereft until *their* city officials developed a sweetheart stadium deal that enticed Cleveland Browns owner Art Modell to move his team to Baltimore in 1996, where it was renamed the Ravens. Angry Cleveland fans vilified Modell for stealing "their team" away from them, but to Baltimore residents, he was a hero. Just as with Indianapolis, they had been willing to pay the going market price and had won in the Browns in open competition.

Like Davis and Irsay before him, Modell had plenty of reasons to smile about the move. In return for providing Baltimore fans with an NFL team, he took home all the publicly financed stadium's revenues from ticket sales, 108 luxury boxes, and parking fees—even for summer rock concerts and other nonfootball events. He also pocketed money from the naming rights to the new stadium. And every time a fan bought a beer and hot dog, Modell's wallet felt a little fuller, since the city's deal gave him all the profits from the stadium's concession stands. Even as they trumpeted the value of the free market, moving to a new city turned out to be mostly about free money for owners.

Sometimes the moves made little sense from a media-market standpoint. The Los Angeles Rams relocated to St. Louis in 1994 and the Raiders moved back to Oakland for the 1995 season, leaving the Los Angeles area—the second-largest city in the country—without an NFL team. Though Los Angeles fans had a reputation for being somewhat lackluster, one devoted Rams fan admitted that he planned to maintain his "Ram shrine, with a helmet and other stuff I've picked up over the years." Another claimed he would "be a Ram fan until I die" and he would try to talk his "wife into going to St. Louis as a little honeymoon."[51] Both the Rams and the Raiders moved to much smaller media markets, especially since the Raiders competed with the San Francisco 49ers for Bay Area fans. New stadiums and the attendant benefits owners received even trumped the potential of television revenues.

As usual, football fans in St. Louis, who had lost the NFL Cardinals to Arizona in 1988, were thrilled with the redemptive power of their new team. The rhetoric from city officials and fans had changed little since the Braves had moved to Milwaukee in 1956. A downtown restaurant owner happily noted that "this brings St. Louis back up to par as a major league city, with three major sports."[52] The *St. Louis Post Dispatch* even set up a phone line for fans who wished to welcome Ram owner Georgia Frontiere and the Rams to town, promising to publish some of the messages in the paper. For most American cities, the emotional and civic benefits—and, to a lesser extent, the perceived economic advantages—of hosting a professional team overcame any cost. Despite the numerous relocations and brokenhearted fans of the previous decade, cities continued to welcome new franchises with open arms and open wallets.

In the case of St. Louis, the wallets opened wide. The NFL-expansion Cardina Panthers had pioneered the use of personal seating licenses (PSLs) the previous year, financing about $100 million for their new stadium by charging fans a fee for the right to buy season tickets. St. Louis officials followed this example and received 74,000 PSL applications within the first two weeks they were offered, raising $73 million. Some took this as a hurdle that the fans had to jump in order to prove they merited a team. One city official called PSLs "put-up or shut-up time," noting that "if we flunk the test, if we can't show we have support for football in this community in a tangible way by buying these," then the city did not deserve to host the Rams.[53] By the mid-1990s, attracting a team had become so competitive that simply paying for the cost of a stadium was not enough.

Ironically, all of this movement—and the deep longing to host a team—happened at a cultural moment that made location less important. Fans could watch multiple national games on network and cable television and follow any team through the nightly highlights available on multiple sport-news shows. But that old desire to be represented by a great team, or even just a great star, made financial sacrifices seem unimportant. "The reality is, St. Louis probably could recruit a medium-sized manufacturing plant to move here from another state, and the long-term permanent financial impact would be greater," admitted a St. Louis fan. "Then again, that company wouldn't appear on national TV several times a year, indirectly promoting the city, with Al Michaels raving about St. Louis in prime-time."[54] Sports provided an emotional boost that money couldn't buy.

For NFL fans, the city that inspired envy in the 1980s was San Francisco. With quarterback Joe Montana, receiver Jerry Rice, and cornerback Ronnie Lott, the 49ers won the Super Bowl four times in eight years. Their first victory, Super Bowl XVI in 1982, trailed only the final episodes of *M*A*S*H*, the miniseries *Roots*, and the much-hyped "Who Shot J.R.?" episode of *Dallas* in all-time television ratings. The game that got them to the Super Bowl featured what came to the called "the Catch," a play in which a scrambling Montana lofted the ball into the end zone to receiver Dwight Clark. With just fifty-one seconds left in the game, Clark caught the pass with his fingertips to give San Francisco a 28–27 victory over Dallas for the 1981 NFC championship. It also became one of the most famous NFL plays in history. For a city, this was publicity that was hard to quantify but easy to appreciate.

Not only did San Francisco enjoy a great team, they became associated with a superstar player. In a hint of things to come, Montana took the University of Notre Dame to a national title in 1977, routing top-ranked Texas 38–10 in the Cotton Bowl. The 6'2" quarterback was such a winner—complete with beautiful blue eyes and a rare sense of style—that most of the Bay Area simply fell in love. "When he came to this organization," 49er owner Edward J. DeBartolo said with an overstatement typical of comments about Montana, "he came as Sir Lancelot came to Camelot."[55] Like Johnny Unitas in the late 1950s, Montana exuded a quiet sense of character that teammates and fans found compelling. "The Joe Montana aura is really an amazing thing," Clark said. "Here's a guy who's shy and quiet off the field—a kid, really—but on the field he was like a general. He was running the show, and you always knew it."[56] He had the kind of cool masculinity that advertisers paid millions to associate themselves with and that the NFL loved to promote.

The NHL had its own cool superstar, Wayne Gretzky, who helped to smooth the dislocations of the decade. Although only five hockey teams moved between 1981 and 1998, the NHL was the most volatile of the professional leagues and added teams with astonishing regularity. The league added four teams from the rival World Hockey Association in 1979, including the Edmonton Oilers and an eighteen-year-old Gretzky. The league, which had expanded from its original six to twenty-one teams, struggled in the late 1970s, but gained a much-needed boost from the coverage of the Olympic "Miracle on Ice." Throughout much of the 1980s, the NHL thrived in Canada and the northern United States, playing to audiences that averaged 90 to 95 percent of arena capacity. But, just as in the NFL, a rapid rise in player salaries made it hard for some owners to bring in the profits they wanted. In addition, unlike the NFL, the NHL did not share revenues between teams, placing small-market owners at a serious disadvantage. New stadiums in new cities proved a ready answer. In the mid-1990s, clubs in Quebec, Winnipeg, Minneapolis, and Hartford all headed south, extending the league's geographic range. And since 1990, the league added more teams for a total of thirty.

Gretzky proved to be a key reason for the league's ability to expand. After helping Edmonton win its fourth Stanley Cup of the 1980s, he was traded to the Los Angeles Kings after the 1988 season. The Kings had averaged just over 10,000 fans per game for most of their history, rarely filling the 16,000 seats in the Great Western Forum. But with Gretzky, who was known as "the Great One," as the star attraction, hockey became a hot ticket in Southern California, despite the ice. The Kings sold out every home game in the 1991 season and demonstrated to league officials that hockey could be popular in warm climates. In Los Angeles, Gretzky passed Gordie Howe to become the NHL's all-time leading scorer. Over his career, he garnered nine MVP awards and was the only player in NHL history to record more than 200 points in a season. Like Montana, Gretzky was attractive and appealing, the kind of player people wanted to watch, even those who didn't care much about hockey. He was the reason many fans were willing to commit hard-earned tax dollars to attract a franchise.

Altogether six NFL teams, two NBA teams, and five NHL teams relocated between 1981 and 1998. Only baseball owners stayed put. Major League Baseball had seen ten franchises move in the period between 1953 and 1972, but though many cities offered major enticements in the 1980s, no other teams moved. Instead, "major-league" cities invested heavily in building new stadiums and arenas to keep their existing teams. Oriole Park at Camden Yards, built in 1992, sparked a national demand for ballpark designs that played to a nostalgia for the past and to memories of local sports heroes. Earl Santee, a partner in the architectural firm that designed Camden Yards, explained that "it was clear to us that each ballclub and each community wanted to have their own brand of baseball, which meant a clear identity."[57] The firm did such a good job that after Camden Yards opened, many owners, and some city officials, clamored for their own new "retro" ballparks. In MLB, fifteen new stadiums broke ground: three for expansion clubs in Denver, Tampa Bay, and Phoenix, the rest part of a determined effort to keep team owners satisfied. In several cities, including Cincinnati, Pittsburgh, and Cleveland, new stadiums replaced all-purpose ones built less than thirty years before.

According to economists Roger Noll and Andrew Zimbalist, state and local governments bore most of the burden for this rush of stadium building. On average, sport facilities cost each city more than $10 million a year; Maryland residents pay $14 million a year for Oriole Park at Camden Yards. Even renovations are costly. Oakland government officials spent approximately $70 million to spruce up the Oakland Coliseum in order to lure the Raiders back to the city in 1995. Nevertheless, most cities proved eager to invest, even though many economists dispute the rosy numbers that new teams and new stadiums are supposed to add to city spending. Before the end of the 1990s, communities had "modernized" or built approximately eighty major-league stadiums and arenas, as well as seventy minor-league stadiums or arenas and twelve motor-sports facilities. Sports teams mattered. Former vice president Hubert Humphrey summed it up best, explaining that Minneapolis needed to make sure it kept the Twins and Vikings because "what do you want to become, a cold Omaha?"[58]

7. High-Priced Heroes Go Global

*I*n August 1989, the Texas Rangers' Nolan Ryan struck out Rickey Henderson to reach 5,000 strikeouts in his career. An editorial from the *Dallas Morning News* gushed that "from work habits that have kept his middle-aged muscles fighting trim, to a clean-cut personal life straight out of the rural Texas he loves, Mr. Ryan is a hero for all ages."[1] The following year, the "hero for all ages" reached 300 wins and pitched his sixth career no-hitter. He wasn't finished, throwing one final no-hitter in 1991 at the age of forty-four. Ryan had broken into the majors with the "Miracle Mets" in 1969, saving the third game of the World Series in New York's victory over the Baltimore Orioles. His reputation as a upstanding straight-shooter attracted companies, including Advil, Wrangler Jeans, Duracell batteries, Southwest Airlines, Nike, and Starter Apparel, who were eager to attach his image to their product. Much like the slogan for Duracell, which assured consumers that "no other battery lasts longer," Ryan played so long that he was the only pitcher to strike out all three of the men who surpassed Babe Ruth's season homerun record: Roger Maris, Mark McGwire, and Barry Bonds.

Ryan was the kind of sports hero that the leaders of professional leagues loved. But in 1994, baseball nearly threw away all of that goodwill when, late in the season, owners declared that ongoing labor negotiations had reached an impasse, and, as a result, they planned to unilaterally impose a salary cap. On August 12, the players went on strike in response. The strike lasted 234 days, canceled the World Series, and delayed the start of the following season. A Baltimore Orioles fan expressed particular disgust with the decision to call off the World Series: "You buy tickets and they tell you to come rain, sleet or shine," he said. "Then they can't get their differences settled, and you are left to deal with it. Everyone is just real bitter."[2] More ominously for the future of the sport was the response of an Atlanta teenager who raged that he was "so mad at the millionaire players and the zillionaire owners. I don't care if they never play again!"[3] America's national game, already surpassed in popularity by the NFL and NBA, seemed to be in deep trouble.

A season-long home-run battle between St. Louis Cardinals first baseman Mark McGwire and Chicago Cubs right fielder Sammy Sosa in 1998 offered near-mystical redemption for the strike and created an outpouring of interest in the sport. Playing for two teams in the American heartland, McGwire and Sosa matched each other home run for home run for most of the season. Both players shattered Roger Maris's record of sixty-one home runs in a season; McGwire slugged seventy-one home runs, while Sosa finished with sixty-six. Sportswriters covered the two sluggers as a pair of mythic heroes from distinctly different backgrounds, and the season-long contest emerged both as a forum for race relations and an example of how sports created powerful men of moral fiber and good character. "We needed a hero in an unheroic time," said Dave Kindred of the *Sporting News* in the kind of language the season inspired. "We needed a star who understood humility, respect, dignity. And the star should do what every great baseball hero has done: Stand in there and whale the bejeezus out of it."[4] Polls showed that white fans overwhelming preferred that McGwire take the title, since, as one woman explained "to me McGwire is so all-American. And this is baseball."[5]

Nevertheless, Sosa emerged as a charismatic superstar with an enormous fan base that spilled over from its source in the Dominican community. By 1998, 30 percent of MLB players were Latino, including many of the game's brightest stars. Japanese and Korean stars also made their mark. "Nomo-mania" swept Los Angeles in 1995 when Japanese pitcher Hideo Nomo won thirteen games for the Dodgers, pitched in the All-Star Game, and won the National League's Rookie of the Year award. The Chicago Bulls, a team whose logo could be found on T-shirts around the world, won the NBA championship in 1998 with an Australian and a Croatian in the starting lineup, signaling that sports had become a global enterprise, with the United States importing players and exporting sports and sporting goods. "The 'swooshification of the world' should more appropriately be deemed the Sportsification of the world," noted Nike's 1997 annual report. "We will mature in tandem with the inexorable penetration of sports into the global psyche."[6]

Basketball remained the hottest sport of the decade, though football drew the top television ratings. But the big three had new competition for fan dollars. Despite the appeal of the 1998 season and the ethnic diversity of the sport, some fans never gave their hearts back to baseball. Teenagers favored top skateboarder Tony Hawk over mainstream stars such as McGwire, and extreme sports—skateboarding, aggressive in-line skating, snowboarding, and the like—attracted a growing number of participants and spectators. Stock car racing completely outgrew its Southern roots, and top racer Jeff Gordon became a national star and top pitchman for a host of products. Even soccer, which had long been the most popular sport in most of the world's countries, began to make inroads into the American psyche. The United States hosted the men's World Cup competition in 1994 and the women's World Cup in 1999, dramatically increasing the game's profile. Like Hawk, soccer star Mia Hamm remained a largely unknown quantity among adults but had an avid fan base in the under-fourteen age group. Hamm and her teammates seemed to embody the changes wrought by Title IX and the accompanying shift in attitudes about women in sports.

But as the widespread admiration for Ryan and McGwire revealed, sports remained a place where many Americans looked for clean-cut, well-behaved male heroes, especially those who could hit prodigious home runs or throw the ball 100 miles per hour. With growing regularity, however, sports stars failed to uphold their part of the bargain, and the sexual indiscretions and sometimes violent behavior of athletes inundated the sports pages. Most famously, O. J. Simpson, the retired running back for the Buffalo Bills who had made a second career as a Hertz Car Rental spokesman, sports announcer, and occasional actor, was accused in 1994 of murdering two people, his wife Nicole Simpson and her friend Ronald Goldman. A jury found Simpson not guilty in October 1995, but a string of other sports-star defendants, including Carolina Panthers wide receiver Rae Carruth, convicted of murdering his pregnant girlfriend, followed.

This chapter will focus on the contested meanings of sports in the 1990s. Proud assertions of homosexual identity and stories of sexual misconduct competed for airtime with athletes who used their sporting fame to preach the gospel of Christianity. Cable television and companies such as Nike and Reebok expanded the global reach of sports, yet teams and athletes remained markers of local distinctiveness and local pride. The major professional leagues saturated the market even as other sports found their niche and drew fans away from the major spectator sports, while minority athletes found monster success in the traditionally lily-white realms of golf and tennis, a development on which marketers quickly capitalized.

The first section of the chapter focuses on the ways that sports reflected—and helped to shape—an emerging discourse about sexuality and morality in the 1990s. With the president of the United States caught in a sexual scandal of his own, the indiscretions of athletes seemed less devastating. Nevertheless, the revelation that Los Angeles Lakers superstar point guard Magic Johnson had tested positive for HIV after years of carefree sexual behavior stunned many fans. And sports, like the military, also became a place to debate the role of gays and lesbians in American society, with some athletes "coming out" while others vocally condemned their behavior. Despite his sexual foibles, President Bill Clinton, elected on a slogan of "it's the economy, stupid," shepherded the country into a sustained period of growth throughout most of the 1990s. The chapter's second section explores how this boom economy helped the sports industry expand its markets but also exacerbated a trend to turn each shining moment of athletic excellence into a consumable product. The ball McGwire blasted for home run number sixty-two went for $3 million at auction, for example. Sometimes it seemed that everything was for sale, as companies and leagues worked to dominate on a global scale. The chapter closes by examining the emergence of new sports—and new heroes—in the American marketplace. Tony Hawk and Mia Hamm represented one kind of changing of the guard; multiracial golfer Tiger Woods and African American tennis players Serena and Venus Williams another.

THE MAGIC MAN AND THE PROMISE KEEPERS

On April 9, 1992, former United States Open and Wimbledon champion Arthur Ashe announced that he had been infected with HIV, most likely through a blood infusion in 1983, and was suffering from AIDS. Ashe was the second major sports figure to publicly reveal his infection status. The thirty-two-year-old Magic Johnson had come forward just six months earlier, announcing his retirement from the Los Angeles Lakers because he had tested positive for HIV. The first diagnosed case of AIDS in the United States had come just ten years before Johnson's disclosure in 1991, and the virus had already killed more than 106,000 people. Johnson joined more than a million other Americans who carried the HIV virus.

When Johnson made his announcement, more than one hundred news articles and editorials covered the story in detail, a majority of them praising Johnson for his disclosure. The Los Angeles Lakers' doctor, Michael Mellman, asserted that Johnson should be "not only commended but held as a modern-day hero" for speaking publicly about his condition.[7] "Magic is a better man now, a bigger hero, a greater agent of good," added *Sports Illustrated* columnist Rick Reilly.[8] Some reporters writing about Johnson did question the sheer amount of sex that basketball player had had in his career. "I confess that after I arrived in L.A. in 1979, I did my best to accommodate as many women as I could—most of them through unprotected sex," admitted Johnson.[9] Tennis player Martina Navratilova argued that if a heterosexual female athlete had announced she had gotten HIV in same way that Johnson contracted the disease, people would say she was a slut or worse. But sexual privilege had long been part of being an elite male athlete. NBA star Wilt Chamberlain, for example, boasted of having slept with over 20,000 women in his life.

After Johnson's announcement, he appeared on the *Arsenio Hall Show*, where the host asked Johnson if he were gay. When Johnson emphatically said no, the studio audience stood up and cheered. The idea that sports stars might be gay made many people uncomfortable, even as the possibility of civil rights for gays and lesbians became an accepted, if quite contentious, part of political debate. During his 1990 campaign, President Clinton had promised to sign a law requiring the military to allow gay and lesbian service members to serve their country openly, but settled for a "don't ask, don't tell" policy for gay service members. The debate continued, as gay Americans demanded the rights of full citizenship. Navratilova, who had come out in the early 1980s, became increasingly visible in the struggle for gay rights, speaking at the 1993 March on Washington and raising money for prominent gay organizations. Tom Waddell, a decathlete in the 1968 Olympics, started the Gay Games in 1982, in part to counter the effeminate stereotype of gay men. By 1994, when the games were held in New York City, over 11,000 athletes from forty countries participated.

But openly gay individuals in sports remained rare, especially among male athletes. As Navratilova quipped in 1993, it was as if professional sports teams had their own "don't ask, don't tell" policy.[10]

The media treatment of three-time Olympic diving gold medalist Greg Louganis helped to explain why this seemed like the case. In 1995, Louganis, who had come out as a gay man the year before, acknowledged that he had AIDS. Public reception of his news proved very different than the hero's welcome that Johnson had received. When Louganis won the springboard and platform diving competitions at the 1988 Olympics, *Newsweek* had called him "the classiest act of the games" and an athlete that "suggested a Greek god beautifully rendered." After the news of his illness became public, the same magazine wrote that Louganis had become "yet another tragic intersection of celebrity and AIDS—and a troubling tale of young gay men competing in big time sports."[11] With few exceptions, the media constructed Johnson as a deeply courageous man who had made a difficult admission of truth. Louganis, on the other hand, was often framed as a carrier of disease and a damaged individual. "For some people," lamented the editor of a gay and lesbian magazine, "Greg got what he deserved. I thought we had broken that barrier."[12] But being a gay athlete continued to carry a heavy stigma.

In part, this was because the media continued to present the sports field as a place where "real" men were made. Sports media depicted aggression and violence on the field as acceptable and necessary, often employing the language of war to describe the action. Sports news shows such as ESPN's *SportsCenter* blissfully replayed incidents of athletes getting clobbered, complete with color commentary that sometimes turned real violence into cartoonlike behavior. A study done in 1999 found that 90 percent of boys aged eight to seventeen watched televised sports at least once a week, meaning that the overt link that sportscasters made between sports and aggressive or even violent behavior most likely contributed to how boys understood the meaning of masculinity. This was a world where "faggot" was the ultimate insult because it connoted a player who was soft, a sissy, afraid of taking a hit. The most popular televised sport featuring female athletes, on the other hand, continued to be figure skating, where federation rules required competitors to wear feminine costumes and makeup on the ice. "Doesn't she look elegant," said announcer Dick Button of top skater Nancy Kerrigan at the U.S. Nationals in 1992. "She looks like a little angel," added Peggy Fleming.[13] Even as female athletes broke new ground in team sports such as basketball and soccer, most television

audiences preferred to see representations of more traditionally feminine behavior. A "little angel" did not sound very athletic.

The line between on-the-field aggression and off-the-field violence
was sometimes crossed in the 1990s, as a growing number of athletes
were charged with abuse of their wives and girlfriends or with sexually
violent acts against women. In part, this represented an evolution in
how Americans viewed violence in the home and sexual violence. Feminists brought the issue of domestic violence into the national spotlight in the mid-1980s, and state and local governments gradually
began to change their approach to handling the problem. No longer
were police officers automatically instructed to try to persuade women
not to press charges. Then came the murder charges against O. J. Simpson, once a hero to millions for his easy smile and electrifying running
ability. Evidence in his trial included photographs of Nicole Simpson
with a blackened eye and the tape of her frantic call for help in 1989.
A police officer testified that "O. J. had slapped her, hit her with his fists
and kicked her—I think pulled her hair."[14] While these revelations
helped put to rest the idea that violence in the home was just a family
squabble, they hardly slowed the news of other athletes arrested for
abuse or the multiple chances they received despite their behavior.

In 1995, as the Simpson trial made daily front-page news, police in
Omaha arrested the University of Nebraska's all-American tailback
Lawrence Phillips for a "confrontation" with his former girlfriend.
According to police reports, Phillips climbed through a window in the
early morning, pulled the woman from her bed and dragged her, by the
hair, down three flights of stairs. He had gained 1,722 yards the previous season for the national-champion Cornhuskers, and even after
Phillips pleaded no contest to the charges, coach Tom Osborne was
reluctant to dismiss the star from the team. Instead, Phillips rejoined
the team in midseason, and helped a juggernaut Nebraska team—the
Cornhuskers averaged more than fifty points per game in 1995—roll to
its second consecutive national title. After the season, the St. Louis
Rams made the troubled but talented player the sixth overall pick in
the NFL draft. As a professional, Phillips's erratic behavior finally
caught up with him; arrested multiple times on assault charges, he
drifted from team to team and finally out of the league.

Phillips was not an isolated case. In 1995 and 1996 alone, over 200
college and professional athletes, almost exclusively football and basketball players, were arrested for sexually or physically abusing women.
One three-year survey of thirty Division I schools by the National Institute of Mental Health concluded that though male athletes made up

only 3.3 percent of the male university population, they constituted 19 percent of the students reported for sexual assault and 35 percent of those accused of domestic violence.

The most extreme example of violent behavior run amuck was heavyweight boxer Mike Tyson. At the age of twenty, "Iron Mike" became the youngest-ever heavyweight champion in 1986. His tough "street" persona and formidable punching ability made Tyson the most frightening boxer in decades, and he dominated the heavyweight division until thirty-five-to-one long-shot Buster Douglas knocked him out in 1990. Even after the defeat, Tyson remained the most compelling draw in boxing; he broke Donovan Ruddock's jaw in a 1991 victory that earned him a fight against Evander Holyfield and a second chance at the title. Before the fight could take place, however, Tyson was accused of raping an eighteen-year-old beauty-contest participant in Indiana. Convicted, he served a three-year jail sentence from 1992 to 1995. Tyson did not help his own case when he boasted that the "best punch he ever threw" was hitting his first wife, actress Robin Givens.[15] During the trial, Tyson's lawyers argued that he was a "sex maniac" and that any woman interested in him would, or should, have known this. In other words, he was not responsible for his own behavior.

Despite the conviction, many boxing fans refused to believe that Tyson had committed rape, and his supporters eagerly awaited his return to the ring in 1995. The National Baptist Convention U.S.A., the largest African American denomination, collected more than 10,000 signatures in a petition drive to keep Tyson out of prison, a sign that support for Tyson often broke down along racial lines. But his behavior grew more erratic. In a 1997 match with Holyfield, Tyson "just snapped" and bit off part of the opposing fighter's ear.[16] The following year, he served three months in prison for a case of road rage where he punched one elderly man and kicked another in the groin. In 2000, Tyson began a war of words with British fighter Lennox Lewis. "I want your heart. I want to eat your children—I want to rip out his heart and feed it to him," he boasted. "I want to kill people. I want to rip their stomachs out and eat their children."[17] Far from making Tyson a pariah, his words and actions helped him remain the biggest attraction in boxing. His 2002 bout with Lewis set a pay-per-view revenue record of $103 million. Moral purity was not *always* the primary attraction for sports fans.

Still, even as some athletes and former athletes found themselves in trouble with the law, others continued to see sports as an ideal platform from which to encourage strong religious values and build character.

The rise of the Christian Right in the 1980s and 1990s had made public expressions of faith much more acceptable in American society. By 1996, every NFL team employed a chaplain, with optional Bible study and chapel services also available for players. In addition, many players on college and professional teams belonged to the Fellowship of Christian Athletes (FCA), which was started in 1954 when college basketball coach Don McClanen realized that companies were using athletes to sell their products. Why, he wondered, couldn't sports stars do the same to promote Christian morals and values? McClanen approached the Dodgers' general manager, Branch Rickey, the same man who signed Jackie Robinson, and together they started FCA. As evangelical Christianity moved toward the mainstream in the 1980s, the group boomed. By the end of the 1990s, the group held about 7,000 of what it called "Huddles"—prayer meetings—at high schools and colleges across the country. Tony Dungy, a head coach in the NFL and long-time member of the FCA, argued the group played a key role in helping players to awaken their spiritual beliefs. "When people can see that some of these players are not afraid to express their Christianity, it can lead others to do the same," he said. "It's a good way to let your Christian testimony get exposed to young kids around the country."[18]

Many players became well known for their religious beliefs. Green Bay Packer Reggie White, a defensive end who was elected to thirteen consecutive Pro Bowls, claimed he knocked down quarterbacks for the glory of the Lord and he encouraged young men to realize that they could be both masculine—aggressive and tough—and good Christians. Known as the "minister of defense," he regularly led his teammates and opposing players in group prayer at the ends of games, creating a visible association between Christianity and sports. White's evangelical mission was aided by Green Bay's 35–21 shellacking of the New England Patriots in the 1997 Super Bowl, where he maintained that God had a hand in the Packer victory. Whatever the truth to that statement, the triumph certainly gave White's crusade more visibility. In response to those who questioned whether the inherent violence of football could be reconciled with Christian values, one of White's teammates maintained that "if Jesus played left tackle for the Green Bay Packers, he'd want to go out and do the best he could, for sure."[19] Another teammate, all-Pro tight end Keith Jackson, explained that players such as himself and White "were willing to take a role model stance, to reach out to kids and say, 'hey, this not what you're supposed to be doing.' "[20] Proselytizing about the importance of Christian faith existed uneasily in the locker room with stories of violence and drugs, but many players insisted that sports and religion were a natural fit and that athletes should be seen as upright, morally engaged role models for children.

Bill McCartney, who served as the head football coach at the University of Colorado from 1982 to 1995, took this longstanding idea of "muscular Christianity" the furthest. McCartney's Colorado Buffalos won the national title for the 1990–1991 season, the same year that McCartney founded a new religious group called the Promise Keepers. McCartney believed that men in U.S. society had been feminized and had grown weak and that they needed guidance from other men, much as a football coach might advise his team, in order to relearn how to lead their families, their wives, and society. "A godly leader in the home is an awesome responsibility," Tim Burke, a former baseball player, revealed to a Promise Keepers gathering in 1994. "God can have anybody pitch in the big leagues. God can only have me lead my family. God has called us to lead our families."[21] The organization sponsored rowdy male-only rallies filled with masculine camaraderie in basketball arenas and football stadiums, urging men to take responsibility for their actions. To increase the appeal to men, the Promise Keepers drew heavily on sports metaphors and athletic experiences, printing T-shirts that read "Lord's Gym: His Pain, Our Gain," for example, and selling a book entitled *Go the Distance*. Both White and McCartney spoke out vehemently against gay rights, arguing that gays and lesbians threatened the social order and were unnatural in the eyes of God. As a result, gay and lesbian groups and many feminist organizations picketed Promise Keeper gatherings, claiming that the group's message was political rather than spiritual and advocated inequality for women and gay people. Sports had become part of the battleground for what presidential candidate Patrick Buchanan called a cultural and "religious war . . . for the soul of America."[22]

GLOBAL MARKETS, LOCAL DEALS

McCartney and White believed that sports were a natural place for reaching young men and shaping their morals and character into a model of the Christian gentleman. But for many others, sports was about creating heroes who could sell products and draw viewers to their television screens. At the 1992 and 1996 Olympics, national pride seemed to fully merge with commercial goals, a fact made particularly clear by the 1992 Dream Team in men's basketball. When the 1988 Olympic basketball team, composed of the top amateur college players, failed to bring home the gold for the first time since the disputed 1972 loss to the Soviets, calls grew louder to send in the professionals. Or at least that was the official story. It was also true that the United States was among the last holdouts against the idea of using professional players in the Olympics, and the European basketball association (FIBA) pushed the USOC hard to change its policy. In addition, for obvious reasons, the NBA strongly supported the change, understanding that the Olympics provided a supreme international stage on which to promote its product. NBA superstars, including Michael Jordan, Charles Barkley, Karl Malone, and Larry Bird, blew away the competition, beating their first opponent, Angola, 116 to 48 and winning the gold medal over Croatia by 32 points. A few writers accused the team of being "bullies," but most Americans reveled in the superior display of talent wearing the red, white, and blue.

All was not rosy, however, for the forces of capitalism. An ongoing and quite acrimonious "shoe war" between Nike and Reebok spilled over into the games when Jordan, Barkley, and other stars signed to Nike refused to wear the logo of the official Olympic sponsor, Reebok, on the victory stand. "I don't believe in endorsing my competition," Jordan declared. "I feel very strongly about my loyalty to my own company."[23] So vociferously did Jordan and Barkley object to wearing Reebok warm-up jackets that there were moments when it became unclear whether the players represented the United States or Nike at the games. In an ingenious compromise, Jordan, Barkley, and other Nike stars wrapped themselves in the American flag at the gold-medal ceremonies, covering the Reebok logo with the stars and stripes.

While nationalistic feelings remained, Barcelona also marked the end of Cold War Summer Olympics. For the first time since 1952, there was no team representing the Soviet Union. After the Berlin Wall came down in 1989, reunifying East and West Germany, the Soviet Union also began to disintegrate. Soviet leader Mikhail Gorbachev recognized the independence of the three Baltic states—Estonia, Latvia, and Lithuania—in August 1991. By December, Gorbachev himself was out of power and the USSR was no more. These radical political developments took place just one month before the start of the 1992 Winter Olympics in Albertville, France. The IOC easily admitted the three Baltic states as independent states and worked out a compromise for both the Winter and Summer Games that created a "Unified Team." These athletes marched under the Olympic flag and heard the Olympic theme when they won, but wore their new countries' colors on their sleeves. Uniforms proved a bit more lax all around; when the Lithuanians appeared for their bronze medal in basketball, they wore T-shirts specially designed by the Grateful Dead.

In 1996, the Summer Olympics returned to the United States, with Atlanta, Georgia, playing host. Muhammad Ali, once reviled by many white Americans for his antiwar stance and his membership in the Nation of Islam, was selected to light the Olympic flame, having been transformed by time into a great American hero. Slowed and trembling from Parkinson's disease, Ali carefully made his way up the steps of the Atlanta Coliseum, giving the opening ceremony a simple dignity. Not everything else went so smoothly. The Games were beset with transportation snafus and overcrowding, especially in the first few days. Then, eight days into the events, a lethal pipe bomb in the Centennial Olympic Park exploded, killing one woman and injuring 110 people. Just as at the 1972 Olympics in Munich, the Games continued. Spectators and athletes vowed that the act of terrorism would not deter their enjoyment, but, after the bombing of the federal building in Oklahoma City the previous year, it was hard not to be uneasy.

Nearly 200 countries attended the Atlanta Games, but the United States team dominated the medal stand, especially in track and field and swimming. Swimmer Amy Van Dyken won golds in four events to lead a strong women's team, while Gary Hall's two golds and two silvers anchored an almost-as-dominant men's squad. The American women's gymnastics team won its first-ever team gold medal when Kerri Strug's final vault on a sprained ankle clinched the U.S. victory. Gail Devers, whose battle with Graves disease in 1989 had almost forced the amputation of her foot, won her second straight gold medal in the 100-meter dash and another as part of the 4x100 relay. And Michael Johnson, running in gold shoes, backed up his pregame boasts that he would "be The Man at these Olympics."[24] He won the 200-meter dash in world-record time and then demonstrated the necessary stamina to take the 400-meter race.

It was thrilling television, even though Strug's courageous vault turned out to have been taped previously instead of broadcast live. An estimated nine-of-ten television viewers worldwide watched some part of the games, and the Nielsen ratings in the United States reached nearly all-time highs. But despite their athletic accomplishments, few of the gold-medal winners found the level of commercial success that previous champions had. "Corporate America wants to be part of the Olympics while it's happening," explained one sports agent who represented several gold-medal winners. "If there is a time to cash in on the Olympics, it's not after the Olympics, it's before."[25] The emphasis on money received mixed reviews from IOC president Juan Antonio Samaranch, who was put off by the sometimes tawdry commercial feeling of the Games. However, Samaranch was not complaining about the nineteen major corporations who paid $40 million each to earn exclusive marketing rights at the Games, or the $456 million NBC paid for the broadcasting rights, but rather the smaller street vendors who were everywhere in Atlanta, hoping to cash in on the excitement. European journalists ridiculed the Atlanta games as a "big flea market." Big capitalism had become the order of the day at the Olympics, but hawking T-shirts on the street still earned a frown.

Though the small vendors in Atlanta lost money, the global audience for the Olympics provided an excellent return on the $40 million that multinational companies invested. The combination of the two "Dream Teams" of 1992 and 1996 and Nike's promotion of Michael Jordan and other stars also helped to promote the NBA as a product around the world. Commissioner David Stern and the league were selling the game itself. The NBA made it a policy to sell television rights even to countries that had no ties to the game. This decision had almost nothing to do with the revenues the rights brought—Mongolia paid $10,350 for the 1997 season, Kuwait $52,375—but was an effort to create new fans for the game who might eventually buy other NBA products. "That's the beauty of television," explained Stern. "Other brands have to buy their way on through advertising. Our core product is a two-hour commercial that someone pays us to run."[26] In Stern's view, Shaquille O'Neal's awe-inspiring dunks, Hakeem Olujawon's "Dream Shake," and Reggie Miller's three-point shooting were part of an exciting American product available for export.

Even as the league marketed itself abroad, an increasing number of foreign players such as Olujawon came to the United States for their chance at international fame (and fortune). Just as a majority of the world's top soccer players played in European leagues, the top basketball players tested their skills in the NBA. By the late 1990s, the European basketball leagues effectively served as far-flung farm teams for the NBA, with the top players heavily scouted and then drafted by the NBA. By 2002, there were sixty-five international players from thirty-four countries playing in the NBA. Fans from Chihuahua, Mexico, willingly traveled seventeen hours by bus to see hometown hero Eduardo Najera play for the Dallas Mavericks. Other international fans followed their stars on local television; at the turn of the century, the NBA was carried in 212 countries, with announcers calling the plays in forty-two languages.

New media also had an impact on the ability of leagues and teams to "go global." Although the Internet has been most popular as a site for viewing pornography, following favorite teams and keeping track of even the most mundane of sports statistics was not far behind. The ESPN Web site attracted 6.3 million visitors in 2000, and CBS's Sportsline.com was second at 5.4 million. The Web meant that information could be accessed by any fan, anywhere, and its influence helped the globalization of sports, though fans who could read English received the greatest benefit.

As the "shoe war" between "Nike athletes" and Reebok revealed, sporting-goods companies had a tremendous investment in the global spread of sports. The Olympics were "the most visible opportunity, period" for sporting goods companies, admitted an executive at Reebok, which aired more than sixty thirty-second advertisements during the Barcelona Games.[27] Sales for both companies surged in European markets, as they pitched a potent combination of athletic gear and American values. Nike continued to benefit from its relationship with Jordan, who became so famous worldwide that Chinese college students chanted "Qiao Dan, Qiao Dan" out their windows when his last-second shot defeated the Utah Jazz in the 1998 finals and the Chinese government replayed the game three times.

Corporations used sports and sports heroes to sell far more than just sneakers. In the 1970s, MLB commissioner Bowie Kuhn had reprimanded Atlanta Braves owner Ted Turner for allowing Burger King to sponsor a bat-day promotion. By the 1990s, owners had moved far beyond permitting companies to sponsor single promotions; franchise owners signed forty-nine naming-rights contracts in the decade. As a result, the Colorado Avalanche claimed the 2001 Stanley Cup on their home ice at the Pepsi Center, the St. Louis Rams won the 2000 Super Bowl after playing its home games at Trans World Stadium, and the Arizona Diamondbacks won the 2001 World Series at Bank One Ballpark. The most ill-fated deal linked Houston's brand-new baseball-only stadium with the Enron Corporation, which paid $100 million for thirty years of naming rights. Unfortunately, in 2001, Enron collapsed amid allegations of massive accounting abuses and became an international symbol of corporate misconduct. The Astros paid approximately $2 million to void the contract and quickly signed up the Minute Maid Corporation as a replacement. The pros were not alone in the search for corporate revenues. By the time the Rose Bowl capitulated in 1999, every postseason college football game had a sponsor whose name featured prominently in the bowl game's title. Federal Express, for example, paid approximately $8 million a year to attach its name to the Orange Bowl.

There were other revenue streams pouring into college sports. By 1996, the sale of licensed goods brought in $2.5 billion a year for colleges and universities. "The schools get dollars, and the corporation gets exposure," said the CEO of Collegiate Licensing Co., which handled licensing arrangements for approximately 150 schools. "It's a sign of the times that's acceptable in other forms of society, and it's creeping into the athletic realm."[28] More than 200 universities had contracts with Nike alone, including the University of Michigan, which signed a six-year contract with the company in 1994. The school received clothing and shoes for its teams—more than 23,000 items—as well as more than $100,000 in additional merchandise, significant scholarship monies for athletes, and a steady advertising revenue. In return, Michigan officials promised that all of their athletes, coaches, and staff would wear only Nike apparel, gave the company exclusive rights to sell "authentic" Michigan products, placed Nike advertisements in the school's sports arenas and programs, and gave the company plenty of game tickets. Nike got to use the vaunted Michigan name; Michigan received revenues that helped keep its programs at the top.

Things had grown more complicated by 2000, when it came time for the contract to be renewed. Although Nike and Michigan eventually signed a second contract in 2001, negotiations grew publicly acrimonious as the two struggled to find common ground. What had happened? Banding together, students at Michigan and other universities across the country mounted a campaign against the exploitation of third world workers, targeting Nike as the biggest offender. Four Nike factories in Indonesia, for example, were discovered to have paid children as little as fifteen cents for an eleven-hour day; the company paid more per year to Michael Jordan alone than to the workers in all four factories. In response to these facts, activists pressured their schools to sign "anti-sweatshop agreements," promising not to sign licensing contracts with companies that used sweatshops to produce their products. Though Michigan allowed Nike to follow less stringent standards, the rules of the sponsorship game had changed, at least a little. And the publicity pushed some to realize that the globalization of sports could have a very seamy underside.

CREATING A NICHE IN THE SPORTS MARKET

ESPN and other cable television channels played a critical role in shifting the viewing habits of American sports fans and helping formerly regional or minor sports grow into national phenomena. During the 1990s, NASCAR outpaced basketball and baseball in television ratings; extreme sports captured the imagination of the next generation of sports fans; and soccer—both men's and women's—finally began to move from participant to spectator sport in the United States. The relationship between these sports and television was symbiotic: more viewers were good for the networks and for the sports, though some purists argued that all the attention—and corporate sponsorships—brought undesirable changes and took "away from the soul of the sport."[29] Despite their clear differences, however, all three worked hard to appeal to families, a practical strategy during a decade in which "family values" played a central role in political debates. Each one was also dominated by white athletes, at least in the United States.

ESPN showed over 200 NASCAR—the National Association for Stock Car Auto Racing—events in 1994, and they routinely attracted larger audiences than broadcasts of college basketball. Crowds at the track grew as well; attendance rose an average of 7 percent annually from 1992 to 1998. The thirty-one Winston Cup races—the sport's most exclusive—drew over 5 million spectators in 1995. Once a sport contested almost solely in the South, by 1997 NASCAR ran races in California, New Hampshire, St. Louis, and Las Vegas. Jeff Gordon, decked out in a distinctive rainbow-hued uniform, was the sports' emerging star in the 1990s, winning the Winston Cup championship for the first time in 1995 when he was only twenty-four. Gordon took top honors again in 1997, 1998, and 2001, and his polished style and Hollywood looks made him a national media darling. "Everything about Jeff Gordon is ideal," claimed one television executive. "He's a family-values man, never one to use profanity, has a beautiful wife, and is the ultimate race-car driver."[30] Named one of *People* magazine's "50 Most Beautiful People," the Indiana-born "Wonder Boy" earned more than $6.6 million in 2001 to become the top-grossing individual athlete of the year, besting even Tiger Woods.

But it was the hard-driving, devil-may-care Dale Earnhardt who was most beloved by racing fans in the 1990s. Earnhardt, known as the "Intimidator" because he would go to any length to win, started his career in 1979, winning his first Winston Cup title in 1980. In fact, for years some fans had viewed him as the ultimate antihero, and "anyone but Earnhardt" signs were common at the track even as his many supporters wore his trademark black and bought models of his no. 3 car. Love or hate him, the native North Carolinian dominated the track in the late 1980s and early 1990s, serving as an emotional bridge between NASCAR's Southern roots and its emergence as a national force. He was forty-nine when he crashed on the final lap of the 2001 Daytona 500, hitting the track wall straight on at about 190mph. Fans across the country grieved. Some compared him to Michael Jordan, others to Elvis Presley. "He was the man everybody loved to hate because he could drive a car," one fan sobbed. "He was the hometown hero."[31]

Despite Earnhardt's aggressive style and the ever-present possibility of death on the track, NASCAR appealed to a family audience because the association's drivers generally maintained squeaky-clean reputations as family men. "They're accessible, they're open, they're modest, and they come out of a Southern culture that's respectful," explained a CBS executive.[32] Earnhardt, for example, was married with four children, including a son who raced with him, one of a large number of father-son combinations in the sport. And until sheer numbers—average attendance in 1999 reached 190,940 spectators for a weekend's events—threatened to overwhelm them, drivers were extraordinarily accessible, signing autographs and shaking hands with their fans after the race.

It might be hard to think of two sports with more differences than stock car racing and extreme sports, but, surprisingly, the two sports shared several things in common. Like NASCAR drivers, extreme sport athletes seemed like "real" people, not aloof superstars too busy to talk to fans. The events and the athletes in both sports also appealed to groups that advertisers were eager to reach. And both sports had long been hugely popular among a small subset of the American population, stock cars in the South and skateboarding, snowboarding, and other extreme sports among a self-styled minority of "Generation X" young men across the country.

Skateboarding and other extreme sports had been around for decades without much financial success when ESPN started the X Games in 1995. ESPN sold the X Games as a sort of sporting eye candy, breathtaking stunts interspersed with hip graphics and interviews for viewers with short attention spans. The first competition featured nine sports, but the network proved willing to tweak the lineup, eliminating some sports in favor of others that ESPN hoped fans would find more appealing. Ron Semiao, the creator of the X Games, admitted that many diehard participants in extreme sports "feel a moral obligation to trash the X Games because ESPN is a large corporation. But when I see more kids buying skateboards, and more skaters doing ads for Pepsi and AT&T, I think, that's a good thing for the skateboard industry."[33] The made-for-TV competitions were so successful that participants complained that ESPN was making money off them without giving enough back and that extreme athletes did not get paid commensurate to their skills and their appeal to fans. Some talked of a union, neatly mirroring the labor struggles that had faced more-established professional athletes in the 1960s and 1970s.

Still, because of ESPN, extreme sports found a wide TV audience almost immediately, and the coverage turned Tony Hawk into an international superstar for the under-eighteen set. Years of developing "street cred" didn't hurt either. A temperamental child who decided that he hated team sports, Hawk was already a skateboard whiz by junior high school, turning professional at fourteen. His ability to create new tricks brought him respect from much older skaters, and, by his senior year in high school, Hawk was earning about $70,000 in competitions. He rode out a dry spell for skateboarding in the early 1990s and then hit it big when ESPN started the X Games. In addition to skating and constantly promoting the sport, he transformed himself into a major sporting goods businessman. By 2000, he took in an estimated $10 million a year selling skateboards and collected another $13 million from his clothing line. Some fans knew Hawk better as a video game character, since his "Tony Hawk's Pro Skater" game sold more than 12.5 million copies in just three years, further diversifying his portfolio and creating an ever-expanding fan base for the sport.

Extreme sports went officially mainstream in 1999 when the U.S. Postal Service issued 150 million stamps featuring in-line skating, snowboarding, BMX biking, and skateboarding. In the same year, Hawk was featured in a "Got Milk" advertisement, along with slugger Mark McGwire and top-ranked tennis player Pete Sampras, marking another major breakthrough into the mainstream. Most Americans over thirty might not have recognized Hawk, but, to their children, he was equal in stature to McGwire and Sampras. Of course, neither ESPN nor the advertisers who bought time during the X Games cared about the moms and dads, and they probably worried about the Postal Service's decision to issue stamps. An ESPN representative explained that the network tried hard to stay "legitimate" to the sports' youthful fans "by using on-air talent that reflects the culture of our athletes, younger voices that know the sports. We don't want to become your father's X Games."[34]

Extreme sports did appeal to kids and teens. A 2001 survey found that the number of boys aged seven to seventeen playing baseball had dropped 13 percent from 1995 to 2000, from 7.9 to 6.9 million, and that participation in football and basketball had also declined slightly. In comparison, the number of boys in the same age group that skateboarded regularly increased almost 130 percent, from 2.7 to 6.2 million. There were more than 800 public skate parks in the United States by 2001. "The individualist nature of the sport is what draws kids to it in the first place," asserted one professional skateboarder. "The reason why we're skaterboarders is we don't want to be organized," said one participant. "We don't like the structure of team sports."[35]

Skaters, snowboarders, and other extreme sport athletes worked hard to create a punk image that put them at odds with more traditional sports. The largest sporting good companies had more difficulty reaching this audience. "There's a big backlash against Nike under way," alleged one industry analyst. "The skateboard generation doesn't want to wear Nike because their fathers wear them."[36] Snowboarders, for example, tended to represent themselves as part of a grunge and hip-hop subculture, with a different style of dress and manner than skiers. Of course, snowboarders often paid just as much for their grunge or hip-hop look as skiers paid for their outfits, and companies drew heavily on this antiestablishment attitude to sell the sport. Promoters also realized the connection between the rebellious attitudes of extreme sports and punk and hip-hop music, first creating the Vans Warped Tour and then the Boom Boom HuckJam tour in the late 1990s. Both were hugely popular. The *Village Voice* called the Boom Boom experience, which featured vert skating, BMX bike stunts, and freestyle motocross events, "the Ice Capades on amphetamines with a punk score."[37]

No one ever made that sort of statement about soccer, but it too found a steadily growing audience among the under-thirty generation, especially as a participant sport. An estimated 18 million Americans played soccer in 1994, many of them under eighteen. So many children played in soccer leagues that "soccer moms" became among the most sought-after voters of the 1996 national elections, replacing the "angry white men" of 1994. The phrase was meant to conjure up white, middle-class mothers who juggled jobs and child care, always making time to take Jessica and Joshua to soccer practice in the Dodge Caravan. The phrase also revealed a shift in the sports that resonated in American society. Politicians were not fighting for the vote of "Little League moms," an ominous sign for the future of America's national pastime.

Soccer had flourished briefly in the United States during the 1970s, when the North American Soccer League (NASL) combined foreign players—especially the Brazilian superstar Pelé, who signed a $4.5 million contract with the New York Cosmos—and homegrown talent to bring in crowds. NASL created one well-known American star, Kyle Rote Jr., but ultimately could not attract enough fans to make the league commercially viable and went out of business in 1985. Nine years later, the sport got another chance to capture the public's imagination when the 1994 World Cup competition was awarded to the United States. Audiences for the games far exceeded the organizers' estimates, and cup matches regularly beat baseball and golf in head-to-head televised matchups. The red-headed, hard-working Alexis Lalas, speedy Cobi Jones, and Earnie Stewart, who scored the winning goal in the American upset over Colombia, were engaging young stars who eagerly promoted their sport.

A second soccer league, called Major League Soccer (MLS), tried to build on the enthusiasm the World Cup had created, starting with ten teams in 1996. Game attendance averaged over 17,000 spectators during the first season, then dropped to approximately 14,200 during the next three. Over 57,000 fans watched Washington's D.C. United win its second straight title in 1997. Despite the drop in attendance, the fledging league attracted only 2,000 fewer spectators to each match than the average for an NBA game. While the men's squad washed out of the 1998 World Cup, failing to win even one game, they came back strong in the 2002 competition, advancing to the second round behind the play of young stars Landon Donovan, DeMarcus Beasley, and Brian McBride. Soccer still did not attract the televised audiences of NASCAR or even baseball, but it finally seemed to be a permanent fixture on the American sporting landscape.

Even with MLS in full swing and with regular appearances on ESPN, the best-known American soccer player in the 1990s remained a woman. Mia Hamm was the sport's first superstar hero, especially among the under-fourteen set. One parent recounted asking his adult friends about Hamm and always getting the same reaction: "Who?" But when he asked his eleven-year-old daughter whether she had heard of the player, "she looked at me as if I were as dumb as fence post."[38] By 1999, girls made up 40 percent of the membership in the American Youth Soccer Organization, which started its girls program in 1971. These players squealed with delight when they saw Hamm in action and spent their allowances on Hamm jerseys, shin guards, and soccer cleats, and even a Mattel Barbie doll designed in the player's image. Twenty-seven-years-old in 1999, Hamm was a twelve-year veteran of the women's national team, and the world's all-time scoring leader in international play. "She has the ability to cause people to hold their breath," exclaimed Tony DiCicco, the U.S. women's team coach. "It's a lot like what Michael Jordan did in basketball. There were other great basketball players, but sometimes he made everybody go, 'Wow!' Mia has that ability, too."[39] Her girl-next-door looks and remarkable scoring abilities also made her an advertising natural, most famously in a series of Gatorade commercials that featured Hamm and Jordan competing against each other in a wide array of sports, each player promising the other that "anything you can do, I can do better."

Just as with NASCAR and extreme sports, soccer emphasized its clean and wholesome appeal, trying to draw families to the stadium. And it was true that crowds were dominated by soccer moms and dads who brought their preteen and teenaged sons and daughters to watch their heroes. Because of the precarious state of their sport, female players always viewed themselves as roles models—salespeople for soccer and for women's sports in general. "We represent women's sports every time we play," Hamm stated. "So you have a responsibility to try to portray what you do in the best light that you can."[40] Corporations also understood the family-based appeal of the sport. Nineteen companies paid a total of $6 million for sponsorship rights to the 1999 Women's World Cup, held in the United States.

The Women's World Cup provided an enormous boost to the future of women's soccer. Over 90,000 spectators attended the sold-out final game between the United States and China, a record for a women's sporting event. The two evenly matched teams played ninety minutes of regulation and thirty minutes of overtime without scoring, so the game came down to a series of spine-tingling penalty kicks. After goalie Briana Scurry stopped the third Chinese attempt, the American team clinched the world championship with a left-footed shot from Brandi Chastain that gave them a 5 to 4 edge. Perhaps the most outgoing member of the women's national team, Chastain had posed nude for *Gear* magazine before the tournament started, wearing just her cleats and a strategically placed soccer ball. When Chastain powered the final kick past Chinese goalie Gao Hong, she raced to corner of the field and ripped off her shirt in exuberant celebration, twirling it over head as she fell to her knees with excitement.

Chastain's postgoal pose in her Nike sports bra made the cover of every major newspaper, *Sports Illustrated*, *Newsweek*, and *Time*, and commentators across the country weighed in on the meaning of her sports bra. Some saw a Nike plot for free advertising, others commented on Chastain's obviously well-toned body and washboard stomach, and still others used the moment to meditate on the place of women in sports. "It was just about being confident and strong and athletic and a woman, and feeling good about myself," said Chastain of her impulse to shed her jersey in celebration.[41] It was also how male players across the globe celebrated the triumph of scoring a goal. Certainly, the celebration of Chastain, Hamm, and other members of the World Cup team was one clear sign of the social changes wrought by Title IX. Women could have muscles, they could sweat, they could be aggressively competitive, they could even rip off their shirts with joy and still be considered feminine and attractive. They could also attract a crowd, an important consideration when the number of spectators often decided the worth of a sport and its athletes. "The legacy that I want to leave . . . is that you can no longer take women's athletics lightly," explained forward Tiffeny Milbrett after the World Cup victory. "There's no more excuses for people to say we're not going to draw. There's no more excuses for people to say we're not marketable. There's no more excuses to say we're not going to put fans in the stands."[42]

The emergence of Venus and Serena Williams in tennis was another marker of social change. When the two first emerged on the tennis scene as teenagers in the mid-1990s, fans and critics read their every move as a commentary on race relations and gender norms, and the symbolism of being powerful black women in a nearly all white game hung heavy in the air. Symbols or not, fans couldn't stop watching and the television networks adored the Williams sisters because they brought in top ratings. The 2001 U.S. Open final, matching the sisters against one another for the title, drew nearly 23 million TV viewers. What spectators saw were two extremely muscular African American women pounding the ball with a sort of power never before seen in women's tennis. The Williams sisters appealed to a global audience who thrilled to their potent combination of speed, strength, and charisma, along with form-fitting outfits that pushed the boundaries of tennis fashion. Together, they redefined how women's tennis could be played, and how it could be marketed. Muscles were cool, and Venus and Serena found themselves hawking an enormous array of products, from American Express to Reebok to Internet start-up companies.

The Williams sisters emerged as tennis superstars at the same cultural moment that Tiger Woods became golf's first black superstar. In just his first major tournament as a professional in 1997, Tiger Woods destroyed the competition and the course at the hallowed grounds of Augusta National. He finished the course at a record eighteen under par, winning by twelve strokes, the largest margin of victory in a major tournament since 1862. Woods became the first black man to ever wear the green jacket, awarded to every Masters' winner. The previous year, Woods had been a nineteen-year-old sophomore at Stanford University, where he won the NCAA individual championship and a remarkable third consecutive U.S. Amateur Championship, coming back from five strokes down with just nine holes to play. The next week, Woods turned professional and signed an endorsement deal with Nike worth nearly $40 million. In 1999, Woods earned a record $6,616,585 to finish as the top money maker on the PGA Tour, recording sixteen top-ten finishes in twenty-one starts. By 2000, at the age of twenty-four, he won the British Open by eight strokes to complete a career Grand Slam, the youngest player to ever accomplish that feat.

Nike was attracted by more than Woods's prodigious skills. By 1990, approximately one in twenty-five married couples in the United States were interracial, and at least three million children were interracial. Responding to pressure and to the reality of many people's lived experiences, in 2000 the Census Bureau began to allow individuals to check more than one box in identifying their racial background. Woods himself was of Thai and African American descent, and Nike played heavily on his racial identity to sell the new star. "I feel very fortunate, and equally proud, to be both African American and Asian," said Woods in 1996. "It does not make a difference to me. The bottom line is that I am an American . . . and proud of it."[43]

Woods was important to repositioning a game that had struggled for decades to overcome racial bias. The Professional Golf Association (PGA) included a "Caucasian only" clause in its bylaws until 1967. In 1990, the PGA selected Shoal Creek Country Club in Birmingham, Alabama, to be the site of the PGA Championships. The club included no African Americans, because, as founder Hall Thompson made clear, "the country club is our home and we pick and choose who we want," adding that even bringing black guests was "just not done in Birmingham."[44] Golfers themselves were not much more sympathetic. "I think it's been blown way out of proportion," declared Payne Stewart, winner of the 1991 U.S. Open. "Discrimination is all over the world. Don't start here at Shoal Creek, go all over the world. The players have probably made more jokes about it than anything else."[45] Despite Stewart's admission that many golfers made jokes about the situation, under pressure from the companies that sponsored the tournaments, the PGA revised its standards for choosing tournament sites.

One of Woods's first Nike commercials painted the young golfer as a crusader for equality, with Woods challenging the camera—and presumably the PGA—with the question "Are you ready for me?" and then deploring the fact that there were golf courses in the United States from which he would barred because of his skin. Like Jordan before him, however, Woods quickly retreated from taking positions on social issues, though he continued to overwhelm golf courses and opponents with his abilities. Nevertheless, he created a new rainbow coalition of fans and sparked a renaissance of interest in the game. For any given tournament, "how'd Tiger do?" has become the most interesting question at hand. His ability to hit the ball straight and far, his massive earnings, his talent for concentrating under extreme pressure, and his domination of the competition was more than enough to make him a hero to many.

In his ability to capture our attention, Woods shares much with Joe DiMaggio, whose exploits in 1941 had a nation asking "did he get a hit today?" Both started off as minority stars and, because of their abilities, quickly found themselves transformed into all-American heroes. Both preferred to let their exploits speak for them, though DiMaggio had the advantage of playing in an era when reporters ignored player transgressions and rarely asked questions about areas not related to sports. When DiMaggio hit safely in fifty-six straight games, nary a television camera recorded his efforts, though he did make the newsreels that appeared before the movies. By comparison, when Woods teed off at the 2002 Masters on his way to a third victory at Augusta, there were at least six all-sports cable channels following the action, as well as five broadcast news stations and an untold number of Internet sites. "Sports has become the dominant entertainment of the world," claimed Nike's Phil Knight, with only a bit of hyperbole.[46] In other words, sports coverage exploded in the sixty-one years between 1941 and 2002.

In fact, every aspect of the sporting world has exploded in the years since 1945. Player salaries, the cost of fielding a team, the hype surrounding games, the number of cameras on the sidelines, the corporate sponsorships, the level of drug use, the number of women and African Americans participating, the global reach of games: all of these have expanded and contributed to a shift in the way that Americans perceive the meaning of sports. Yet some aspects haven't changed much at all. We continue to create heroes out of sports stars, despite a growing number of stories that make it clear that not all athletes deserve the label. We loyally root for the home team, though owner after owner has snatched our teams away. We use sports to talk about complex racial and gender issues, and we view the achievements of individual athletes as a referendum on social change. When Woods won the Masters in Augusta, Georgia, and when Jackie Robinson joined the Brooklyn Dodgers at second base, these were read as moments of racial progress. Whether it was Joan Benoit's victory at the first women's marathon at the 1984 Olympics, or the women's national soccer team attracting over 90,000 spectators to the Rose Bowl, these moments were understood as symbols of social change for women.

Of course, sports both reflect and shape American society. The money that has poured into sports and the association between athletic and financial success are examples of what Americans hold to be important, even when we bemoan the fact that weak-hitting second basemen make more than kindergarten teachers. But there's a better market for second basemen, even light-hitting ones, than there is for teachers, and Americans traditionally respect what can be bought and sold on the open market. Similarly, corporate sponsorships and the tight links between athletes and a host of consumer products only reinforces the importance of the market in American society. Sports stars are judged not just on their athletic abilities but on their facility to promote themselves, to turn their skills into something that sells. As Rod Tidwell, the cocky wide receiver in the 1996 movie *Jerry Maguire*, said, "SHOW! ME! THE! MONEY!"[47] That the media routinely reports on how much a shoe contract is worth, the number of endorsements an athlete has, or whether he has earned a Wheaties cereal box reveals something about what we value.

"Money is what people respect and when you are a professional athlete, they want to know how much you have made," said Billie Jean King, trying to explain why the rewards for tournament victories for female tennis players needed to be equal to male players. "[Americans] judge you on that."[48] She was right. Player paychecks mattered, and the fight to equalize prize money in tennis played a small role in the ongoing struggle to achieve equality for women in the workplace. The debates over the impact of Title IX similarly revealed the complex interplay between financial worth and sporting opportunity for women. For many, women did not deserve equal treatment—even if mandated by law—unless they could pack the stands with screaming fans, just like the men. In the postwar period, revenue streams and fan bases were the true markers of achievement.

Maybe the importance of sports—and the making of sports heroes— can be attributed largely to the impact of television. Hank Aaron, baseball's all-time career home-run leader, certainly thought so. "TV is what creates the heroes today," he declared. "If people turn on the TV and see you all the time, they're going to think you're something special."[49] Americans value celebrity, people who make a splash and capture the imagination, even if only for a moment. Roone Arledge understood this way back in the 1960s, and he pioneered the now-common practice of turning a sporting event into a compelling narrative, complete with background on players' families, educations, and the obstacles they had overcome. Ironically, however, as sports heroes grew ever larger than life and more spectacular, many fans craved a sense of intimacy that television could not provide.

So why do we continue to talk about the purity of sport even as it has been compromised by consumer impulses or by drug use or player violence? "Every time we tip it off or tee it up, there's always the chance of something exhilarating happening. It doesn't happen 90 percent of the time, but there's always that chance," explained longtime CBS sportscaster Verne Lundquist. "It's the attraction of the unknown."[50] Sports are a soap opera, but they are a soap opera in which the ending cannot be predicted. And even as televised spectacle, even as a prepackaged entertainment that exists to sell consumer goods, sports offer moments of transcendence and a sense of wonderful possibility. At their best, sports provide us with a sense of wonder at what the human body can achieve and a feeling of awe at what a group of people can accomplish together. They give us a chance to think and relax at the same time, the opportunity to argue happily with total strangers, and a bridge with which to connect across generational, racial, ethnic, and class lines. Watching games sometimes creates moments of untrammeled delight for fans and a set of intimate memories that can be shared with family members, friends, communities, and, sometimes, the entire country. Sports aren't perfect, but then, neither are we.

Notes

INTRODUCTION

1. James Bennet, "President Leads TV Discussion on Role of Race in Sports," *New York Times*, 15 April 1998.

2. James A. Michener, *Sports in America* (New York: Random House, 1976), 42.

3. Quoted in "Men-Medals-Marxism," *Newsweek*, 9 August 1960, 79.

4. Bob Ottum, "BYU: Land of Cuties and 12 Tall Cougars," *Sports Illustrated*, 4 January 1965, 26.

5. Lance Armstrong and Sally Jenkins, *It's Not About the Bike: My Journey Back to Life* (New York: Berkley Books, 2000), 9.

6. Michael Hall, "Lance Armstrong Has Something to Get off His Chest," *Texas Monthly* (July 2001): 72.

7. Ibid.

8. Vicki Michaelis, "Hero Worship," *Denver Post*, 17 January 1999.

1. SPORTS, THE AMERICAN WAY

1. Richard Ben Cramer, *Joe DiMaggio: The Hero's Life* (New York: Simon and Schuster, 2000), 175–76.

2. G. Edward White, *Creating the National Pastime: Baseball Transforms Itself, 1903–1953* (Princeton, N.J.: Princeton University Press, 1996), 263–64.

3. Quoted in Charles C. Alexander, *Breaking the Slump: Baseball in the Depression Era* (New York: Columbia University Press, 2002), 280.

4. Franklin Delano Roosevelt to Commissioner Kenesaw M. Landis, 15 January 1942, National Baseball Hall of Fame; available from www.baseball-halloffame.org/education/primary_sources/world_war_ii/letter_01_Transcript.htm.

5. Jim Sargent, "Helen 'Gig' Smith: Remembering the All-American Girls Baseball League," available from www.aapbl.org/aticles/arti_hs.html; Susan K. Cahn, *Coming on Strong: Gender and Sexuality in Twentieth-Century Women's Sport* (New York: Free Press, 1994), 155.

6. *Federal Baseball Club of Baltimore, Inc. v. National Baseball Clubs*, 42 Supreme Court 465 (1922).

7. Quoted in Marc Pachter, ed., *Champions of American Sport* (Washington D.C.: Smithsonian Institute, 1981), 165.

8. John Tunis, *All-American* (1942; reprint, New York: Odyssey Classics, 1989), 56.

9. John D. Fair, "Bob Hoffman, the York Barbell Company, and the Golden Age of American Weightlifting, 1945–1960," *Journal of Sport History* 14, no. 2 (1987): 174.

10. Ibid., 174.

11. Maya Angelou, *I Know Why the Caged Bird Sings* (New York: Random House, 1970).

12. Frederick Lewis Allen, *Only Yesterday: An Informal History of the Nineteen Twenties* (New York: Harper and Brothers, 1931), 21.

13. Quoted in David Maraniss, *When Pride Still Mattered: A Life of Vincent Lombardi* (New York: Simon and Schuster, 1999), 76–77.

14. Ibid.

15. Robert Liston, *The Pros* (New York: Platt and Munk, 1968), 77.

16. Will Herberg, *Protestant, Catholic, Jew: An Essay in American Religious Sociology* (Garden City, N.Y.: Doubleday, 1955), 31, 75.

17. Joe Louis Jr. with Edna and Art Rust, *Joe Louis: My Life* (New York: Harcourt Brace Jovanovich, 1978).

18. Quoted in Will Grimsley, ed., *The Sports Immortals* (Englewood Cliffs, N.J.: Prentice-Hall, 1972), 125.

19. Jules Tygiel, *Baseball's Great Experiment: Jackie Robinson and His Legacy* (New York: Oxford University Press, 1983), 43.

20. Ibid., 66.

21. Ibid., 197.

22. William Simons, "Jackie Robinson and the American Mind: Journalistic Perceptions of the Reintegration of Baseball," *Journal of Sport History* 12, no. 1 (1985): 52.

23. John Keim, *Legends by the Lake: The Cleveland Browns at Municipal Stadium* (Akron, Ohio: University of Akron Press, 2001).

24. Thomas G. Smith, "Outside the Pale: The Exclusion of Blacks from Organized Professional Football, 1934–1946," *Journal of Sports History* 15, no. 3 (1988): 273.

25. "Freedom to Play: The Life and Times of Basketball's African-American Pioneers." Basketball Hall of Fame, www.hoophall.com/exhibits/freedom_ nba.htm.

26. Murray Sperber, *Onward to Victory: The Crises That Shaped College Sports* (New York: Henry Holt and Company, 1998), 139.

27. Robert L. Kerr, "The Great White Father and the Antichrist: *Bud Wilkinson's Football Letter* as Cultural History," *American Journalism* 18, no. 3 (2001): 39.

28. Ibid., 39.

29. Ibid., 293.

30. Randy Roberts and James Olson, *Winning is the Only Thing: Sports in America Since 1945* (Baltimore, Md.: Johns Hopkins University Press, 1989), 84.

31. Sperber, *Onward to Victory*, 311.

32. Sperber, *Onward to Victory*, 334.

33. Kerr, "The Great White Father and the Antichrist," 46.

2. *AN ATHLETIC COLD WAR*

1. Jacques Barzun, "God's Country and Mine: A Declaration of Love Spiced with a Few Harsh Words," 1954; reprint, in *Baseball: A Literary Anthology*, ed. Nicholas Dawidoff (Washington, D.C.: Library of America, 2002).

2. Quoted in Richard Schapp, *An Illustrated History of the Olympics* (New York: Alfred Knopf, 1963), 235.

3. Ibid.

4. Quoted in William Oscar Johnson, *100 Years of Change* (Time International, vol. 147, no. 22, 27 May 1996); available from www.time.com/time/international/1996/960527/olympics.history.html.

5. Quoted in Allen Guttmann, *The Olympics: A History of the Modern Games* (Urbana: University of Illinois Press, 1992), 97.

6. John D. Fair, "Bob Hoffman, the York Barbell Company, and the Golden Age of American Weightlifting, 1945–1960," *Journal of Sport History* 14, no. 2 (1987): 179.

7. Arthur Daley, "Every Little Bit Helps," *New York Times*, 10 June 1952.

8. "Melbourne Concluded," *Newsweek*, 17 December 1956, 96; "End of the Affair," *Time*, 17 December 1956, 80.

9. "Our Flag on Wings," *Newsweek*, 10 December 1956, 98.

10. Mary Jo Festle, *Playing Nice: Politics and Apologies in Women's Sports* (New York: Columbia University Press, 1996), 90.

11. Jeremiah Tax, "First Sputnik, Now This," *Sports Illustrated*, 9 February 1959, 11.

12. John D. Fair, "Isometrics or Steroids? Exploring New Frontiers of Strength in the Early 1960s," *Journal of Sport History* 20, no. 1 (1993): 20.

13. Susan K. Cahn, *Coming on Strong: Gender and Sexuality in Twentieth-Century Women's Sport* (New York: Free Press, 1994), 137.

14. Quoted in Arthur Daley, "Somber Second Thoughts," *New York Times*, 13 September 1960.

15. John F. Kennedy, "The Soft American," *Sports Illustrated*, 26 December 1960, 16.

16. John Lardner, "We Hung in the Stretch," *Newsweek*, 17 December 1956, 98.

17. Walter Imbiorski, "Convention Speeches," 1958, Box 57, CCFM Collection, Archives of the University of Notre Dame, South Bend, Ind.

18. Quoted in Donald M. Fisher, "Lester Harrison and the Rochester Royals, 1945–1957: A Jewish Entrepreneur in the NBA," in *Sports and the American Jew*, ed. Steven A. Riess (Syracuse, N.Y.: Syracuse University Press, 1998), 220.

19. "George W. Bush Is First Former Little Leaguer To Become U.S. President," Little League Online; available from www.littleleague.org/media/ bush.htm.

20. "CYO Pledge," Stritch Papers, Archives of the Archdiocese of Chicago, box 1, folder 21.

21. Gay Talese, "Alleys a la Mode," *New York Times Magazine*, 11 November 1956, 77.

22. Quoted in Nicole Cohen, "The 1950s Bowling Alley: An American Landscape," unpublished paper, Barnard College, 2002.

23. Ibid.

24. Festle, *Playing Nice*, 38.

25. Bil Gilbert, "Sis-Boom-Bah! For Amalgamated Sponge," *Sports Illustrated*, 25 January, 1965, 56.

26. Susan E. Cayleff, *Babe: The Life and Legend of Babe Didrikson Zaharias* (Urbana: University of Illinois Press, 1995), 151.

27. Ray Cave, "Sportsman of the Year: Arnold Palmer," *Sports Illustrated*, 9 January 1961, 24.

28. Jules Tygiel, *Baseball's Great Experiment: Jackie Robinson and His Legacy* (1983; reprint, New York: Oxford University Press, 1997), 280.

29. Jack E. Davis, "Baseball's Reluctant Challenge: Desegregating Major League Spring Training Sites, 1961–1964," *Journal of Sport History* 19, no. 2 (1992): 154.

30. Ibid., 155.

31. Ibid., 158.

32. Quoted in Robert H. Boyle, "The Latins Storm Las Grandes Ligas," *Sports Illustrated*, 9 August 1965, 26.

33. Quoted in Leonard Koppett, "The Dark Controversy," *New York Times*, 4 August 1964.

34. Samuel O. Regaldo, *Viva Baseball! Latin Major Leaguers and Their Special Hunger* (Urbana: University of Illinois Press, 1998), 123.

35. Quoted in Rob Ruck, "Roberto Clemente," American National Biography Online, February 2000, available from www.anb.org/articles/19/19– 00299.html.

36. Charles Ross, *Outside the Lines: African Americans and the Integration of the National Football League* (New York: New York University Press, 1999), 135.

37. Charles H. Martin, "Integrating New Year's Day: The Racial Politics of College Bowl Games in the American South," *Journal of Sport History* 24, no. 3 (1997): 364.

38. Ibid., 370.

39. Ronald E. Marcello, "The Integration of Intercollegiate Athletics in Texas: North Texas State College as a Test Case, 1956," *Journal of Sport History* 14, no. 3 (1987): 308.

40. Kevin Pierce Thornton, "Symbolism at Ole Miss and the Crisis of Southern Identity," *South Atlantic Quarterly* 86, no. 3 (1987).

41. Patricia Vertinsky, "More Myth than History: American Culture and Representations of the Black Female's Athletic Ability," *Journal of Sport History* 25, no. 3 (1998): 545.

42. Daniel A. Nathan, "Sugar Ray Robinson, the Sweet Science, and the Politics of Meaning," *Journal of Sport History* 26, no. 1 (1999): 166.

3. A BRAVE NEW WORLD

1. Glen Gendzel, "Competitive Boosterism: How Milwaukee Lost the Braves," *Business History Review* 69, no. 4 (1995): 536.

2. Jules Tygiel, *Past Time: Baseball as History* (New York: Oxford University Press, 2000), 172.

3. Gendzel, "Competitive Boosterism," 538.

4. Ibid., 458.

5. Ibid., 556.

6. Bruce Kuklick, *To Every Thing a Season: Shibe Park and Urban Philadelphia, 1909–1976* (Princeton, N.J.: Princeton University Press, 1991), 112–26.

7. Andrew Zimbalist, *Baseball and Billions: A Probing Look Inside the Big Business of Our National Pastime* (New York: BasicBooks, 1992).

8. Tygiel, *Past Time*, 180.

9. Arthur Daley, "Long Way from New York," *New York Times*, 15 April 1958.

10. Roy Terrell, "Fast Man with a .45," *Sports Illustrated*, 22 December 1962, 32.

11. Ibid.

12. Baseball Almanac, *Quotations from Roger Maris*, 1997–2003; available from http://www.baseball-almanac.com/quotes/quomari.shtml.

13. Jeff Neal-Lunsford, "Sport in the Land of Television: The Use of Sport in Network Prime-Time Schedules, 1946–50," *Journal of Sports History* 19, no. 1 (1992): 67.

14. David A. Klatell and Norman Marcus Klatell, *Sports for Sale: Television, Money, and the Fans* (New York: Oxford University Press, 1988), 119–20.

15. Will Grimsley, ed., *The Sports Immortals* (Englewood Cliffs, N.J.: Prentice-Hall, 1972), 167.

16. Ibid., 196.

17. Gary T. Brown, "The Electronic Free Ticket," *The NCAA News*, 22 November 1999; available from www.ncaa.org/news/1999/19991122/active/3624n30.html.

18. William Oscar Johnson, "TV Made It All a New Game," *Sports Illustrated*, 22 December 1969, 89.

19. Benjamin G. Rader, *In Its Own Image: How Television Has Transformed Sports* (New York: Free Press, 1984), 106.

20. Tex Maule, "The Coaches Take Over," *Sports Illustrated*, 22 December 1962, 42.

21. Frederick Klein, "In This Corner . . . AAU, NCAA, Each Old and Strong, Vie to Run U.S. Amateur Sports," *Wall Street Journal*, 24 February 1970.

22. Edward L. Lach, *Povich, Shirley*, American National Biography Online, September 2000 update; available from www.anb.org/articles/16/16-03377.html.

23. Jack Olsen, "The Black Athlete. Part 4: In the Back of the Bus," *Sports Illustrated*, 22 July 1968, 39.

24. Kenneth Rudeen, "Sportsman of the Year: Pete Rozelle," *Sports Illustrated*, 6 January 1964, 24.

25. Jim Minter, "The Mayor Surrenders Atlanta," *Sports Illustrated*, 12 July 1965, 17.

26. Edwin Shrake, "What Are They Doing with the Sacred Game of Pro Football?," *Sports Illustrated*, 25 October 1971, 99.

4. MAKING SENSE OF THE SIXTIES

1. Jack Newfield, "The Meaning of Muhammad," *The Nation*, 4 February 2002, 25.

2. Mike Marqusee, *Redemption Song: Muhammad Ali and the Spirit of the Sixties* (London: Verso Press, 1999), 8.

3. Jack Olsen, "The Black Athlete. Part 4: In the Back of the Bus," *Sports Illustrated*, 22 July 1968, 28.

4. Quoted in Henry Hampton, ed., *Voices of Freedom: An Oral History of the Civil Rights Movement* (New York: Bantam Books, 1990), 322.

5. Ron Mix, "Was This Their Freedom Ride?" *Sports Illustrated*, 18 January 1965, 24–25.

6. Quoted in Marqusee, *Redemption Song*, 142.

7. Quoted in ibid., 214.

8. Quoted in Robert Lipsyte and Peter Levine, *Idols of the Games: A Sporting History of the American Century* (Atlanta: Turner Publishing, 1995), 258.

9. Eldridge Cleaver, *Soul on Ice* (New York: Dell, 1968).

10. From *When We Were Kings*, prod. and dir. Leon Gast, 89 mins. Polygram Video, New York, 1997.

11. Quoted in Robert W. Creamer, "Scorecard," *Sports Illustrated*, 1 November 1971, 13.

12. Quoted in Olsen, "The Black Athlete. Part 4: In the Back of the Bus," 28.

13. "Scorecard," *Sports Illustrated*, 17 June 1968, 17.

14. William Wallace, "Poverty and Grambling Provide Top Prospects for Pro Football," *New York Times* 9 January 1968, 51.

15. "Scorecard," *Sports Illustrated*, 6 May 1968, 8.

16. Jack Olsen, "The Black Athlete. Part 3: In An Alien World," *Sports Illustrated*, 15 July 1968, 30.

17. Ibid., 34.

18. David K. Wiggins, "'The Future of College Athletics is at Stake': Black Athletes and Racial Turmoil on Three Predominantly White University Campuses, 1968–1972," *Journal of Sport History* 15, no. 3 (1988): 308.

19. William Johnson, "Collision on the New Underground Railroad," *Sports Illustrated*, 12 February 1968, 52–53.

20. Quoted in Olsen, "The Black Athlete. Part 3: In An Alien World," 31.

21. Jack Olsen, "The Black Athlete. Part 1: The Cruel Deception," *Sports Illustrated*, 1 July 1968, 27.

22. Harry Edwards, *The Revolt of the Black Athlete* (New York: Free Press, 1969), 44.

23. Ibid.

24. "Scorecard," *Sports Illustrated*, 18 March 1968, 14.

25. Edwards, *The Revolt of the Black Athlete*, 69.

26. Pete Axthelm, "Boos and a Beating for Tommie," *Sports Illustrated*, 29 January 1968, 58.

27. "Scorecard," *Sports Illustrated*, 15 April 1968, 21.

28. Bob Ottum, "Grim Countdown to the Games," *Sports Illustrated*, 14 October 1968, 38.

29. Ibid., 43.

30. Leola Johnson and David Roediger, "'Hertz, Don't It?' Becoming Colorless and Staying Black in the Crossover of O.J. Simpson," in *Reading Sport: Critical Essays on Power and Representation*, ed. Susan Birrell and Mary G. McDonald (Boston: Northeastern University Press, 2000), 50.

31. Ibid., 49.

32. Robert M. Collins, "Richard M. Nixon: The Psychic, Political, and Moral Use of Sport," *Journal of Sport History* 10, no. 2 (1983): 81.

33. Carlton Stowers, "A Pride of Lions in Cattle Country," *Sports Illustrated*, 1 November 1971, 40.

34. Lipsyte and Levine, *Idols of the Games*, 231.

35. Quoted in Edwin Shrake, "What Are They Doing with the Sacred Game of Pro Football?" *Sports Illustrated*, 25 October 1971, 104.

36. Robert Lipsyte, "A Brand New Ball Game?" *New York Times*, 1 January 1968.

37. David Maraniss, *When Pride Still Mattered: A Life of Vincent Lombardi* (New York: Simon and Schuster, 1999), 422.

38. Quoted in Marc Pachter, ed., *Champions of American Sport* (Washington D.C.: Smithsonian Institute, 1981), 135.

39. Tex Maule, "Say It's So, Joe," *Sports Illustrated*, 20 January 1969, 10.

40. Quoted in John D. Bloom, "Joe Namath and Super Bowl III: An Interpretation of Style," *Journal of Sport History* 15, no. 1 (1988): 70–71.

41. Lipsyte and Levine, *Idols of the Games*, 231.

42. Ron Flatter, "Russell Was Proud, Fierce Warrior," *ESPN SportsCentury*, available from espn.go.com/sportscentury/features/00016449.html; Stan Isaacs, "January 20: Bill Russell's State Of the Union Message," *The 1969 Chronicles: A Sports Writer's Notes*, available from www.izix.com/stan/index.php?chapter=5&column=6.

43. Terry Pluto, *Loose Balls: The Short, Wild Life of the American Basketball Association as Told by the Players, Coaches, and Movers and Shakers who Made It Happen* (New York: Simon and Schuster, 1990), 206.

44. Frank Deford, "Push Comes to Shove," *Sports Illustrated*, 15 April 1968, 34.

45. Pluto, *Loose Balls*, 367.

46. Nelson George, *Elevating the Game: The History and Aesthetics of Black Men in Basketball* (New York: Simon and Schuster, 1992), 185.

5. WALKING THE PICKET LINE AND FIGHTING FOR RIGHTS

1. Dave Anderson, "Coach Nixon Sends in Play to the Miami Dolphins," in *At the Super Bowl*, ed. Leonard Koppett (New York: Quadrangle Books, 1974), 233.

2. Jim McKay, *The Real McKay: My Wide World of Sports* (New York: Penguin Press, 1998), 16.

3. Jerry Kirshenbaum, "On Your Mark, Get Set, Sell," *Sports Illustrated* 14 May 1973, 37.

4. William Oscar Johnson, "What's Happened To Our Heroes?" *Sports Illustrated*, 15 August 1983, 33.

5. *Breaking Away*, prod. and dir. Peter Yates, 100 mins. Twentieth-Century Fox, 1979.

6. Murray Chass, "Steinbrenner Proposes Diluting Kuhn's Power," *New York Times*, 23 March 1977.

7. "George Steinbrenner Sent to the Bleachers for Next Two Years," *Wall Street Journal*, 29 November 1974.

8. *Baseball*, prod. and dir. Ken Burns, Atlanta, PBS Home Video, 1994.

9. *Flood v. Kuhn*, 407 U.S. 258 (1972).

10. Murray Chass, "Turner Barred as Manager But Sees Team Triumph 6–1," *New York Times* 1977.

11. Kenneth M. Jennings, *Balls and Strikes: The Money Game in Professional Baseball* (New York: Praeger, 1990), 51.

12. Quoted in ibid., 67.

13. Jack Tatum, *They Call Me Assassin* (New York: Avon Publishing, 1980).

14. Stephanie Twin, *Out of the Bleachers: Writings on Women and Sport* (New York: McGraw-Hill Book Co., 1979), xxxvi.

15. Quoted in ibid., xxxiv.

16. Bob Ottum, "Dolls on the Move to Mexico," *Sports Illustrated*, 2 September 1968, 16, 17.

17. Pamela Cooper, "Marathon Women and the Corporation," *Journal of Women's History* 7, no. 4 (1995): 63.

18. Bobby Riggs, *Court Hustler* (Philadelphia: J. P. Lippincott, 1973), 11; Gerald Eskenazi, "$100,000 Tennis Match: Bobby Riggs vs. Mrs. King," *New York Times*, 12 July 1973.

19. Riggs, *Court Hustler*, 174–75.

20. Susan K. Cahn, *Coming on Strong: Gender and Sexuality in Twentieth-Century Women's Sport* (New York: Free Press, 1994), 250.

21. Paula D. Welch, *Silver Era, Golden Moments: A Celebration of Ivy League Women's Athletics* (Lanham, Md.: Madison Books, 1999), 26.

22. See, for example, Felice M. Duffy, "Twenty-Seven Years Post Title IX: Why Gender Equity in College Athletics Does Not Exist," *Quinnipiac Law Review* 67, no. 10 (2000): 67–124; Cahn, *Coming on Strong*; Mary Jo Festle, *Playing Nice: Politics and Apologies in Women's Sports* (New York: Columbia University Press, 1996).

23. John Underwood, "The NCAA Goes on the Defense," *Sports Illustrated*, 27 February 1978, 23.

24. House Committee on Education and Labor, *Hearings Before the Subcom-*

mittee on Postsecondary Education on "Sex Discrimination Regulations," 94th Cong., 1st sess., 17–26 June 1975, 47.

25. "Women's Sports Boom—Too Slow for Some," *U.S. News and World Report,* 10 July 1978, 79.

26. House Committee on Education and Labor, *Hearings on "Sex Discrimination Regulations,"* 60.

27. Senate Committee on Labor and Public Welfare, *"Prohibition of Sex Discrimination,"* 1975: Hearings Before the Subcommittee on Education S.2106 to Amend Title IX, 94th Cong., 1st sess., 16 and 18 September 1975.

28. Festle, *Playing Nice,* 181.

29. Quoted in Kent, "Too Far, Too Fast," *Sports Illustrated,* 20 March 1978, 35.

30. Steve Springer, "After 16 Years, Title IX's Goals Remain Unfulfilled," *Los Angeles Times,* 30 October 1988.

31. Bart Barnes, "Lack of Money Halts Boom in Women's Sports," *Washington Post,* 5 July 1981.

32. Ibid.

33. Quoted in Robert Lipsyte and Peter Levine, *Idols of the Games: A Sporting History of the American Century* (Atlanta: Turner Publishing, 1995), 287.

34. Quoted in Allen Guttmann, *Women's Sports: A History* (New York: Columbia University Press, 1991), 211.

35. Sarah Pileggi, "This Martina Tests 100 Proof," *Sports Illustrated,* 6 March 1978, 20.

36. Quoted in Barry McDermott, "Wrong Image But The Right Touch," *Sports Illustrated,* 25 July 1983, 38.

37. Barry McDermott, "All Smiles While She Tears Up The Tour," *Sports Illustrated,* June 19 1978, 23.

38. William P. Lineberry, ed., *The Business of Sports* (New York: H. H. Holt Company, 1973), 183–85.

39. Parton Keese, "To Frisbee Fans, It's the Ultimate," *New York Times,* 7 August 1977.

40. "Scorecard," *Sports Illustrated,* 18 March 1968, 14.

41. Pamela L. Cooper, "The 'Visible Hand' on the Footrace: Fred Lebow and the Marketing of the Marathon," *Journal of Sport History* 19, no. 3 (1992): 245.

42. Kenny Moore, "She Runs and We Are Lifted," *Sports Illustrated,* 26 December 1983 and 3 January 1984, 34.

43. Cooper, "The 'Visible Hand' on the Footrace," 253.

6. COMPETING ON THE OPEN MARKET

1. Dudley Clendinen, "U.S. Hockey Victory Stirs National Celebration," *New York Times,* 25 February 1980.

2. Alexander J. LaRosa, "Diverging Ideologies: The 1980 Summer Olympic Boycott as an Illumination of Differences in Cold War History," thesis paper, Barnard College, 2003.

3. Jim McKay, *The Real McKay: My Wide World of Sports* (New York: Penguin Press, 1998), 127.

4. "Wall Street," prod. and dir. Oliver Stone, 125 mins. 20th Century Fox, 1987.

5. Ronald Reagan, "Address at Commencement Exercises at the University of Notre Dame," 17 May 1981, *Public Papers of the Presidents of the United States: Ronald Reagan* (Washington, D.C.: Government Printing Office, 1982), 431–35.

6. Ibid.

7. Gordon S. White Jr., "Review of Title IX Is No Surprise," *The New York Times*, 15 August 1981.

8. Thomas Boswell, "Sprit of Title IX Survives," *The Bergen Record*, 5 February 1987.

9. Jerrold K. Footlick, "Of Sports, Sex and Money," *Newsweek*, 16 March 1981, 98.

10. "Judge Alters Title IX Outlook," *New York Times*, 1 March 1981.

11. By 1984, this was the federal government's official position. Grove City College, a small conservative Christian institution in Pennsylvania, had argued that indirect federal funding, largely through grants and loans to students, should not compel them to enforce federal regulations with which they did not agree. The Supreme Court denied Grove City's claim, but nevertheless radically narrowed the interpretation of Title IX regulations. For a more detailed description of the case, see Mary Jo Festle, *Playing Nice: Politics and Apologies in Women's Sports* (New York: Columbia University Press, 1996), 217–21.

12. *Congressional Record*, 100th Cong., 2d sess., 17 March 1988, vol. 134, no. 33, S 2409.

13. Debra E. Blum, "Big-Time Football Confronts a Threat," *Chronicle of Higher Education*, 16 June 1993, 41.

14. Curtis Tong, "The Reawakening Discrimination Against Women in Sports," *Christian Science Monitor*, 23 January 1986.

15. Steve Springer, "After 16 Years, Title IX's Goals Remain Unfulfilled," *Los Angeles Times*, 30 October 1988.

16. Ed Fowler, "Title IX Fails in Real-Life World," *Houston Chronicle*, 9 July 1992.

17. Frank Litsky, "Women's Game Draws Rising Crowd Support," *New York Times*, 14 February 1990.

18. Steve Rock, "Women Attempt to Carve Niche," *Kansas City Star*, 28 March 1998.

19. Walter Byers, *Unsportsmanlike Conduct: Exploiting College Athletes* (Ann Arbor, Mich.: University of Michigan Press, 1995), 281; John Sayle Watterson, *College Football: History, Spectacle, Controversy* (Baltimore, Md.: Johns Hopkins University Press, 2000), 338–39.

20. Rick Telander, *The Hundred Yard Lie: The Corruption of College Football and What We Can Do To Stop It* (New York: Simon and Schuster, 1989), 196.

21. Byers, *Unsportsmanlike Conduct*, 282.

22. Jimmie L. Reeves and Richard Campbell, *Cracked Coverage: Television News, the Anti-Cocaine Crusade, and the Reagan Legacy* (Durham, N.C.: Duke University Press, 1994), 145.

23. William Oscar Johnson, "What's Happened To Our Heroes?" *Sports Illustrated*, 15 August 1983, 42.

24. Ibid., 42.

25. Terry Todd, "Anabolic Steroids: The Gremlins of Sport," *Journal of Sport History* 14, no. 1 (1987): 103.

26. Michael Janofsky and Peter Alfano, "Drug Use by Athletes Runs Free Despite Tests," *New York Times*, 17 November 1988.

27. Ibid.

28. Michael Janofsky and Peter Alfano, "Steroids in Sports, Part 5," *New York Times*, 21 November 1988.

29. Ibid.

30. Telander, *The Hundred Yard Lie*, 158.

31. Jane Leavy, *Sandy Koufax: A Lefty's Legacy* (New York: HarperCollins, 2002), 239.

32. Michael Janofsky and Peter Alfano, "Victory at Any Cost: Drug Pressure Growing," *New York Times*, 21 November 1988.

33. Stephen Kindel, "Anatomy of a Sports Promotion," *Financial World*, 13 April 1993, 49.

34. Marc Gunther, "They All Want to be Like Mike," *Fortune*, 21 July 1997, 51.

35. Paul Weiler, *Leveling the Playing Field: How the Law Can Make Sports Better for Fans* (Cambridge, Mass.: Harvard University Press, 2000), 67.

36. Frederick Klein, "The NBA's No. 1 Cheerleader," *Wall Street Journal*, 26 October 1984.

37. Phil Patton, "The Selling of Michael Jordan," *New York Times Magazine*, 9 November 1986.

38. Quoted in ibid., 48.

39. Kenny Moore, "Very Fancy, Very Fast," *Sports Illustrated*, 14 September 1988, 158.

40. Neil Amdur, "The Television Dollars Foster New Perceptions," *New York Times*, 30 October 1982.

41. Quoted in Kenneth M. Jennings, *Balls and Strikes: The Money Game in Professional Baseball* (New York: Praeger, 1990), 169.

42. Quoted in Francis X. Dealy, *Win at Any Cost: The Sell Out of College Athletics* (New York: Birch Lane Press, 1990), 98–99.

43. Quoted in Rick Telander, "Senseless," *Sports Illustrated*, 14 May 1990.

44. *The Los Angeles Times*, editorial, "The Rams Look Like Something Else," 12 February 1980.

45. Lionel J. Wilson, "Why Oakland Needs the Raiders," in *Major Problems in American Sports History*, ed. Steven Riess (Boston: Houghton Mifflin, 1997), 415.

46. Michael Janofsky, "Football's Place Under the Sun," *New York Times*, 26 October 1984.

47. Earl Gustkey, "Coliseum, Sports Arena Try to Regain Spotlight," *Los Angeles Times*, 20 June 1982.

48. Jeffrey Kluger, "The Seduction of the Colts: Decision to Leave Baltimore," *New York Times*, 9 December 1984.

49. Quoted in Frank Ahrens, "In NFL-Starved Baltimore, Long Drought Ends Today," *Washington Post*, 1 September 1996.

50. Frank Deford, "The Colts Were Ours . . . They Were One with the City," *Sports Illustrated*, 9 April 1984, 13.

51. Helene Elliott, "Rams and Raiders Are Gone, but They're Not Forgotten," *Los Angeles Times*, 2 September 1995.

52. "Euphoria Ram-pant Among Fans," *St. Louis Post Dispatch*, 16 January 1995.

53. Jim Thomas, "St. Louis Lands Rams; Now It's In Fans' Hands," *St. Louis Post Dispatch*, 18 January 1995.

54. Bernie Miklasz, "The Rams Aren't Worth Big Money, Just Our Trust," *St. Louis Post Dispatch*, 15 January 1995.

55. Carl Nolte, "Sweet 16," SFGate.com, 16 December 1997; available from www.sfgate.com/cgi-bin/article.cgi?file=/chronicle/archive/1997/12/16/MN45280.DTL.

56. Tim Koewn, "Joe's Mystical Cool Couldn't Be Duplicated," SFGate.com, 15 December 1997; available from www.sfgate.com/cgi-bin/article.cgi?file=/chronicle/archive/1997/12/15/SP35988.DTL.

57. Quoted in Gregg Krupa, "Going Downtown: A Concentration on Design of Old-Time City Ballparks Puts Kansas City's HOK Into a League of Its Own," *Boston Globe*, 30 May 1999.

58. "Suddenly Everyone Wants to Build a Superdome," *Business Week*, 5 December 1983, 110.

7. HIGH-PRICED HEROES GO GLOBAL

1. Quoted in Nick Trujillo, "Hegemonic Masculinity on the Mound," in *Reading Sport: Critical Essays on Power and Representation*, ed. Susan Birrell and Mary G. McDonald (Boston: Northeastern University Press, 2000), 28.

2. Quoted in Thom Loverro and Kevin Lyons, "Inevitable End Leaves O's Fans Jilted, Angry," *Washington Times*, 15 September 1994.

3. Quoted in Tim Tucker, "Baseball Fans Are Fed Up," *Atlanta Journal and Constitution*, 20 September 1994.

4. Dave Kindred, "The Class of '98," *Sporting News*, 21 December 1998, 10.

5. Quoted in Tony Emerson and Alan Zarembo, "Sosa's Streak," *Newsweek*, 5 October 1998, 66.

6. Quoted in Toby Miller et al., "Modifying the Sign: Sport and Globalization," *Social Text* 17, no. 3 (1999): 22.

7. Quoted in Richard W. Stevenson, "Magic Johnson Ends His Career, Saying He Has AIDS Infection," *New York Times*, 8 November 1991.

8. Quoted in Richard K. Cacioppo, "This Magic Moment: Earvin Johnson's HIV Announcement and Its Effect on Athletes' Behavior," term paper, American Sports History Since 1945, Barnard College, 2002.

9. Quoted in Stevenson, "Magic Johnson Ends His Career."

10. Quoted in Kimberly McLarin, "Center-Court Star at Center Stage," *New York Times*, 1 August 1993.

11. Quoted in Erika Rose, "From Athlete to Anything But: The Life of Greg Louganis as a Commentary on Homosexuals and Their Portrayal in the Media," term paper, American Sports History Since 1945, Barnard College, 2002.

12. Peter Alfano, "AIDS in the Age of Hype," *New York Times*, 5 March 1995.

13. Quoted in Abigail M. Feder-Kane, "'A Radiant Smile from the Lovely Lady': Overdetermined Femininity in 'Ladies' Figure Skating," in *Reading Sport: Critical Essays on Power and Representation*, ed. Susan Birrell and Mary G. McDonald (Boston: Northeastern University Press, 2000), 213.

14. Quoted in William Carlsen, "Cop Details Nicole's '89 Beating," *San Francisco Chronicle*, 1 February 1995.

15. Gerald Early, "Mike's Brilliant Career: Mike Tyson and the Riddle of Black Cool," *Transition*, no. 71 (1996): 57.

16. Mark Starr and Allison Samuels, "Ear Today, but Gone Tomorrow," *Newsweek*, 14 July 1997, 58.

17. Quoted in Ira Berkow, "Tyson's Aura Says a Lot," *New York Times*, 26 June 2000.

18. Maureen Byrne, "Huddles Help Youth Bring Faith Into Play," *St. Petersburg Times*, 12 September 1997.

19. Quoted in Mark O'Keefe, "Packers Among Those Spreading Faith," *Milwaukee Journal Sentinel*, 27 December 1997.

20. Timothy G. Smith, "White Wants Pulpit Between Hash Marks," *New York Times*, 23 January 1997.

21. Quoted in Michael Romano, "50,800 Gather to Pray, Praise," *Rocky Mountain News*, 31 July 1994.

22. Pat Buchanan, "1992 Republican National Convention Speech," 17 August 1992; available from www.buchanan.org/pa-92–0817-rnc.html.

23. Quoted in Walter LeFeber, *Michael Jordan and the New Global Capitalism* (New York: W. W. Norton, 1999), 100.

24. Larry Schwartz, "Johnson Doubled the Difficulty," *ESPN SportsCentury*; available from espn.go.com/sportscentury/features/00016046.html.

25. Quoted in David Barboza, "The Summer Olympics Failed to Vault Any Gold Medal Winners Into Major Endorsement Deals," *New York Times*, 13 November 1996.

26. Quoted in Marc Gunther, "They All Want to be Like Mike," *Fortune*, 21 July 1997, 52.

27. Frederic Biddle, "Sneaker Wars," *Boston Globe*, 26 July 1992.

28. Quoted in Nancy Armour, "Notre Dame Unique in Sports Marketing," *Marketing News*, 20 May 1996, 13.

29. Rebecca Heino, "What Is So Punk About Snowboarding?" *Journal of Sport and Social Issues* 24, no. 2 (2000): 187.

30. Luke Cyphers, "The Gordon Rules: Jeff Wants to Be Like Mike," *New York Daily News*, 21 February 1999.

31. Quoted in Chris Burritt, "Neighbors Mourn for Fallen Hero," *Atlanta Journal Constitution*, 20 February 2001.

32. Joseph Siano, "How NASCAR's Power Figure Keeps Everybody Happy," *New York Times*, 20 October 1999.

33. Bill Donahue, "For New Sports, ESPN Rules as the X-treme Gatekeeper," *New York Times*, 11 March 1998.

34. Quoted in Sal Ruibal, "X-tremely Overexposed? Burnout Likely Without Change," *USA Today*, 23 June 1999.

35. Quoted in Ryan Wilner, "The Evolution of the X Games and Their Impact on Twenty-first-Century Sports and Culture," term paper, American Sports History Since 1945, Barnard College, 2002.

36. Timothy Egan, "The Swoon of the Swoosh," *New York Times*, 13 September 1998.

37. Matt Higgins, "Chairman of the Board," *Village Voice*, 5 November 2002, 36.

38. Egan, "The Swoon of the Swoosh."

39. Quoted in Jill Lieber, "Reluctant Soccer Icon Tries to Deflect the World Cup Spotlight," *USA Today*, 14 June 1999.

40. Quoted in Patrick Hruby, "The Heat is On," *Washington Times*, 18 June 1999.

41. Quoted in Lisa Olson, "Changing the Image is Everything," *New York Daily News*, 18 July 1999.

42. Barbara Huebner, "So, What's Next," *Boston Globe*, 14 July 1999.

43. Quoted in Joe Concannon, "Fore! It's Tiger Time," *Boston Globe*, 24 October 1996.

44. Quoted in "P.G.A. Site Bars Blacks," *New York Times*, 22 June 1990.

45. Quoted in Sally Jenkins, "Stewart's Comments Spark Shoal Creek Anew," *Washington Post*, 8 August 1990.

46. Quoted in LeFeber, *Michael Jordan and the New Global Capitalism*, 143.

47. Quoted in Huebner, "So, What's Next."

48. Quoted in Marc Pachter, ed., *Champions of American Sport* (Washington, D.C.: Smithsonian Institute, 1981), 165.

49. Quoted in Vicki Michaelis, "Hero Worship," *Denver Post*, 17 January 1999.

50. Quoted in Jim Armstrong, "The Difference Between Maris and McGwire," *Denver Post*, 23 May 1999.

Ahrens, Frank. "In NFL-Starved Baltimore, Long Drought Ends Today." *Washington Post*, 1 September 1996.

Alexander, Charles C. *Breaking the Slump: Baseball in the Depression Era*. New York: Columbia University Press, 2002.

Alfano, Peter. "AIDS in the Age of Hype." *New York Times*, 5 March 1995.

Amdur, Neil. "The Television Dollars Foster New Perceptions." *New York Times*, 30 October 1982.

Anderson, Dave. "Coach Nixon Sends in Play to the Miami Dolphins." In *At the Super Bowl*, ed. Leonard Koppett. New York: Quadrangle Books, 1974.

Angelou, Maya. *I Know Why the Caged Bird Sings*. New York: Random House, 1970.

Armour, Nancy. "Notre Dame Unique in Sports Marketing." *Marketing News*, 20 May 1996, 13.

Armstrong, Jim. "The Difference Between Maris and McGwire." *Denver Post*, 23 May 1999.

Armstrong, Lance, and Sally Jenkins. *It's Not About the Bike: My Journey Back to Life*. New York: Berkley Books, 2000.

Axthelm, Pete. "Boos and a Beating for Tommie." *Sports Illustrated*, 29 January 1968, 56, 59.

Barboza, David. "The Summer Olympics Failed To Vault Any Gold Medal Winners Into Major Endorsement Deals." *New York Times*, 13 November 1996.

Barnes, Bart. "Lack of Money Halts Boom in Women's Sports." *Washington Post*, 5 July 1981.

Baseball. Prod. and dir. Ken Burns. Atlanta, PBS Home Video, 1994.

Baseball Almanac, *Quotations from Roger Maris*, 1997–2003; available from http://www.baseball-almanac.com/quotes/quomari.shtml.

Barzun, Jacques. "God's Country and Mine: A Declaration of Love Spiced with a Few Harsh Words." 1954. Reprint, in *Baseball: A Literary Anthology*, edited by Nicholas Dawidoff. Washington, D.C.: Library of America, 2002.

Bennet, James. "President Leads TV Discussion on Role of Race in Sports." *New York Times*, 15 April 1998.

Berkow, Ira. "Tyson's Aura Says a Lot." *New York Times*, 26 June 2000.

Biddle, Frederic. "Sneaker Wars." *Boston Globe*, 26 July 1992.

Bloom, John D. "Joe Namath and Super Bowl III: An Interpretation of Style." *Journal of Sport History* 15, no. 1 (1988): 64–74.

Blum, Debra E. "Big-Time Football Confronts a Threat." *Chronicle of Higher Education*, 16 June 1993.

Boswell, Thomas. "Sprit of Title IX Survives." *The Bergen Record*, 5 February 1987.

Boyle, Robert H. "The Latins Storm Las Grandes Ligas." *Sports Illustrated*. 9 August 1965, 24–26, 29–30.

"Breaking Away." Prod. and dir. Peter Yates. 100 mins. Twentieth-Century Fox, 1979.

Brown, Gary T. "The Electronic Free Ticket." *The NCAA News*, 22 November 1999. Available from www.ncaa.org/news/1999/19991122/active/3624n30.html.

Buchanan, Pat. "1992 Republican National Convention Speech." 17 August 1992. Available from www.buchanan.org/pa-92-0817-rnc.html.

Burritt, Chris. "Neighbors Mourn for Fallen Hero." *Atlanta Journal Constitution*, 20 February 2001.

Byers, Walter. *Unsportsmanlike Conduct: Exploiting College Athletes*. Ann Arbor, Mich.: University of Michigan Press, 1995.

Byrne, Maureen. "Huddles Help Youth Bring Faith Into Play." *St. Petersburg Times*, 12 September 1997.

Cacioppo, Richard K. "This Magic Moment: Earvin Johnson's HIV Announcement and Its Effect on Athletes' Behavior." Term paper, American Sports History Since 1945, Barnard College, 2002.

Cahn, Susan K. *Coming on Strong: Gender and Sexuality in Twentieth-Century Women's Sport*. New York: Free Press, 1994.

Carlsen, William. "Cop Details Nicole's '89 Beating." *San Francisco Chronicle*, 1 February 1995.

Cave, Ray. "Sportsman of the Year: Arnold Palmer." *Sports Illustrated*. 9 January 1961, 23–30.

Cayleff, Susan E. *Babe: The Life and Legend of Babe Didrikson Zaharias*. Urbana: University of Illinois Press, 1995.

Chass, Murray. "Steinbrenner Proposes Diluting Kuhn's Power." *New York Times*, 23 March 1977.

——. "Turner Barred as Manager But Sees Team Triumph 6–1." *New York Times* 1977.

Cleaver, Eldridge. *Soul on Ice*. New York: Dell, 1968.

Clendinen, Dudley. "U.S. Hockey Victory Stirs National Celebration." *New York Times*, 25 February 1980.

Cohen, Nicole. "The 1950s Bowling Alley: An American Landscape." Unpublished paper, Barnard College, 2002.

Collins, Robert M. "Richard M. Nixon: The Psychic, Political, and Moral Use of Sport." *Journal of Sport History* 10, no. 2 (1983): 77–84.

Congressional Record, 100th Cong., 2d sess., 17 March 1988. Vol. 134, no. 33, S 2409.

Concannon, Joe. "Fore! It's Tiger Time." *Boston Globe*, 24 October 1996.

Cooper, Pamela L. "Marathon Women and the Corporation." *Journal of Women's History* 7, no. 4 (1995): 62–78.

———. "The 'Visible Hand' on the Footrace: Fred Lebow and the Marketing of the Marathon." *Journal of Sport History* 19, no. 3 (1992): 244–56.

Cramer, Richard Ben. *Joe DiMaggio: The Hero's Life*. New York: Simon and Schuster, 2000.

Creamer, Robert W. "Scorecard." *Sports Illustrated*, 1 November 1971, 13.

"CYO Pledge." Stritch Papers. Archives of the Archdiocese of Chicago. Box 1, folder 21. Chicago.

Cyphers, Luke. "The Gordon Rules: Jeff Wants to Be Like Mike." *New York Daily News*, 21 February 1999.

Daley, Arthur. "Every Little Bit Helps." *New York Times*, 10 June 1952.

———. "Long Way from New York." *New York Times*, 15 April 1958.

———. "Somber Second Thoughts." *New York Times*, 13 September 1960.

Davis, Jack E. "Baseball's Reluctant Challenge: Desegregating Major League Spring Training Sites, 1961–1964." *Journal of Sport History* 19, no. 2 (1992): 144–62.

Dealy, Francis X. *Win at Any Cost: The Sell Out of College Athletics*. New York: Birch Lane Press, 1990.

Deford, Frank. "Push Comes to Shove." *Sports Illustrated*, 15 April 1968, 34–39.

———. "The Colts Were Ours . . . They Were One with the City." *Sports Illustrated*, 9 April 1984, 13.

Donahue, Bill. "For New Sports, ESPN Rules as the X-treme Gatekeeper." *New York Times*, 11 March 1998.

Duffy, Felice M. "Twenty-Seven Years Post Title IX: Why Gender Equity in College Athletics Does Not Exist." *Quinnipiac Law Review* 67, no. 10 (2000): 67–124.

Early, Gerald. "Mike's Brilliant Career: Mike Tyson and the Riddle of Black Cool." *Transition*, no. 71 (1996): 46–59.

Edwards, Harry. *The Revolt of the Black Athlete*. New York: Free Press, 1969.

Egan, Timothy. "The Swoon of the Swoosh." *New York Times*, 13 September 1998.

Elliott, Helene. "Rams and Raiders Are Gone, but They're Not Forgotten." *Los Angeles Times*, 2 September 1995.

Emerson, Tony, and Alan Zarembo. "Sosa's Streak." *Newsweek*, 5 October 1998, 66.

"End of the Affair." *Time*. 17 December 1956, 80.

Eskenazi, Gerald. "$100,000 Tennis Match: Bobby Riggs vs. Mrs. King." *New York Times*, 12 July 1973.

"Euphoria Ram-pant Among Fans." *St. Louis Post Dispatch*, 16 January 1995.

Fair, John D. "Bob Hoffman, the York Barbell Company, and the Golden Age of American Weightlifting, 1945–1960." *Journal of Sport History* 14, no. 2 (1987): 164–88.

———. "Isometrics or Steroids? Exploring New Frontiers of Strength in the Early 1960s." *Journal of Sport History* 20, no. 1 (1993): 1–24.

Feder-Kane, Abigail M. " 'A Radiant Smile from the Lovely Lady': Overdetermined Femininity in 'Ladies' Figure Skating." In *Reading Sport: Critical Essays on Power and Representation*, edited by Susan Birrell and Mary G. McDonald, 206–33. Boston: Northeastern University Press, 2000.

Festle, Mary Jo. *Playing Nice: Politics and Apologies in Women's Sports*. New York: Columbia University Press, 1996.

Fisher, Donald M. "Lester Harrison and the Rochester Royals, 1945–1957: A Jewish Entrepreneur in the NBA." In *Sports and the American Jew*, ed. Steven A. Riess, 208–40. Syracuse, N.Y.: Syracuse University Press, 1998.

Flatter, Ron. "Russell Was Proud, Fierce Warrior." *ESPN SportsCentury*. Available from espn.go.com/sportscentury/features/00016449.html.

Footlick, Jerrold K. "Of Sports, Sex and Money." *Newsweek*, 16 March 1981, 98.

Fowler, Ed. "Title IX Fails in Real-Life World." *Houston Chronicle*, 9 July 1992.

"Freedom to Play: The Life and Times of Basketball's African-American Pioneers." Basketball Hall of Fame. www.hoophall.com/exhibits/freedom_nba.htm.

Gendzel, Glen. "Competitive Boosterism: How Milwaukee Lost the Braves." *Business History Review* 69, no. 4 (1995): 530–66.

"George W. Bush Is First Former Little Leaguer To Become U.S. President." Little League Online. Available from www.littleleague.org/media/bush.htm.

George, Nelson. *Elevating the Game: The History and Aesthetics of Black Men in Basketball*. New York: Simon and Schuster, 1992.

"George Steinbrenner Sent to the Bleachers for Next Two Years." *Wall Street Journal*, 29 November 1974.

Gilbert, Bil. "Sis-Boom-Bah! For Amalgamated Sponge." *Sports Illustrated*. 25 January 1965, 54–60, 64–65.

Grimsley, Will, ed. *The Sports Immortals*. Englewood Cliffs, N.J.: Prentice-Hall, 1972.

Gunther, Marc. "They All Want to be Like Mike." *Fortune*, 21 July 1997, 51–53.

Gustkey, Earl. "Coliseum, Sports Arena Try to Regain Spotlight." *Los Angeles Times*, 20 June 1982.

Guttmann, Allen. *The Olympics: A History of the Modern Games*. Urbana: University of Illinois Press, 1992.

———. *Women's Sports: A History*. New York: Columbia University Press, 1991.

Hall, Michael. "Lance Armstrong Has Something to Get off His Chest." *Texas Monthly* (July 2001): 72.

Hampton, Henry, ed. *Voices of Freedom: An Oral History of the Civil Rights Movement*. New York: Bantam Books, 1990.

Hannon, Kent. "Too Far, Too Fast." *Sports Illustrated*, 20 March 1978, 34–35.

Heino, Rebecca. "What Is So Punk About Snowboarding?" *Journal of Sport and Social Issues* 24, no. 2 (2000): 176–91.

Herberg, Will. *Protestant, Catholic, Jew: An Essay in American Religious Sociology.* Garden City, N.Y.: Doubleday, 1955.

Higgins, Matt. "Chairman of the Board." *Village Voice,* 5 November 2002, 36.

House Committee on Education and Labor. *Hearings Before the Subcommittee on Postsecondary Education on "Sex Discrimination Regulations."* 94th Cong., 1st sess., 17–26 June 1975.

Hruby, Patrick. "The Heat is On." *Washington Times,* 18 June 1999.

Huebner, Barbara. "So, What's Next." *Boston Globe,* 14 July 1999.

Imbiorski, Walter. "Convention Speeches." 1958. Box 57, CCFM Collection, Archives of the University of Notre Dame, South Bend, Ind.

Isaacs, Stan. "January 20: Bill Russell's State Of the Union Message." *The 1969 Chronicles: A Sports Writer's Notes.* Available from www.izix.com/stan/index.php?chapter=5&column 6.

Janofsky, Michael. "Football's Place Under the Sun." *New York Times,* 26 October 1984.

Janofsky, Michael, and Peter Alfano. "Drug Use by Athletes Runs Free Despite Tests." *New York Times,* 17 November 1988.

———. "Steroids in Sports, Part 5." *New York Times,* 21 November 1988.

———. "Victory at Any Cost: Drug Pressure Growing." *New York Times,* 21 November 1988.

Jenkins, Sally. "Stewart's Comments Spark Shoal Creek Anew." *Washington Post,* 8 August 1990.

Jennings, Kenneth M. *Balls and Strikes: The Money Game in Professional Baseball.* New York: Praeger, 1990.

Johnson, Leola, and David Roediger. " 'Hertz, Don't It?' Becoming Colorless and Staying Black in the Crossover of O. J. Simpson." In *Reading Sport: Critical Essays on Power and Representation,* ed. Susan Birrell and Mary G. McDonald, 40–73. Boston: Northeastern University Press, 2000.

Johnson, William Oscar. "Collision on the New Underground Railroad." *Sports Illustrated,* 12 February 1968, 52–53.

———. *100 Years of Change.* Time International, 27 May 1996. Available from www.time.com/time/international/1996/960527/olympics.history.html.

———. "TV Made It All a New Game." *Sports Illustrated* 22 December 1969, 86–90, 98–102.

———. "What's Happened To Our Heroes?" *Sports Illustrated,* 15 August 1983, 32–34, 38, 40, 42.

"Judge Alters Title IX Outlook." *New York Times,* 1 March 1981.

Keese, Parton. "To Frisbee Fans, It's the Ultimate." *New York Times,* 7 August 1977.

Keim, John. *Legends by the Lake: The Cleveland Browns at Municipal Stadium.* Akron, Ohio: University of Akron Press, 2001.

Kennedy, John F. "The Soft American." *Sports Illustrated.* 26 December 1960, 15–17.

Kerr, Robert L. "The Great White Father and the Antichrist: *Bud Wilkinson's*

Football Letter as Cultural History." *American Journalism* 18, no. 3 (2001): 35–60.

Kindel, Stephen. "Anatomy of a Sports Promotion." *Financial World*, 13 April 1993, 49.

Kindred, Dave. "The Class of '98." *Sporting News*, 21 December 1998, 10.

Kirshenbaum, Jerry. "On Your Mark, Get Set, Sell." *Sports Illustrated*, 14 May 1973, 36–47.

Klatell, David A., and Norman Marcus Klatell. *Sports for Sale: Television, Money, and the Fans*. New York: Oxford University Press, 1988.

Klein, Frederick. "In This Corner . . . AAU, NCAA, Each Old and Strong, Vie to Run U.S. Amateur Sports." *Wall Street Journal*, 24 February 1970.

———. "The NBA's No.1 Cheerleader." *Wall Street Journal*, 26 October 1984.

Kluger, Jeffrey. "The Seduction of the Colts: Decision to Leave Baltimore." *New York Times*, 9 December 1984.

Koewn, Tim. "Joe's Mystical Cool Couldn't Be Duplicated." SFGate.com, 15 December 1997. Available from www.sfgate.com/cgi-bin/article.cgi?file=/chronicle/archive/1997/12/15/SP35988.DTL.

Koppett, Leonard. "The Dark Controversy." *New York Times*, 4 August 1964.

Krupa, Gregg. "Going Downtown: A Concentration on Design of Old-Time City Ballparks Puts Kansas City's HOK Into a League of Its Own." *Boston Globe*, 30 May 1999.

Kuklick, Bruce. *To Every Thing a Season: Shibe Park and Urban Philadelphia, 1909–1976*. Princeton, N.J.: Princeton University Press, 1991.

Lach, Edward L. *Povich, Shirley*. American National Biography Online, September 2000 update. Available from www.anb.org/articles/16/ 16–03377.html.

Lardner, John. "We Hung in the Stretch." *Newsweek*. 17 December 1956, 98.

LaRosa, Alexander J. "Diverging Ideologies: The 1980 Summer Olympic Boycott as an Illumination of Differences in Cold War History." Thesis paper, Barnard College, 2003.

Leavy, Jane. *Sandy Koufax: A Lefty's Legacy*. New York: HarperCollins, 2002.

LeFeber, Walter. *Michael Jordan and the New Global Capitalism*. New York: W. W. Norton, 1999.

Lieber, Jill. "Reluctant Soccer Icon Tries to Deflect the World Cup Spotlight." *USA Today*, 14 June 1999.

Lineberry, William P., ed. *The Business of Sports*. New York: H. H. Holt Company, 1973.

Lipsyte, Robert. "A Brand New Ball Game?" *New York Times*, 1 January 1968.

Lipsyte, Robert, and Peter Levine. *Idols of the Games: A Sporting History of the American Century*. Atlanta: Turner Publishing, 1995.

Liston, Robert. *The Pros*. New York: Platt and Munk, 1968.

Litsky, Frank. "Women's Game Draws Rising Crowd Support." *New York Times*, 14 February 1990.

The Los Angeles Times. Editorial. "The Rams Look Like Something Else." 12 February 1980.

Louis, Joe, Jr., with Edna and Art Rust. *Joe Louis: My Life*. New York: Harcourt Brace Jovanovich, 1978.

Loverro, Thom, and Kevin Lyons. "Inevitable End Leaves O's Fans Jilted, Angry." *Washington Times*, 15 September 1994.

Maraniss, David. *When Pride Still Mattered: A Life of Vincent Lombardi*. New York: Simon and Schuster, 1999.

Marcello, Ronald E. "The Integration of Intercollegiate Athletics in Texas: North Texas State College as a Test Case, 1956." *Journal of Sport History* 14, no. 3 (1987): 286–316.

Marqusee, Mike. *Redemption Song: Muhammad Ali and the Spirit of the Sixties*. London: Verso Press, 1999.

Martin, Charles H. "Integrating New Year's Day: The Racial Politics of College Bowl Games in the American South." *Journal of Sport History* 24, no. 3 (1997): 358–77.

McDermott, Barry. "All Smiles While She Tears Up The Tour," *Sports Illustrated*, 19 June 1978, 22–23.

———. "The Coaches Take Over." *Sports Illustrated*, 22 December 1962, 12–13, 46–47.

———. "Say It's So, Joe." *Sports Illustrated*, 20 January 1969, 10.

———. "Wrong Image But The Right Touch." *Sports Illustrated*, 25 July 1983, 38–41, 44.

McKay, Jim. *The Real McKay: My Wide World of Sports*. New York: Penguin Press, 1998.

McLarin, Kimberly. "Center-Court Star at Center Stage." *New York Times*, 1 August 1993.

"Melbourne Concluded." *Newsweek*, 17 December 1956, 96.

"Men-Medals-Marxism." *Newsweek*, 9 August 1960, 79.

Michaelis, Vicki. "Hero Worship." *Denver Post*, 17 January 1999.

Michener, James A. *Sports in America*. New York: Random House, 1976.

Miklasz, Bernie. "The Rams Aren't Worth Big Money, Just Our Trust." *St. Louis Post-Dispatch*, 15 January 1995.

Miller, Toby, Geoffrey Lawrence, Jim McKay, and David Rowe. "Modifying the Sign: Sport and Globalization." *Social Text* 17, no. 3 (1999): 15–33.

Minter, Jim. "The Mayor Surrenders Atlanta." *Sports Illustrated*, 12 July 1965, 14–17.

Mix, Ron. "Was This Their Freedom Ride?" *Sports Illustrated*, 15 January 1965, 24–25.

Moore, Kenny. "She Runs and We Are Lifted." *Sports Illustrated*, 26 December 1983 and 3 January 1984, 33–44.

———. "Very Fancy, Very Fast." *Sports Illustrated*, 14 September 1988, 158–61.

Nathan, Daniel A. "Sugar Ray Robinson, the Sweet Science, and the Politics of Meaning." *Journal of Sport History* 26, no. 1 (1999): 163–74.

Neal-Lunsford, Jeff. "Sport in the Land of Television: The Use of Sport in Network Prime-Time Schedules 1946–50." *Journal of Sports History* 19, no. 1 (1992): 56–76.

Newfield, Jack. "The Meaning of Muhammad." *The Nation*, 4 February 2002, 25.

"19th Hole: The Readers Take Over." *Sports Illustrated* 1962, 69–70.

Nolte, Carl. "Sweet 16." SFGate.com, 16 December 1997. Available from www.sfgate.com/cgi-bin/article.cgi?file=/chronicle/archive/1997/12/16/MN45280.DTL.

O'Keefe, Mark. "Packers Among Those Spreading Faith." *Milwaukee Journal Sentinel,* 27 December 1997.

Olsen, Jack. "The Black Athlete. Part 1: The Cruel Deception." *Sports Illustrated,* 1 July 1968, 15–27.

———. "The Black Athlete. Part 3: In An Alien World." *Sports Illustrated,* 15 July 1968, 28–36, 41–43.

———. "The Black Athlete. Part 4: In the Back of the Bus." *Sports Illustrated,* 22 July 1968, 28–34, 39–41.

Olson, Lisa. "Changing the Image is Everything." *New York Daily News,* 18 July 1999.

Ottum, Bob. "BYU: Land of Cuties and 12 Tall Cougars." *Sports Illustrated,* 4 January 1965, 26–29.

———. "Dolls on the Move to Mexico." *Sports Illustrated,* 2 September 1968, 16–19.

———. "Grim Countdown to the Games." *Sports Illustrated,* 14 October 1968, 36–38, 43.

"Our Flag on Wings." *Newsweek.* 10 December 1956, 98.

"P.G.A. Site Bars Blacks." *New York Times,* 22 June 1990.

Pachter, Marc, ed. *Champions of American Sport.* Washington D.C.: Smithsonian Institute, 1981.

Patton, Phil. "The Selling of Michael Jordan." *New York Times,* 9 November 1986.

Pileggi, Sarah. "This Martina Tests 100 Proof." *Sports Illustrated,* 6 March 1978, 20–22.

Pluto, Terry. *Loose Balls: The Short, Wild Life of the American Basketball Association as Told by the Players, Coaches, and Movers and Shakers who Made It Happen.* New York: Simon and Schuster, 1990.

Rader, Benjamin G. *In Its Own Image: How Television Has Transformed Sports.* New York: Free Press, 1984.

Reagan, Ronald. "Address at Commencement Exercises at the University of Notre Dame." 17 May 1981. *Public Papers of the Presidents of the United States: Ronald Reagan,* 431–35. Washington, D.C.: Government Printing Office, 1982.

Reeves, Jimmie L., and Richard Campbell. *Cracked Coverage: Television News, the Anti-Cocaine Crusade, and the Reagan Legacy.* Durham, N.C.: Duke University Press, 1994.

Regaldo, Samuel O. *Viva Baseball! Latin Major Leaguers and Their Special Hunger.* Urbana: University of Illinois Press, 1998.

Riggs, Bobby. *Court Hustler.* Philadelphia: J. P. Lippincott, 1973.

Roberts, Randy, and James Olson. *Winning is the Only Thing: Sports in America Since 1945.* Baltimore, Md.: Johns Hopkins University Press, 1989.

Rock, Steve. "Women Attempt to Carve Niche." *Kansas City Star,* 28 March 1998.

Romano, Michael. "50,800 Gather to Pray, Praise." *Rocky Mountain News,* 31 July 1994.

Roosevelt, Franklin Delano. Letter to Commissioner Kenesaw M. Landis. 15

January 1942. National Baseball Hall of Fame. Available from www.baseball-halloffame.org/education/primary_sources/world_war_ii/letter_01_Transcript.htm.

Rose, Erika. "From Athlete to Anything But: The Life of Greg Louganis as a Commentary on Homosexuals and Their Portrayal in the Media." Term paper, American Sports History Since 1945, Barnard College, 2002.

Ross, Charles. *Outside the Lines: African Americans and the Integration of the National Football League*. New York: New York University Press, 1999.

Ruck, Rob. "Roberto Clemente." American National Biography Online, February 2000. Available from www.anb.org/articles/19/19–00299.html.

Rudeen, Kenneth. "Sportsman of the Year: Pete Rozelle." *Sports Illustrated*, 6 January 1964, 23–29.

Ruibal, Sal. "X-tremely Overexposed? Burnout Likely Without Change." *USA Today*, 23 June 1999.

Sargent, Jim. "Helen 'Gig' Smith: Remembering the All-American Girls Baseball League." AAGPBL Web site, 1999. Available from www.aapbl.org/articles/arti_hs.html.

Schapp, Richard. *An Illustrated History of the Olympics*. New York: Alfred Knopf, 1963.

Schwartz, Larry. "Johnson Doubled the Difficulty." *ESPN SportsCentury*. Available from espn.go.com/sportscentury/features/00016046.html.

"Scorecard." *Sports Illustrated*, 18 March 1968, 14.

"Scorecard." *Sports Illustrated*, 15 April 1968, 21.

"Scorecard." *Sports Illustrated*, 6 May 1968, 8.

"Scorecard." *Sports Illustrated*, 17 June 1968, 9.

Senate Committee on Labor and Public Welfare. *"Prohibition of Sex Discrimination," 1975: Hearings before the Subcommittee on Education S.2106 to Amend Title IX*. 94th Cong., 1st sess., 16 and 18 September 1975.

Shrake, Edwin. "What Are They Doing with the Sacred Game of Pro Football?" *Sports Illustrated*, 25 October 1971, 96–99, 101–2, 104, 106.

Siano, Joseph. "How NASCAR's Power Figure Keeps Everybody Happy." *New York Times*, 20 October 1999.

Simons, William. "Jackie Robinson and the American Mind: Journalistic Perceptions of the Reintegration of Baseball." *Journal of Sport History* 12, no. 1 (1985): 39–64.

Smith, Thomas G. "Outside the Pale: The Exclusion of Blacks from Organized Professional Football, 1934–1946." *Journal of Sports History* 15, no. 3 (1988): 255–81.

———. "White Wants Pulpit Between Hash Marks." *New York Times*, 23 January 1997.

Sperber, Murray. *Onward to Victory: The Crises That Shaped College Sports*. New York: Henry Holt and Company, 1998.

Springer, Steve. "After 16 Years, Title IX's Goals Remain Unfulfilled." *Los Angeles Times*, 30 October 1988.

Starr, Mark, and Allison Samuels. "Ear Today, but Gone Tomorrow." *Newsweek*, 14 July 1997, 58.

Stevenson, Richard W. "Magic Johnson Ends His Career, Saying He Has AIDS Infection." *New York Times*, 8 November 1991.

Stowers, Carlton. "A Pride of Lions in Cattle Country." *Sports Illustrated*, 1 November 1971, 38–42.

"Suddenly Everyone Wants to Build a Superdome." *Business Week*, 5 December 1983, 110.

Talese, Gay. "Alleys á la Mode." *New York Times Magazine*, 11 November 1956, 77.

Tatum, Jack. *They Call Me Assassin*. New York: Avon Publishing, 1980.

Tax, Jeremiah. "First Sputnik, Now This." *Sports Illustrated*, 9 February 1959, 11.

Telander, Rick. *The Hundred Yard Lie: The Corruption of College Football and What We Can Do To Stop It*. New York: Simon and Schuster, 1989.

———. "Senseless." *Sports Illustrated*, 14 May 1990, 36.

Terrell, Roy. "Fast Man with a .45." *Sports Illustrated*, 22 December 1962, 32–36, 41–42.

Thomas, Jim. "St. Louis Lands Rams; Now It's In Fans' Hands." *St. Louis Post Dispatch*, 18 January 1995.

Thornton, Kevin Pierce. "Symbolism at Ole Miss and the Crisis of Southern Identity." *South Atlantic Quarterly* 86, no. 3 (1987).

Todd, Terry. "Anabolic Steroids: The Gremlins of Sport." *Journal of Sport History* 14, no. 1 (1987): 87–107.

Tong, Curtis. "The Reawakening Discrimination Against Women in Sports." *Christian Science Monitor*, 23 January 1986.

Trujillo, Nick. "Hegemonic Masculinity on the Mound." In *Reading Sport: Critical Essays on Power and Representation*, ed. Susan Birrell and Mary G. McDonald, 14–39. Boston: Northeastern University Press, 2000.

Tucker, Tim. "Baseball Fans Are Fed Up." *Atlanta Journal and Constitution*, 20 September 1994.

Tunis, John. *All-American*. 1942. Reprint, New York: Odyssey Classics, 1989.

Twin, Stephanie. *Out of the Bleachers: Writings on Women and Sport*. New York: McGraw-Hill Book Co., 1979.

Tygiel, Jules. *Baseball's Great Experiment: Jackie Robinson and His Legacy*. 1983. Reprint, New York: Oxford University Press, 1997.

———. *Past Time: Baseball as History*. New York: Oxford University Press, 2000.

Underwood, John. "The NCAA Goes on the Defense." *Sports Illustrated*, 27 February 1978, 20–24, 29.

Vertinsky, Patricia. "More Myth than History: American Culture and Representations of the Black Female's Athletic Ability." *Journal of Sport History* 25, no. 3 (1998): 532–61.

"Wall Street." Prod. and dir. Oliver Stone. 125 mins. Twentieth Century Fox, 1987.

Wallace, William. "Poverty and Grambling Provide Top Prospects for Pro Football." *New York Times*, 9 January 1968.

Watterson, John Sayle. *College Football: History, Spectacle, Controversy*. Baltimore, Md.: Johns Hopkins University Press, 2000.

Weiler, Paul. *Leveling the Playing Field: How the Law Can Make Sports Better for Fans*. Cambridge, Mass.: Harvard University Press, 2000.

Welch, Paula D. *Silver Era, Golden Moments: A Celebration of Ivy League Women's Athletics*. Lanham, Md.: Madison Books, 1999.

When We Were Kings. Prod. and dir. Leon Gast. 89 mins. Polygram Video, 1997.

White, G. Edward. *Creating the National Pastime: Baseball Transforms Itself, 1903–1953*. Princeton, N.J.: Princeton University Press, 1996.

White, Gordon S., Jr. "Review of Title IX Is No Surprise." *The New York Times*, 15 August 1981.

Wiggins, David K. " 'The Future of College Athletics is at Stake': Black Athletes and Racial Turmoil on Three Predominantly White University Campuses, 1968–1972." *Journal of Sport History* 15, no. 3 (1988): 304–33.

Wilner, Ryan. "The Evolution of the X Games and Their Impact on Twenty-first-Century Sports and Culture." Term paper, American Sports History Since 1945, Barnard College, 2002.

Wilson, Lionel J. "Why Oakland Needs the Raiders." In *Major Problems in American Sports History*, ed. Steven Riess, 415. Boston: Houghton Mifflin, 1997.

"Women's Sports Boom—Too Slow for Some." *U.S. News and World Report*, 10 July 1978, 79.

Zimbalist, Andrew. *Baseball and Billions: A Probing Look Inside the Big Business of Our National Pastime*. New York: BasicBooks, 1992.